高一同學的目

- 1. 熟背「高中常用7000字」
- 2. 月期考得高分
- 3. 會說流利的英語

1.「用會話背7000字①」書＋CD 280元

以三個極短句為一組的方式，讓同學背了會話，同時快速增加單字。高一同學要從「國中常用2000字」挑戰「高中常用7000字」，加強單字是第一目標。

2.「一分鐘背9個單字」書＋CD 280元

利用字首、字尾的排列，讓你快速增加單字。一次背9個比背1個字簡單。

3. rival

rival [5] ('raɪvl̩) n. 對手
arrival [3] (ə'raɪvl̩) n. 到達 } 都有 rival
festival [2] ('fɛstəvl̩) n. 節日；慶祝活動

revival [6] (rɪ'vaɪvl̩) n. 復甦
survival [3] (sə'vaɪvl̩) n. 生還 } 字尾是 vival
carnival [6] ('karnəvl̩) n. 嘉年華會

carnation [5] (kar'neʃən) n. 康乃馨
donation [6] (do'neʃən) n. 捐贈 } 字尾是 nation
donate [6] ('donet) v. 捐贈

3.「一口氣考試英語」書＋CD 280元

把大學入學考試題目編成會話，背了以後，會說英語，又會考試。

例如：

What a nice surprise! (真令人驚喜！)【常考】
I can't believe my eyes.
(我無法相信我的眼睛。)
Little did I dream of seeing you here.
(做夢也沒想到會在這裡看到你。)【駒澤大】

4. 「一口氣背文法」書＋CD 280元
   英文文法範圍無限大，規則無限多，誰背得完？
   劉毅老師把文法整體的概念，編成216句，背完
   了會做文法題、會說英語，也會寫作文。既是一
   本文法書，也是一本會話書。

1. 現在簡單式的用法

I *get up* early every day.　　我每天早起。

I *understand* this rule now.　　我現在了解這條規定了。

Actions *speak* louder than　　行動勝於言辭。
   words.

【二、三句強調實踐早起】

5. 「高中英語聽力測驗①」書＋MP3 280元
6. 「高中英語聽力測驗進階」書＋MP3 280元
   高一月期考聽力佔20%，我們根據大考中心公布的
   聽力題型編輯而成。

7. 「高一月期考英文試題」書 280元
   收集建中、北一女、師大附中、中山、成功、景
   美女中等各校試題，並聘請各校名師編寫模擬試
   題。

8. 「高一英文克漏字測驗」書 180元

9. 「高一英文閱讀測驗」書 180元
   全部取材自高一月期考試題，英雄
   所見略同，重複出現的機率很高。
   附有翻譯及詳解，不必查字典，對
   錯答案都有明確交待，做完題目，
   一看就懂。

高二同學的目標——提早準備考大學

1.「用會話背7000字①②」
書+CD，每冊280元

「用會話背7000字」能夠解決
所有學英文的困難。高二同學
可先從第一冊開始背，第一冊
和第二冊沒有程度上的差異，
背得越多，單字量越多，在腦
海中的短句越多。每一個極短句大多不超過5個字，1個字或
2個字都可以成一個句子，如：「用會話背7000字①」p.184，
每一句都2個字，好背得不得了，而且與生活息息相關，是
每個人都必須知道的知識，例如：成功的祕訣是什麼？

11. What are the keys to success?

Be *ambitious*.	要有**雄心**。
Be *confident*.	要有**信心**。
Have *determination*.	要有**決心**。
Be *patient*.	要有**耐心**。
Be *persistent*.	要有**恆心**。
Show *sincerity*.	要有**誠心**。
Be *charitable*.	要有**愛心**。
Be *modest*.	要**虛心**。
Have *devotion*.	要**專心**。

當你背單字的時候，就要有「雄心」，要「決心」背好，對
自己要有「信心」，一定要有「耐心」和「恆心」，背書時
要「專心」。

背完後，腦中有2,160個句子，那不得了，無限多的排列組
合，可以寫作文。有了單字，翻譯、閱讀測驗、克漏字都難
不倒你了。高二的時候，要下定決心，把7000字背熟、背
爛。雖然高中課本以7000字為範圍，編書者為了便宜行事，
往往超出7000字，同學背了少用的單字，反倒忽略真正重要
的單字。千萬記住，背就要背「高中常用7000字」，背完之
後，天不怕、地不怕，任何考試都難不倒你。

2.「時速破百單字快速記憶」書 250元

3.「高二英文克漏字測驗」書 180元

4.「高二英文閱讀測驗」書 180元
全部選自各校高二月期考試題精華，
英雄所見略同，再出現的機率很高。

5.「7000字學測試題詳解」書 250元
唯有鎖定7000字為範圍的試題，才會對準備考試
有幫助。每份試題附有詳細解答，對錯答案都有
明確交待，做完題目，再看詳解，快樂無比。

6.「高中常用7000字(錄音版)」書附錄音QR碼 280元
英文唸2遍，中文唸1遍，穿腦記憶，中英文同時
背。不用看書、不用背，只要聽一聽就背下來了。

7.「高中常用7000字解析【豪華版】」書 390元
按照「大考中心高中英文參考詞彙表」編輯而成
。難背的單字有「記憶技巧」、「同義字」及
「反義字」，關鍵的單字有「典型考題」。大學
入學考試核心單字，以紅色標記。

8.「高中7000字測驗題庫」書 180元
取材自大規模考試，解答詳盡，節省查字典的時間。

9.「英文一字金」系列：①成功勵志經 (How to Succeed) ②人見
人愛經 (How to Be Popular) ③金玉良言經 (Good Advice :
What Not to Do) ④快樂幸福經 (How to Be Happy) ⑤養生救
命經 (Eat Healthy) ⑥激勵演講經 (Motivational Speeches)
書每冊 280元
以「高中常用7000字」為範圍，每
一句話、每一個單字都能脫口而
出，自然會寫作文、會閱讀。

劉 毅 主編

TEST 1

Read the following passage and choose the best answer for each question.

During the summer session there will be a revised schedule of services for the university campus. Specific changes for intercampus bus services and the cafeteria, and summer hours for the infirmary and recreational and athletic facilities will be posted on the bulletin board outside of the cafeteria. Weekly movie and concert schedules, which are in the process of being arranged, will be posted each Wednesday outside of the cafeteria.

Intercampus buses will leave the main hall every hour on the half hour and make all of the regular stops on their route around the campus. The cafeteria will serve breakfast, lunch and dinner from 7 a.m. to 7 p.m. during the week and from noon to 7 p.m. on weekends. The library will maintain regular hours during the week, but shorter hours on Saturdays and Sundays. Weekend hours are from noon to 7 p.m.

All students who want to use the library borrowing services and the recreational, athletic and entertainment facilities must have a valid summer identification card. This announcement will also appear in the next issue of the student newspaper.

1. Which of the following is the main purpose of this announcement?
   (A) To tell people of the new library services.
   (B) To announce the new movies on campus this summer.
   (C) To notify people of the important schedule changes.
   (D) To remind students to validate their identification cards.

2. Times for movies and concerts are not listed in the announcement because ＿＿＿＿＿＿＿.
   (A) they will be announced via broadcast
   (B) students have to call and check in person
   (C) they belong to the private service
   (D) the full list is not ready yet

3. Which of the following facilities are listed for specific schedule changes?
   (A) Bulletin board.
   (B) Food and transportation.
   (C) Bookstore and post office.
   (D) Movies and concerts.

4. According to the passage, a valid identification card is required to ＿＿＿＿＿＿＿.
   (A) ride on intercampus buses
   (B) make use of the infirmary
   (C) borrow equipment from the school
   (D) check books out of the library

TEST 1 詳解

During the summer session there will be a revised schedule of services for the university campus.

在暑修期間，大學校區的各項服務時間表將有所變更。

* session[6] ('sɛʃən) n. 授課時間；開會　　**summer session** 暑修
  revised[4] (rɪ'vaɪzd) adj. 修訂過的
  schedule[3] ('skɛdʒʊl) n. 時間表　　service[1] ('sɜvɪs) n. 服務
  university[4] (,junə'vɜsətɪ) n. 大學　　campus[3] ('kæmpəs) n. 校園
  university campus 大學校園

Specific changes for intercampus bus services **and** the cafeteria, **and** summer hours for the infirmary **and** recreational **and** athletic facilities will be posted on the bulletin board outside of the cafeteria.

跨校區公車和自助餐廳有特定的時間變更，醫務室和休閒、運動設施的暑期開放時間，將張貼於自助餐廳外的佈告欄。

* specific[3] (spɪ'sɪfɪk) adj. 特定的
  intercampus (,ɪntɚ'kæmpəs) adj. 跨校區的
  cafeteria[2] (,kæfə'tɪrɪə) n. 自助餐廳
  hours[1] (aʊrz) n. pl. 辦公時間
  infirmary (ɪn'fɜmərɪ) n. (學校的) 醫務室
  recreational[6] (,rɛkrɪ'eʃənl) adj. 娛樂的；休閒的
  athletic[4] (æθ'lɛtɪk) adj. 運動選手用的；體育的
  facilities[4] (fə'sɪlətɪz) n. pl. 設施　　post[2] (post) v. 張貼
  bulletin[4] ('bʊlətn) n. 佈告　　**bulletin board** 佈告欄
  outside of 在…的外面

Weekly movie *and* concert schedules, *which are in the process of*
being arranged, will be posted *each Wednesday outside of the cafeteria.*
每週放映的電影和音樂會的時間表還在安排中,將於每週三張貼在自助
餐廳外。

> * weekly[4] (ˈwiklɪ) *adj.* 每週一次的　　process[3] (ˈprɑsɛs) *n.* 過程
> *in the process of* 在…過程中　　arrange[2] (əˈrendʒ) *v.* 安排

Intercampus buses will leave the main hall *every hour on the*
half hour and make all *of the regular stops on their route around the*
campus.

跨校區公車每小時的 30 分於大禮堂發車,環校區的路線上固定的
各站皆停。

> * *main hall* 大禮堂
> *every hour on the half hour* 每小時的半點;每小時的 30 分
> 　　(如 6:30、7:30 等)
> 【比較】*every hour on the hour* 每小時的整點 (如 6:00、7:00 等)
> regular[2] (ˈrɛgjələ) *adj.* 正常的;規律的;固定的
> *make a stop* 停止;停靠　　route[4] (rut) *n.* 路線
> *on one's route* 在…路線上

The cafeteria will serve breakfast, lunch *and* dinner *from 7 a.m. to*
7 p.m. during the week and from noon to 7 p.m. on weekends.
自助餐廳平日於上午七點至晚上七點間供應早、午餐,及晚餐,週末
則於中午至晚上七點供應。

> * serve[1] (sɝv) *v.* 服務;供應
> *during the week* 平日【即週一至週五】
> noon[1] (nun) *n.* 正午;中午

The library will maintain regular hours *during the week*, ***but*** shorter

hours *on Saturdays **and** Sundays*. Weekend hours are from noon to

7 p.m.

圖書館平日維持正常的開放時間，但週六、週日的開放時間會縮短。週末的開放時間，是從中午到晚上七點。

> * maintain² 〔men'ten〕 *v.* 維持　　hours¹ 〔aʊrz〕 *n. pl.* 時間

All students ***who*** *want to use the library borrowing services **and***

*the recreational, athletic **and** entertainment facilities* must have a

valid summer identification card.

所有想利用圖書館借書服務，和休閒、運動及娛樂設施的學生，都必須持有效的暑期學生證。

> * borrow² 〔'bɑro〕 *v.* 借（出）
> entertainment⁴ 〔ˌɛntɚ'tenmənt〕 *n.* 娛樂
> valid⁶ 〔'vælɪd〕 *adj.* 有效的
> identification⁴ 〔aɪˌdɛntəfə'keʃən〕 *n.* 身份證明（文件）
> ***identification card*** 識別證；身分證；學生證（= *student identicication card*）

This announcement will *also* appear *in the next issue of the student*

newspaper.

本公告也將刊登在下一期的學生報上。

> * announcement³ 〔ə'naʊnsmənt〕 *n.* 通告；公告
> appear¹ 〔ə'pɪr〕 *v.* 出現　　issue⁵ 〔'ɪʃʊ〕 *n.* （刊物的）一期

1.(**C**) 下列何者為這則公告的主要目的？

    (A) 告知人們新的圖書館服務。

    (B) 公告今年夏天校園的新電影。

    (C) <u>通知人們重要的時間表變更。</u>

    (D) 提醒學生確認他們的學生證是有效的。

    * main^2〔men〕*v.* 主要的   purpose^1〔'pɝpəs〕*n.* 目的
    announce^3〔ə'naʊns〕*v.* 宣布；公布
    notify^5〔'notə,faɪ〕*v.* 通知   remind^3〔rɪ'maɪnd〕*v.* 提醒
    validate^6〔'vælə,det〕*v.* 使有效；確認…有效

2.(**D**) 電影和音樂會的時間沒有列在公告裡，因為 _____。

    (A) 他們會經由廣播的方式公告

    (B) 學生必須親自打電話確認

    (C) 它們屬於私人服務   (D) <u>完整的時間表還沒準備好</u>

    * list^1〔lɪst〕*v.* 列表 *n.* 清單   via^5〔'vaɪə〕*prep.* 經由
    broadcast^2〔'brɔd,kæst〕*n.* 廣播   check^1〔tʃɛk〕*v.* 確認
    in person 親自   ***belong to*** 屬於
    private^2〔'praɪvɪt〕*adj.* 私人的   full^1〔fʊl〕*adj.* 完整的
    not…yet 尚未

3.(**B**) 下列哪些設施被列在特定變更的時間表裡？

    (A) 佈告欄。   (B) <u>食物和交通。</u>

    (C) 書店和郵局。   (D) 電影和音樂會。

4.(**D**) 根據本文，_____ 需要一張有效的學生證。

    (A) 搭乘跨校區公車   (B) 使用醫務室

    (C) 借用學校的設備   (D) <u>借出圖書館的書</u>

    * require^2〔rɪ'kwaɪr〕*v.* 需要   ***make use of*** 利用
    equipment^4〔ɪ'kwɪpmənt〕*n.* 設備
    check out（在圖書館）辦理借（書）手續

TEST 2

Read the following passage and choose the best answer for each question.

Introducing others will make you seem gracious and well-connected, but be sure to follow the proper ***protocol***.

In social situations the order in which you introduce two people is based on gender and age (women and older people first). In business settings the order is determined by rank.

Think of it as a circle. Begin the introduction by addressing the higher-ranking person and presenting the lower-ranking person. Then reverse the order, so you say each person's name two times. Try to add some interesting information to start the conversation.

If you were introducing Mrs. Smith, a vice president of the company, and Mr. Jones, a junior associate, for example, you might say:

"Mrs. Smith, I would like to introduce you to Mr. Jones, a junior associate. Mr. Jones, this is Mrs. Smith. Mr. Jones just returned from Thailand."

If you're unsure who the more important person is, follow the gender and age guideline.

Don't panic if you forget a name. Most people will be happy to remind you and appreciate the introduction.

1. The best title for this passage would be _____.

   (A) Making Connections

   (B) Presenting Yourself

   (C) Making a Presentation

   (D) Introductions Etiquette

2. We can replace *protocol* with _____.

   (A) fault

   (B) attachment

   (C) practice

   (D) image

3. In social situations the order in which you introduce two people will be _____.

   (A) Ms. Chang, this is Chen Meling. She is a student of mine. Meling, this is Ms. Chang. We're teaching at the same school.

   (B) Ms. Xue, this is Ms. Chen. We're in the same office. Ms. Chen, Ms. Xue, a student of mine.

   (C) Mr. Wang, this is Ms. Chao. Ms. Chao, Mr. Wang.

   (D) Mr. Tan, this is Ms. Lee. Ms. Lee just returned from the U.S.

4. While you're introducing others, if you forget a name, _____.

   (A) it will make you more gracious

   (B) you should stay calm

   (C) it makes you seem well-connected

   (D) happy folks will look at the bright side

TEST 2 詳解

Introducing others will make you seem gracious *and*

well-connected, *but* be sure to follow the proper *protocol*.

　　介紹別人會讓使你看起來很親切、社會關係良好，不過，請務必
要遵守正確的禮節。

* introduce[2] (ˌɪntrəˈdjus) *v.* 介紹
  gracious[4] (ˈgreʃəs) *adj.* 親切的；誠摯的
  connected[3] (kəˈnɛktɪd) *adj.* 有關係的
  well-connected (ˌwɛlkəˈnɛktɪd) *adj.* 與權貴人物有交情的；
  　有良好社會關係的
  be sure to V. 務必～ (= *be certain to V.* = *must V.*)
  follow[1] (ˈfɑlo) *v.* 遵守
  proper[3] (ˈprɑpɚ) *adj.* 適當的；正確的
  protocol (ˈprɑtəˌkɔl) *n.* 禮節 (= *manners*[3])

In social situations the order *in which* you introduce two people is

based on gender *and* age (*women and older people first*). *In business*

settings the order is determined *by rank*.

　　在社交場合，介紹兩個人的順序，要視性別和年齡而定（女性以
及較年長的先介紹）。在商業場合中，介紹順序由地位來決定。

* social[2] (ˈsoʃəl) *adj.* 社會的；社交的
  situation[3] (ˌsɪtʃuˈeʃən) *n.* 情況；位置
  social situation 社會環境；社交場合　　order[1] (ˈɔrdɚ) *n.* 順序
  be based on 視…而定；根據　　gender[5] (ˈdʒɛndɚ) *n.* 性別
  setting[5] (ˈsɛtɪŋ) *n.* 環境　　*business setting* 商業場合
  determine[3] (dɪˈtɝmɪn) *v.* 決定　　rank[3] (ræŋk) *n.* 地位；階級

Think of it as a circle. Begin the introduction *by addressing the higher-ranking person **and** presenting the lower-ranking person.*

把介紹別人想成是一個循環。開始先向地位較高的人介紹並引見地位較低的人。

* ***think of A as B*** 認為 A 是 B　　circle[2] ('sɜkḷ) *n.* 圓圈；循環
introduction[3] (͵ɪntrə'dʌkʃən) *n.* 介紹
address[1] (ə'drɛs) *v.* 對…說話
high-ranking ('haɪ'ræŋkɪŋ) *adj.* 等級高的；職位高的
present[2] (prɪ'zɛnt) *v.* 介紹
low-ranking ('lo'ræŋkɪŋ) *adj.* 等級低的；職位低的

Then reverse the order, *so* you say each person's name *two times.*

Try to add some interesting information *to start the conversation.*

然後把順序倒過來,所以每個人的名字你都要說兩次。試著在開始對話時,加上一些有趣的資訊。

* reverse[5] (rɪ'vɜs) *v.* 使顛倒　　time[1] (taɪm) *n.* 次數
add[1] (æd) *v.* 增加　　interesting[1] ('ɪntərɪstɪŋ) *adj.* 有趣的
information[4] (͵ɪnfə'meʃən) *n.* 資訊
conversation[2] (͵kɑnvə'seʃən) *n.* 對話

If you were introducing Mrs. Smith, a vice president of the company, **and** Mr. Jones, *a junior associate, for example,* you might say:

例如,如果你要介紹公司的副總裁史密斯太太,給新進同事瓊斯先生認識,你可能會說:

* vice[6]〔vaɪs〕*adj.* 副的　　***vice president*** 副總裁

junior[4]〔'dʒunjɚ〕*adj.* 後進的；資淺的

associate[4]〔ə'soʃɪɪt〕*n.* 同事

"Mrs. Smith, I would like to introduce you *to Mr. Jones, a junior associate*. Mr. Jones, this is Mrs. Smith.　Mr. Jones *just* returned *from Thailand*."

「史密斯太太，我想向妳介紹瓊斯先生，他剛進公司服務。瓊斯先生，這位是史密斯太太。瓊斯先生才剛從泰國回來。」

* ***would like to** V.* 想要～【禮貌用法】

return[1]〔rɪ'tɝn〕*v.* 返回　　Thailand〔'taɪlənd〕*n.* 泰國

***If** you're unsure **who** the more important person is*, follow the gender *and* age guideline.

如果你不確定誰比較重要，就用性別跟年齡作為介紹的依據。

* unsure[1]〔ʌn'ʃur〕*adj.* 不確定的

guideline[5]〔'gaɪd,laɪn〕*n.* 準則；指導方針

Don't panic *if you forget a name*.　Most people will be happy to remind you *and* appreciate the introduction.

如果你忘了名字，別驚慌。大部分的人都會很樂意提醒你，並感謝你的介紹。

* panic[3]〔'pænɪk〕*v.* 驚慌　　***be happy to** V.* 樂意…

remind[3]〔rɪ'maɪnd〕*v.* 提醒；使想起

appreciate[3]〔ə'priʃɪ,et〕*v.* 感激

1. (**D**) 本文最好的標題會是 ＿＿＿＿＿＿ 。

    (A) 建立關係   (B) 表現自己

    (C) 發表演說   (D) 介紹的禮節

    * connections[3] 〔 kəˋnɛkʃən 〕 n. pl. 社會關係
    present[2] 〔 prɪˋzɛnt 〕 v. 呈現；表現
    presentation[4] 〔 ͵prɛznˋteʃən 〕 n. 報告；演講
    etiquette 〔 ˋɛtɪ͵kɛt 〕 n. 禮儀；禮節 (= *manners*[3])

2. (**C**) 我們可以把 *protocol* 代換成 ＿＿＿＿＿＿ 。

    (A) fault[2] 〔 fɔlt 〕 n. 過錯

    (B) attachment[4] 〔 əˋtætʃmənt 〕 n. 附屬物；附件

    (C) *practice*[1] 〔 ˋpræktɪs 〕 n. 常規；慣例；做法

    (D) image[3] 〔 ˋɪmɪdʒ 〕 n. 形象

    * replace[3] 〔 rɪˋples 〕 v. 取代

3. (**A**) 在社交場合，介紹兩個人互相認識的順序會是 ＿＿＿＿＿＿ 。

    (A) 張女士，這是陳梅琳。她是我的學生。梅琳，這是張女士。我們在同一間學校教書。

    (B) 薛女士，這是陳小姐。我們是同事。陳小姐，這是薛女士，我的學生。

    (C) 王先生，這是趙女士。趙女士，王先生。

    (D) 譚先生，這是李女士。李女士剛從美國回來。

    * Ms.[1] 〔 mɪs 〕 n. …女士

4. (**B**) 當你正在介紹他人時，如果你忘記名字，＿＿＿＿＿＿ 。

    (A) 會讓你更有親切感   (B) 你應該保持冷靜

    (C) 會讓你看起來社會關係良好

    (D) 快樂的人會往好處著想

    * calm[2] 〔 kɑm 〕 adj. 冷靜的   *stay calm* 保持冷靜
    look at the bright side 看事情的光明面；往好處著想

TEST 3

Read the following passage and choose the best answer for each question.

Have you ever wondered what ancient books were like? The first books were stories, poems, histories, and prayers. Writers made them by scratching words on cakes of moist clay. When the clay was baked, it formed hard tablets that lasted a long time.

Egyptians made books of two kinds. Record books, which people used and handled over and over, were written on leather. For ordinary reading a more fragile material called papyrus was used instead. Writers used brushes and ink to paint words on long strips of papyrus. Then the strips were rolled up and stored in containers.

The Greeks and Romans used a material called parchment. Parchment was made either from goatskin or calfskin, which was scraped with a special knife until it was very thin. The finished product was white and so strong that the Romans used it for permanent record scrolls.

The Maya Indians wrote their books on paper made of bark that they pulled in long strips from wild fig trees. After the bark had been soaked and washed, it was beaten with paddles to stretch it out thin and wide.

Early Chinese books were handwritten in a kind of varnish on slabs of wood or strips of bamboo. Later, perhaps about A.D. 100, a Chinese inventor made paper from bark and rags. Books in China were soon being written on paper—a millennium before the idea finally reached Europe.

1. Where was papyrus made?
   (A) Egypt.   (B) Greece.
   (C) China.   (D) Central America.

2. Egyptians made their record books with leather because leather was _____.
   (A) durable   (B) valuable
   (C) fragile   (D) white

3. Maya Indians obtained material for their paper from _____.
   (A) goats   (B) trees
   (C) clay   (D) papyrus

4. How long were the Chinese writing on paper before the idea finally reached Europe?
   (A) 100 years.   (B) 200 years.
   (C) 1000 years.   (D) 2000 years.

TEST 3 詳解

Have you *ever* wondered ***what** ancient books were like*?

你曾經對於古代書本是什麼樣子感到好奇嗎？

* wonder² 〔'wʌndɚ 〕 *v.* 想知道；好奇
ancient² 〔'enʃənt 〕 *adj.* 古代的

The first books were stories, poems, histories, ***and*** prayers.

最早的書本是故事、詩集、史書，還有祈禱文。

* poem² 〔'poɪm 〕 *n.* 詩　　history¹ 〔'hɪstrɪ 〕 *n.* 歷史；史書
prayer³ 〔'prɛɚ 〕 *n.* 祈禱；祈禱文

Writers made them *by scratching words on cakes of moist clay.* ***When**
the clay was baked*, it formed hard tablets ***that** lasted a long time*.

作者將字刻在一塊潮濕的黏土上做成書。等黏土被烘烤後，就變成一塊
可以持續存在很久的硬字板。

* scratch⁴ 〔skrætʃ 〕 *v.* 刮；潦草書寫　　cake⁴ 〔kek 〕 *n.* 塊狀物
moist³ 〔mɔɪst 〕 *adj.* 潮濕的　　clay² 〔kle 〕 *n.* 黏土
bake² 〔bek 〕 *v.* 烘烤；曬乾變硬　　form² 〔fɔrm 〕 *v.* 形成
hard¹ 〔hɑrd 〕 *adj.* 硬的　　tablet³ 〔'tæblɪt 〕 *n.* 平板；寫字板
last¹ 〔læst 〕 *v.* 持續；持續存在

Egyptians made books *of two kinds.* Record books, ***which**
people used **and** handled over **and** over*, were written *on leather*.

埃及人做了兩種書。做爲記錄的書是寫在皮革上，人們能一再使用的。

* Egyptian〔ɪ'dʒɪpʃən〕*n.* 埃及人　　kind[1]〔kaɪnd〕*n.* 種類
handle[2]〔'hændl̩〕*v.* 處理；觸摸
over and over 一再地　　leather[3]〔'lɛðɚ〕*n.* 皮革

For ordinary reading a *more* fragile material *called papyrus* was used

instead. Writers used brushes ***and*** ink *to paint words on long strips*

of papyrus. Then the strips were rolled up ***and*** stored *in containers.*

而一般的讀本則會用較脆弱的莎草紙。書寫者用毛筆跟墨水把字畫在一張細長的莎草紙上，然後將莎草紙捲起來，存放在容器裡。

* ordinary[2]〔'ɔrdn̩͵ɛrɪ〕*adj.* 普通的；一般的
reading〔'ridɪŋ〕*n.* 閱讀；讀本
fragile[6]〔'frædʒəl〕*adj.* 脆弱的　　material[2]〔mə'tɪrɪəl〕*n.* 材料
papyrus〔pə'paɪrəs〕*n.* 莎草紙
instead[3]〔ɪn'stɛd〕*adv.* 更換；代替
brush[2]〔brʌʃ〕*n.* 刷子；毛筆　　ink[2]〔ɪŋk〕*n.* 墨水
paint[1]〔pent〕*v.* 畫；油漆　　strip[3]〔strɪp〕*n.*（細長的）一條
roll up 捲起　　store[1]〔stor〕*v.* 貯存
container[4]〔kən'tenɚ〕*n.* 容器

The Greeks ***and*** Romans used a material *called parchment.*

Parchment was made *either from goatskin **or** calfskin, **which** was*

*scraped with a special knife **until** it was very thin.*

希臘人跟羅馬人會用一種叫作羊皮紙的材料。羊皮紙是用山羊皮或小牛皮做成的，會用特別的刀片一直刮到它變成非常薄爲止。

* Greek〔grik〕*n.* 希臘人　　Roman〔'romən〕*n.* 羅馬人
parchment〔'portʃmənt〕*n.* 羊皮紙
either…or~ 不是…就是~　　goatskin〔'got,skɪn〕*n.* 山羊皮
calfskin〔'kæf,skɪn〕*n.* 小牛皮　　scrape⁵〔skrep〕*v.* 刮；削；擦
knife¹〔naɪf〕*n.* 刀子

The finished product was white ***and*** *so* strong ***that*** *the Romans used it for permanent record scrolls.*

完成的產品會是白色的，而且非常堅固，羅馬人會把它拿來做永久紀錄的紙卷。

* finished¹〔'fɪnɪʃt〕*adj.* 完工的　　product³〔'prɑdəkt〕*n.* 產品
strong¹〔strɔŋ〕*adj.* 堅固的
permanent⁴〔'pɝmənənt〕*adj.* 永久的（= *eternal*⁵）
scroll⁵〔skrol〕*n.* 紙卷；捲軸

The Maya Indians wrote their books *on paper made of bark* ***that*** *they pulled in long strips from wild fig trees.* ***After*** *the bark had been soaked **and** washed*, it was beaten *with paddles to stretch it out thin **and** wide.*

馬雅印地安人用樹皮製成的紙來寫書，他們將野生無花果樹的樹皮拉開成長條狀，然後將樹皮浸泡、清洗，再用槳狀物的工具將樹皮打成又薄又寬。

* Maya〔'majə〕*n.* 馬雅人　　Indian〔'ɪndɪən〕*n.* 印地安人
bark[2]〔bɑrk〕*n.* 樹皮　　pull[1]〔pʊl〕*v.* 拉；揪下
wild[2]〔waɪld〕*adj.* 野生的　　fig〔fɪg〕*n.* 無花果
soak[5]〔sok〕*v.* 浸泡　　beat[1]〔bit〕*v.* 打；擊
paddle[5]〔'pædl〕*n.* 槳；槳狀物
stretch[2]〔strɛtʃ〕*v.* 拉長；延伸　　wide[1]〔waɪd〕*adj.* 寬的

Early Chinese books were handwritten *in a kind of varnish on*

slabs of wood **or** *strips of bamboo.*

早期中國的書籍，是手寫在一種光滑厚木板或是長條竹片上。

* handwritten〔'hænd,rɪtn̩〕*adj.* 手寫的
varnish〔'vɑrnɪʃ〕*n.* 亮光漆　　slab〔slæb〕*n.* 厚板
wood[1]〔wʊd〕*n.* 木材　　bamboo[2]〔bæm'bu〕*n.* 竹子

Later, perhaps about A.D. 100, a Chinese inventor made paper *from*

bark **and** *rags.* Books *in China* were *soon* being written *on paper—*

a millennium **before** *the idea finally reached Europe.*

後來，大約西元一百年時，一位中國的發明家用樹皮跟破布造紙。很快
地，中國的書就被寫在紙上了——這個想法一千年後才傳到歐洲。

* **A.D.** 西元後　　inventor[3]〔ɪn'vɛntə〕*n.* 發明家
rag[3]〔ræg〕*n.* 破布　　millennium〔mə'lɛnɪəm〕*n.* 一千年
idea[1]〔aɪ'diə〕*n.* 想法；主意　　reach[1]〔ritʃ〕*v.* 抵達；傳到
Europe〔'jʊrəp〕*n.* 歐洲

1. (**A**) 莎草紙是在哪裡製成的？
　(A) 埃及。　　(B) 希臘。　　(C) 中國。　　(D) 中美洲。
　* Greece〔gris〕*n.* 希臘

2. (**A**) 埃及人用皮革製成他們的紀錄書，因爲皮革是 ＿＿＿＿＿＿。
　(A) ***durable***⁴〔'djurəbḷ〕*adj.* 耐用的
　(B) valuable³〔'væljuəbḷ〕*adj.* 有價值的
　(C) fragile⁶〔'frædʒəl〕*adj.* 脆弱的
　(D) white¹〔hwaɪt〕*adj.* 白色的

3. (**B**) 馬雅印地安人從 ＿＿＿＿＿＿ 得到他們製紙的材料。
　(A) 山羊　　(B) 樹　　(C) 黏土　　(D) 莎草紙
　* obtain⁴〔əb'ten〕*v.* 獲得

4. (**C**) 中國人書寫在紙上的這種想法，過了多久，才終於傳到歐洲？
　(A) 一百年。　(B) 二百年。　(C) 一千年。　(D) 二千年。

【補充資料】

　　莎草紙又稱爲草紙，是古埃及人廣泛採用的書寫介質，它用盛產於尼羅河三角洲的紙莎草的莖製成。大約在西元前 3000 年，古埃及人就開始使用莎草紙，並將這種特產出口到古希臘等古代地中海文明地區，甚至遙遠的歐洲內陸和西亞。

　　莎草紙一直使用到 8 世紀左右，後來由於造紙術的傳播而退出歷史舞台。在埃及，莎草紙一直使用到 9 世紀才被從阿拉伯傳入的廉價紙張代替。在此之前，洋皮紙和牛皮紙已經在很多領域代替了莎草紙，因爲它們在潮濕的環境下更耐用，而且在任何地方都能生產。在歐洲，教會直到 11 世紀左右依然在正式文件中使用莎草紙。

　　現在留存下來最近的具有確切年代的莎草紙實物文件，是一份 1057 年的教宗敕令，和一卷書寫於 1087 年的阿拉伯文獻。拜占庭帝國直到 12 世紀依然在使用莎草紙，但是沒能留下實物。

　　莎草紙消亡以後，製作莎草紙的技術也因缺乏記載而失傳。後來跟隨拿破崙遠征埃及的法國學者雖然收集到古埃及莎草紙的實物，也沒能復原其製造方法。直到 1962 年，埃及工程師哈桑拉賈（Hassan Ragab）利用 1872 年從法國引種回埃及的紙莎草，重新發明了製作莎草紙的技術。

TEST 4

Read the following passage and choose the best answer for each question.

Amnesty International is a worldwide movement that works to promote human rights. Amnesty International campaigns include efforts to free all prisoners of conscience; to ensure fair and prompt trials for political prisoners; to abolish the death penalty, torture and other cruel treatment of prisoners; to end political killings and "disappearances"; and to oppose human rights abuses by governments.

Amnesty International has around a million members and supporters in 162 countries and territories. Activities range from public demonstrations to letter-writing, from human rights education to fundraising concerts, from individual appeals on a particular case to global campaigns on a particular issue.

Amnesty International is independent of any government, political persuasion or religious creed. Amnesty International is financed largely by subscriptions and donations from its worldwide membership.

1. What is Amnesty International's purpose?

   (A) To campaign for human rights.

   (B) To free prisoners.

   (C) To earn a profit.

   (D) To oppose governments.

2. Which of the following is an activity Amnesty International participates in?

   (A) Political elections.

   (B) Demonstrations.

   (C) The spreading of computer viruses.

   (D) Bombings.

3. Which of the following is NOT listed as one of Amnesty International's campaigns?

   (A) Animal abuse.

   (B) Anti-torture.

   (C) Opposing capital punishment.

   (D) Freeing political prisoners.

4. What is the number of Amnesty International members and supporters?

   (A) One hundred and sixty-two.

   (B) One million.

   (C) One billion.

   (D) Not mentioned.

TEST 4 詳解

Amnesty International is a worldwide movement *that works to*

promote human rights.

「國際特赦組織」是個全球性的組織，致力於提倡人權。

* amnesty〔'æm,nɛstɪ〕*n.* 大赦；特赦
  international[2]〔,ɪntə'næʃənļ〕*adj.* 國際的
  Amnesty International 國際特赦組織【簡稱 AI，是全世界最大的國際性非政府人權組織，1961 年創立，宗旨爲「預防及終止肆意侵犯身體以至精神方面的健全、表達良心的自由，以及免受歧視的自由」，廢除死刑爲該組織主要訴求之一，該組織在 1977 年獲得諾貝爾和平獎】
  worldwide〔'wɜld'waɪd〕*adj.* 全世界的
  movement[1]〔'muvmənt〕*n.*（政治、社會、思想等方面的）運動
  promote[3]〔prə'mot〕*v.* 促進；提倡　　***human rights*** 人權

Amnesty International campaigns include efforts *to free all prisoners*

of conscience; *to ensure fair **and** prompt trials for political prisoners*; *to*

*abolish the death penalty, torture **and** other cruel treatment of prisoners*;

*to end political killings **and** "disappearances"; **and** to oppose human*

rights abuses by governments.

「國際特赦組織」的行動包括努力於釋放所有有良知的犯人；確保政治犯公平和立即的審判；廢除死刑、虐囚，及其他對囚犯的殘忍對待；終止政治謀殺和政治「失蹤案」；並且反對政府侵犯人權。

* campaign[4]〔kæm'pen〕*n. v.* 運動；宣傳活動
  include[2]〔ɪn'klud〕*v.* 包括　　effort[2]〔'ɛfət〕*n.* 努力

free[1] 〔fri〕 *v.* 釋放　　prisoner[2] 〔'prɪznə〕 *n.* 犯人
conscience[4] 〔'kɑnʃəns〕 *n.* 良心
prisoner of conscience　良心犯【簡稱 POC，是 1960 年代初期，「國
　際特赦組織」創造的名詞，與政治犯不同。是指沒有做出國際人權組
　織所認定的犯罪行為，並通常沒有做出教唆暴力及仇恨，而往往因為
　種族、宗教、膚色、語言、性取向，以及信仰等問題而被拘禁】
ensure〔ɪn'ʃʊr〕 *v.* 確保　　fair[2] 〔fɛr〕 *adj.* 公平的
prompt[4] 〔prɑmpt〕 *adj.* 立即的；迅速的
trial[2] 〔'traɪəl〕 *n.* 審判　　political[3] 〔pə'lɪtɪkl̩〕 *adj.* 政治的
abolish[5] 〔ə'bɑlɪʃ〕 *v.* 廢除　　penalty[4] 〔'pɛnl̩tɪ〕 *n.* 刑罰
death penalty 死刑　　torture[5] 〔'tɔrtʃə〕 *n.* 折磨；拷問
cruel[2] 〔'kruəl〕 *adj.* 殘忍的　　treatment[5] 〔'tritmənt〕 *n.* 對待
killing[1] 〔'kɪlɪŋ〕 *n.* 殺害　　disappearance〔ˌdɪsə'pɪrəns〕 *n.* 消失
oppose[4] 〔ə'poz〕 *v.* 反對
abuse[6] 〔ə'bjus〕 *n.* 濫用；虐待；傷害
government[2] 〔'gʌvənmənt〕 *n.* 政府

Amnesty International has around a million members ***and***

supporters *in 162 countries **and** territories.*

　「國際特赦組織」在一百六十二個國家與區域中，大約有一百萬名
成員和支持者。

　　* member[2] 〔'mɛmbə〕 *n.* 成員　　supporter[2] 〔sə'portə〕 *n.* 支持者
　　territory[3] 〔'tɛrəˌtorɪ〕 *n.* 領土；領域

Activities range *from public demonstrations to letter-writing, from*

human rights education to fundraising concerts, from individual

appeals on a particular case to global campaigns on a particular issue.

活動從公開示威遊行到寫信、從人權教育到募款演唱會、從特定案件的個人訴求到特定議題的全球宣傳都有。

* activity[3] 〔æk'tɪvətɪ〕 *n.* 活動　　range[2] 〔rendʒ〕 *v.* (範圍) 包括
  range from A to B (範圍) 從 A 到 B 都有
  public[1] 〔'pʌblɪk〕 *adj.* 公開的
  demonstration[4] 〔‚dɛmən'streʃən〕 *n.* 示威
  letter-writing *n.* 寫信　　education[2] 〔‚ɛdʒə'keʃən〕 *n.* 教育
  fundraising 〔'fʌnd‚rezɪŋ〕 *adj.* 募款的【raise[1] 〔rez〕 *v.* 籌募】
  concert[3] 〔'kɑnsɝt〕 *n.* 演唱會;音樂會
  individual[3] 〔‚ɪndə'vɪdʒuəl〕 *adj.* 個人的　　appeal[3] 〔ə'pil〕 *n.* 懇求
  particular[2] 〔pɚ'tɪkjələ〕 *adj.* 特定的　　case[1] 〔kes〕 *n.* 案例
  global[3] 〔'globḷ〕 *adj.* 全球的　　issue[5] 〔'ɪʃʊ〕 *n.* 議題

Amnesty International is independent *of any government, political persuasion **or** religious creed.* Amnesty International is financed *largely by subscriptions **and** donations from its worldwide membership.*

「國際特赦組織」獨立於任何政府、政黨派別或是宗教信條之外。「國際特赦組織」的資金來源,大多是來自全世界會員的會費跟捐款。

* independent[2] 〔‚ɪndɪ'pɛndənt〕 *adj.* 獨立的 < *of* >
  persuasion[4] 〔pɚ'sweʒən〕 *n.* 說服力;派別;教派
  religious[3] 〔rɪ'lɪdʒəs〕 *adj.* 宗教的
  creed 〔krid〕 *n.* 宗教信條;教義 (= *doctrine*[4])
  finance[4] 〔fə'næns〕 *v.* 資助
  largely[4] 〔'lɑrdʒlɪ〕 *adv.* 大多;主要地
  subscription[6] 〔səb'skrɪpʃən〕 *n.* 捐款;會費
  donation[6] 〔do'neʃən〕 *n.* 捐贈;捐款
  membership[3] 〔'mɛmbɚ‚ʃɪp〕 *n.* 會員身分;全體會員

1. (**A**) 「國際特赦組織」的目的是？

    (A) 從事人權運動。

    (B) 釋放犯人。

    (C) 賺取利潤。

    (D) 反對政府。

    * earn[2] 〔 ɝn 〕 v. 賺得；掙得   profit[3] 〔'prɑfɪt 〕 n. 利潤；收益

2. (**B**) 下列何者是國際特赦組織所參與的活動？

    (A) 政治性的選舉。

    (B) 示威遊行。

    (C) 散播電腦病毒。

    (D) 轟炸。

    * participate[3] 〔 par'tɪsə‚pet 〕 v. 參加；參與 < in >
    election[3] 〔 ɪ'lɛkʃən 〕 n. 選舉
    spreading[2] 〔'sprɛdɪŋ 〕 n. 散布   virus[4] 〔'vaɪrəs 〕 n. 病毒
    bombing[2] 〔'bɑmɪŋ 〕 n. 轟炸

3. (**A**) 下列何者「沒有」被列入「國際特赦組織」的活動？

    (A) 動物虐待。   (B) 反嚴刑拷打。

    (C) 反對死刑。   (D) 釋放政治犯。

    * list[1] 〔 lɪst 〕 v. 將…列於名單上
    capital[3,4] 〔'kæpət̩l 〕 adj. 致命的
    punishment[2] 〔'pʌnɪʃmənt 〕 n. 處罰
    capital punishment 死刑 (= *death penalty*)

4. (**B**) 「國際特赦組織」的會員和支持者的人數是多少？

    (A) 一百六十二。   (B) 一百萬。

    (C) 十億。   (D) 本文沒有提到。

    * billion[3] 〔'bɪljən 〕 n. 十億   mention[3] 〔'mɛnʃən 〕 v. 提到

TEST 5

Read the following passage and choose the best answer for each question.

Intelligent machines are a part of our daily lives. They handle Internet searches, talk to us on the phone, and plan schedules for companies. These machines all use some kind of Artificial Intelligence (AI).

AI gives machines the power to work intelligently. The *term* was first used in 1956 by scientists at Dartmouth University. They were interested in programming computers to think like people.

That's easier said than done. In movies like *I, Robot*, we often see thinking machines. They're very smart and can do almost anything people can. Of course, the real world is quite different. It's not yet possible to build computers with brains like ours.

However, we can program machines to be good at certain skills. For example, in 1997, a supercomputer beat the world's best chess player. Eight years later, several robot cars finished a race across a desert. Also, many computer games have built-in AI to make them more exciting.

And that's just the beginning. In the future, computers with AI will handle many more jobs. They'll help out at banks, stores, and police departments. Also, expect to see more robots (like Sony's AIBO) that use AI. All these changes will make the world a very different yet very interesting place.

1. What does the passage suggest about intelligent machines?
   (A) They are programmed by computers.
   (B) Many of them are made at Dartmouth University.
   (C) Only scientists are interested in them.
   (D) We have worked on them for more than 50 years.

2. How are thinking machines often shown in movies?
   (A) They are unlike real-world robots.
   (B) They sometimes have more than one brain.
   (C) They are not as smart as today's machines.
   (D) They usually fight against people.

3. What are computers still unable to do?
   (A) Drive cars across a desert.
   (B) Beat excellent chess players.
   (C) Think the same way as people.
   (D) Play computer games well.

4. What does the word "*term*" in the second paragraph mean?
   (A) Phrase.   (B) Length.
   (C) Period.   (D) Rule.

TEST 5 詳解

Intelligent machines are a part *of our daily lives*. They handle Internet searches, talk to us *on the phone*, **and** plan schedules *for companies*. These machines all use some kind *of Artificial Intelligence (AI)*.

聰明的機器是我們日常生活的一部分。它們處理網路搜尋、在電話中跟我們對話,而且替公司安排日程表。這些機器全都使用某種人工智慧(AI)。

* intelligent[4] 〔ɪnˈtɛlədʒənt〕 *adj.* 有理解力的;聰明的
  daily[2] 〔ˈdelɪ〕 *adj.* 每日的;日常的　　***daily life*** 日常生活
  handle[2] 〔ˈhændḷ〕 *v.* 處理　　Internet[4] 〔ˈɪntɚˌnɛt〕 *n.* 網際網路
  search[2] 〔sɝtʃ〕 *n.* 搜尋　　***on the phone*** 在電話中
  schedule[3] 〔ˈskɛdʒul〕 *n.* 時間表;行事曆
  company[2] 〔ˈkʌmpənɪ〕 *n.* 公司
  artificial[4] 〔ˌɑrtəˈfɪʃəl〕 *adj.* 人造的;人工的
  intelligence[4] 〔ɪnˈtɛlədʒəns〕 *n.* 智能;理解力;智力
  Artificial Intelligence 人工智慧(= *AI*)【是指由人打造出來,能展現智慧的機器,又叫作機器智能,如電算機、電腦、機器人等】

AI gives machines the power *to work intelligently*. The **term** was *first* used *in 1956 by scientists at Dartmouth University*. They were interested in programming computers *to think like people*.

　　人工智慧讓機器有權限可以聰明地運作。這個用詞最先在 1956 年，為達特茅斯大學的科學家們所使用。他們對設計程式，使電腦像人類一樣思考感興趣。

* power¹〔'pauɚ〕*n.* 職權；權限 < *to* >
　work¹〔wɝk〕*v.*（機器等）運作
　intelligently⁴〔ɪn'tɛlədʒəntlɪ〕*adv.* 聰明地
　term²〔tɝm〕*n.* 用詞；術語
　scientist²〔'saɪəntɪst〕*n.* 科學家
　Dartmouth University 達特茅斯大學【位於美國東北部新罕布夏州，
　　是全美最著名的私立大學之一】
　be interested in 對…感興趣
　program³〔'prog ræm〕*v.* 設計程式

That's easier said ***than*** *done*.
但說比做容易。

* ***It's easier said than done***. 【諺】說比做容易。

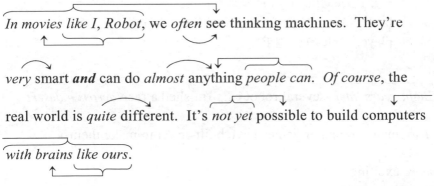

In movies like I, Robot, we *often* see thinking machines. They're

very smart ***and*** can do *almost* anything *people can*. *Of course*, the

real world is *quite* different. It's *not yet* possible to build computers

with brains like ours.

像在電影《機械公敵》中，我們常常看到會思考的機器。它們絕頂聰明，而且幾乎可以做任何人類能做的事情。當然，真實世界跟電影大不相同，還不能創造出有著像我們頭腦一樣的電腦。

* robot¹ 〔ˈrobət〕 n. 機器人
I, Robot 機械公敵【2004 年上映的美國科幻動作片，改編自同名短篇
　小説《*I, Robot*》。小説作者 Isaac Asimov 是美國科幻小説代表作者
　之一】
thinking¹ 〔ˈθɪŋkɪŋ〕 adj. 會思考的　　brain² 〔bren〕 n. 頭腦

However, we can program machines *to be good at certain skills.*

For example, *in 1997*, a supercomputer beat the world's best chess
player.

然而，我們可以替機器設計程式，使它們專精於某些技能。例如，
在 1997 年，一台超級電腦打敗了世界頂尖的西洋棋選手。

* *be good at* 擅長於　　certain¹ 〔ˈsɝtn̩〕 adj. 某種；某些
skill¹ 〔skɪl〕 n. 技能
supercomputer 〔ˈsupɚˌkəmˈpjutɚ〕 n. 超級電腦【也叫超高速電腦，
　指計算速度跟容量都領先世界的電腦，每秒計算速度達一兆筆以上。
　文中打敗西洋棋高手的超級電腦，是特別專精於下西洋棋，名為「深
　藍（Deep Blue）」的超級電腦】
beat¹ 〔bit〕 v. 打敗　　chess² 〔tʃɛs〕 n. 西洋棋
player¹ 〔ˈpleɚ〕 n. 選手

Eight years later, several robot cars finished a race *across a desert.*

Also, many computer games have built-in AI to make them

more exciting.

八年後，有好幾台機器車完成了一場橫越沙漠的比賽。而且，很多
電腦遊戲有內建的人工智慧，能使遊戲更刺激。

* race¹ 〔res〕 n. 比賽　　across¹ 〔əˈkrɔs〕 prep. 橫越

desert² 〔ˈdɛzɚt 〕 *n.* 沙漠　　also¹ 〔ˈɔlso 〕 *adv.* 也；此外
built-in 〔ˈbɪltˈɪn 〕 *adj.* 內建的　　exciting² 〔 ɪkˈsaɪtɪŋ 〕 *adj.* 刺激的

And that's *just* the beginning. *In the future*, computers *with AI*
will handle many more jobs.

而那都只是開始而已。在未來，有人工智慧的電腦，將能處理更多
多工作。

* beginning¹ 〔 bɪˈgɪnɪŋ 〕 *n.* 開始　　future² 〔ˈfjutʃɚ 〕 *n.* 未來

They'll help out *at banks*, *stores*, ***and*** *police departments*. *Also,*
expect to see more robots (*like Sony's AIBO*) ***that*** *use AI.*

它們能在銀行、商店，和警察局裡幫忙。而且預計會看到更多使用
人工智慧的機器人（像是新力公司的愛寶寵物狗）。

* ***help out*** 幫助　　***police department*** 警局
expect² 〔 ɪkˈspɛkt 〕 *v.* 預計；預料
Sony 〔ˈsonɪ 〕 *n.* 新力公司【日本科技公司】
AIBO 〔ˈaɪbo 〕 *n.* 愛寶寵物狗【新力公司開發的電子寵物狗】

All these changes will make the world a *very* different ***yet***
very interesting place.

所有這些改變會讓世界變成一個非常很不一樣，但卻很有趣的地方。

* yet¹ 〔 jɛt 〕 *conj.* 但是；然而

1. (**D**) 關於聰明的機器，本文暗示什麼？

　　(A) 它們會照著電腦的指令運作。

(B) 它們多數都是在達特茅斯大學製成。

(C) 只有科學家才對它們有興趣。

(D) 我們已經研究它們超過五十年了。

* ***work on*** 從事；致力於

2. (**A**) 通常會思考的機器在電影中是如何呈現？

(A) 它們和現實世界中的機器人不同。

(B) 它們有時候會有不只一個頭腦。

(C) 它們不如現今的機器聰明。

(D) 它們經常對抗人類。

* show¹〔ʃo〕v. 顯現；描述
unlike¹〔ʌn'laɪk〕n. 不像
real-world n. 存在於現實世界的；真實的
smart¹〔smɑrt〕adj. 聰明的　　***fight against*** 對抗

3. (**C**) 電腦仍然不能做什麼？

(A) 駕車橫越沙漠。

(B) 打敗優秀的西洋棋選手。

(C) 像人一樣思考。

(D) 很會玩電腦遊戲。

* unable¹〔ʌn'ebḷ〕adj. 不能夠的
excellent²〔'ɛksḷənt〕adj. 優秀的

4. (**A**) 第二段的 "**term**" 是什麼意思？

(A) ***phrase***²〔frez〕n. 措辭；說法；片語

(B) length²〔lɛŋθ〕n. 長度

(C) period²〔'pɪrɪəd〕n. 時期；期間

(D) rule¹〔rul〕n. 規則；規定

* mean¹〔min〕v. 意思是

TEST 6

Read the following passage and choose the best answer for each question.

Scientists are struggling to find the cause of a terrifying disease that is killing off numerous species of starfish on both the Pacific and Atlantic coasts of North America. Researchers said that they have ruled out some of the possible **_culprits_**, including fungi, some parasites and certain types of microbes. Now they're considering whether viruses or bacteria may be to blame.

The starfish, also called sea stars, are being wiped out by an unexplained tissue-weakening disease that causes white wounds to appear. The animal's body eventually breaks, spilling out its internal organs and leaving a hollow shell. This epidemic is very likely to cause some of these species to go extinct.

The mysterious infectious illness is affecting 18 different West Coast species along their entire range. The disease appeared last year and is showing no indication of diminishing. Scientists and biologists are worried about its origin and pattern of progression. They are even afraid that the disease could be a sign of another devastating affliction in the future for other marine species. Scientists are also wondering whether the starfish have been infected by a virus, bacterium or something else unwittingly imported to the region, or whether a pre-existing unfound disease somehow has evolved into such a dangerous one.

Since sea stars are significant predators, if they go extinct, there will be some really huge impacts on the ecosystems they live in.

1. What is the passage mainly about?
   (A) Scientists found that fungi are not responsible for the fatal disease.
   (B) Starfish will spill out their organs before they die.
   (C) Some species of starfish may go extinct because of a deadly disease.
   (D) Eighteen species of starfish are affected by an unknown disease.

2. Which of the following is closest in meaning to the word *culprits*?

   (A) solutions

   (B) criminals

   (C) events

   (D) chances

3. If a starfish contracts the disease, what happens after it develops white wounds?

   (A) It spills out its organs.

   (B) It lives.

   (C) It goes extinct.

   (D) Its infects other starfish.

4. According to the third paragraph, what are scientists worried about?

   (A) What is causing the disease to diminish.

   (B) How starfish recover.

   (C) How people import goods from overseas.

   (D) How the ecosystem will be affected.

TEST 6 詳解

Scientists are struggling to find the cause *of a terrifying disease*

*that is killing off numerous species of starfish on **both** the Pacific **and***

Atlantic coasts of North America.

科學家正努力找出，造成可怕疾病的原因，這種在北美太平洋和大西洋岸邊的疾病，正殺光許多種海星。

* scientist[2]〔ˈsaɪəntɪst〕*n.* 科學家
  struggle[2]〔ˈstrʌgl̩〕*v.* 努力；掙扎
  cause[1]〔kɔz〕*n.* 原因　*v.* 造成
  terrifying[4]〔ˈtɛrəˌfaɪɪŋ〕*adj.* 可怕的 (= *horrible*[3])
  disease[3]〔dɪˈziz〕*n.* 疾病　　***kill off*** 殺光
  numerous[4]〔ˈnjumərəs〕*adj.* 許多的 (= *many*[1])
  species[4]〔ˈspiʃɪz〕*n.* 物種【單複數同形】
  starfish[3]〔ˈstɑrˌfɪʃ〕*n.* 海星
  Pacific〔pəˈsɪfɪk〕*adj.* 太平洋的
  Atlantic〔ətˈlæntɪk〕*adj.* 大西洋的
  coast[1]〔kost〕*n.* 海岸；沿岸地區

Researchers said *that* they have ruled out some *of the possible*

*culprits, including fungi, some parasites **and** certain types of microbes.*

研究人員說，他們已經排除一些可能的罪犯，包括真菌、一些寄生蟲，以及某些類型的微生物。

* researcher[4]〔rɪ'sɝtʃɚ〕 *n.* 研究人員　　***rule out*** 排除
culprit〔'kʌprɪt〕 *n.* 罪犯（ = *criminal*[3]）
including[4]〔ɪn'kludɪŋ〕*prep.* 包括
fungi[3]〔'fʌŋgaɪ〕*n. pl.* 眞菌類【單數 fungus〔'fʌŋgəs〕】
parasite〔'pærə,saɪt〕*n.* 寄生蟲
certain[1]〔'sɝtn̩〕*adj.* 某些　　type[2]〔taɪp〕*n.* 類型
microbe〔'maɪkrob〕*n.* 微生物；病菌

Now they're considering ***whether*** *viruses **or** bacteria may be to blame.*
現在他們認爲，原因可能是病毒或是細菌。

* consider[2]〔kən'sɪdɚ〕*v.* 認爲；考慮
whether···or··· 是···或是···　　virus[4]〔'vaɪrəs〕*n.* 病毒
bacteria[3]〔bæk'tɪrɪə〕*n. pl.* 細菌【單數 bacterium[3]〔bæk'tɪrɪəm〕】
blame[3]〔blem〕*v.* 責備
be to blame 該受責備；應負責任；是（某種不良後果的）原因

The starfish, *also called sea stars*, are being wiped out *by an*

*unexplained tissue-weakening disease **that** causes white wounds to*

appear.

　　海星也稱爲 sea stars，正被一種不知名的弱化組織疾病所消滅，
這種疾病會造成海星出現白色傷口。

* ***wipe out*** 消滅；使···死亡
unexplained〔ʌnɪk'splend〕*adj.* 未解釋的；未說明的；原因不明的
tissue[3]〔'tɪʃju〕*n.* 組織　　weaken[3]〔'wikən〕*v.* 使虛弱
tissue-weakening *adj.* 弱化組織的
wound[2]〔wund〕*n.* 傷口　　appear[1]〔ə'pɪr〕*v.* 出現

The animal's body *eventually* breaks, *spilling out its internal organs*
and *leaving a hollow shell.*

海星的身體最後會裂開，內部的器官流出來，然後剩下空殼。

* eventually[4] (ɪ'vɛntʃʊəlɪ) *adv.* 最後
  break[1] (brek) *v.* 破裂　　spill[3] (spɪl) *v.* 灑出 < *out* >
  internal[3] (ɪn'tɝnḷ) *adj.* 內部的
  organ[2] ('ɔrgən) *n.* 器官　　hollow[3] ('halo) *adj.* 中空的
  shell[2] (ʃɛl) *n.* 貝殼；甲殼

This epidemic is *very* likely to cause some *of these species* to go
extinct.

這種傳染病很有可能會造成某些種類的海星絕種。

* epidemic[6] (ˌɛpɪ'dɛmɪk) *n.* 傳染病
  likely[1] ('laɪklɪ) *adj.* 可能的
  go[1] (go) *v.* 變得 (= *become*[1])
  extinct[5] (ɪk'stɪŋkt) *adj.* 絕種的

The mysterious infectious illness is affecting 18 different West
Coast species *along their entire range.*

這種神祕的傳染病，正影響著西岸十八個不同的物種和牠們的整個
生存區域。

* mysterious[4] (mɪs'tɪrɪəs) *adj.* 神祕的
  infectious[6] (ɪn'fɛkʃəs) *adj.* 傳染的 (= *contagious*[5])
  illness[2] ('ɪlnɪs) *n.* 疾病　　affect[3] (ə'fɛkt) *v.* 影響
  entire[2] (ɪn'taɪr) *adj.* 整個的
  range[2] ('rendʒ) *n.* 範圍；區域；（動植物的）分布

The disease appeared *last year **and*** is showing no indication *of*

diminishing.

這個疾病去年出現，而且現在並沒有減少的跡象。

* indication[4] 〔͵ɪndə'keʃən〕 *n.* 指標；跡象 (= *sign*[2])
  diminish[6] 〔də'mɪnɪʃ〕 *v.* 減少 (= *decrease*[4])

Scientists ***and*** biologists are worried about its origin ***and*** pattern *of*

progression.

科學家和生物學家擔心，此疾病的來源以及它發展的模式。

* biologist 〔baɪ'ɑlədʒɪst〕 *n.* 生物學家
  origin[3] 〔'ɔrədʒɪn〕 *n.* 起源　　pattern[2] 〔'pætən〕 *n.* 模式
  progression 〔prə'grɛʃən〕 *n.* 發展；連續

They are *even* afraid ***that*** *the disease could be a sign of another*

devastating affliction in the future for other marine species.

他們甚至擔心，此疾病對其他海洋物種而言，可能是未來另一種毀滅性
疾病的徵兆。

* afraid[1] 〔ə'frɛd〕 *adj.* 害怕的；擔心的
  sign[2] 〔saɪn〕 *n.* 徵兆；跡象
  devastating 〔'dɛvəs͵tetɪŋ〕 *adj.* 毀滅性的
  affliction 〔ə'flɪkʃən〕 *n.* 疾病；折磨
  in the future 將來的
  marine[5] 〔mə'rin〕 *adj.* 海洋的

Scientists are *also* wondering **whether** the starfish have been infected

by a virus, bacterium **or** something else unwittingly imported to the

region, **or whether** a pre-existing unfound disease somehow has

evolved into such a dangerous one.

科學家們也想知道，海星是否已經受到由病毒、細菌或其他不經意被帶入此地區的東西所感染了，或是否是之前就早已存在，卻未被發現而不知爲何演化成如此危險的疾病。

* wonder[2]（'wʌndɚ）v. 想知道　infect[4]（ɪn'fɛkt）v. 傳染；感染
　unwittingly（ˌʌn'wɪtɪŋlɪ）adv. 不經意地；不知不覺地
　import[3]（ɪm'port）v. 進口；輸入；引進
　region[2]（'ridʒən）n. 地區　exist[2]（ɪg'zɪst）v. 存在
　pre-existing adj. 早已存在的
　unfound（ʌn'faʊnd）adj. 未被發現的
　somehow[3]（'sʌm,haʊ）adv. 不知爲什麼
　evolve[6]（ɪ'vɑlv）v. 進化；演化

Since sea stars are significant predators, **if** they go extinct, there

will be some *really* huge impacts *on the ecosystems they live in*.

　　因爲海星是相當重要的捕食者，如果牠們絕種，那將會對牠們所生存的生態系統造成一些極大的衝擊。

* significant[3]（sɪg'nɪfəkənt）adj. 重要的
　predator（'prɛdətɚ）n. 捕食者　huge[1]（hjudʒ）adj. 巨大的
　impact[4]（'ɪmpækt）n. 衝擊；影響（= influence[2] = effecft[2]）
　ecosystem（'ɛko,sɪstəm）n. 生態系統

1. (**C**) 本文主要是關於什麼？
   (A) 科學家發現真菌類不是這致命疾病的原因。
   (B) 海星在死之前會使牠們的器官流出。
   (C) 某些種類的海星可能會因為一種致命的疾病而絕種。
   (D) 有十八種海星受到不知名疾病的影響。

   * mainly² 〔'menlɪ 〕*adv.* 主要地
   responsible² 〔 rɪ'spɑnsəbḷ 〕*adj.* 應負責任的
   be responsible for 應對…負責；是…的原因；導致；造成
   fatal⁴ 〔'fetḷ 〕*adj.* 致命的 (= *deadly*⁶)
   unknown 〔 ʌn'non 〕*adj.* 不知道的；未知的

2. (**B**) 下列何者最接近 "**culprits**" 的意思？
   (A) solutions² 〔 sə'luʃənz 〕*n. pl.* 解決之道
   (B) *criminals*³ 〔'krɪmənḷz 〕*n. pl.* 罪犯
   (C) events² 〔 ɪ'vɛnts 〕*n. pl.* 事件；大事
   (D) chances¹ 〔 tʃæns 〕*n. pl.* 機會

3. (**A**) 如果一隻海星感染此疾病，在牠形成白色傷口後會發生什麼
   事？
   (A) 牠會流出牠的器官。　　(B) 牠會存活。
   (C) 牠會絕種。　　　　　　(D) 牠會傳染給其他的海星。

   * contract³ 〔 kən'trækt 〕*v.* 感染　　develop² 〔 dɪ'vɛləp 〕*v.* 形成

4. (**D**) 根據第三段，科學家擔心什麼？
   (A) 是什麼造成此疾病減少。
   (B) 海星如何復原。
   (C) 人們如何從海外進口貨物。
   (D) 生態系統將如何被影響。

   * recover³ 〔 rɪ'kʌvɚ 〕*v.* 恢復　　goods⁴ 〔 gʊdz 〕*n. pl.* 貨物
   overseas² 〔'ovɚ'siz 〕*adv.* 海外

TEST 7

Read the following passage and choose the best answer for each question.

Going to school means learning new skills and facts in subjects such as math, reading, science, history or geography. Many scientists have been interested in the relationship between how teacher behaviors are related to student learning. In a new study about how children learn math in elementary schools, Beilock and Levine, psychologists at the University of Chicago, found a surprising relationship between what female teachers think and what female students learn in terms of math learning.

The subjects of the study included 65 girls, 52 boys and 17 first- and second-grade teachers in elementary schools in the American Midwest. The students were asked to take math achievement tests at the beginning and also the end of the school year. The researchers then asked teachers how they felt when they came across math such as when reading a sales receipt. A teacher who got nervous when looking at the numbers on a sales receipt was probably anxious about math.

The test scores were later compared by the researchers. The result suggests that when female teachers feel anxious about math or uncomfortable with their own math skills, their female students tend to believe that boys are better at math than girls. Consequently, if this kind of belief persists, these girls may not do as well as they would have done if they were more confident. On the contrary, boys, on average, seem to be less affected by a teacher's anxiety.

The scale of the study, however, is too small to see large patterns. For later research, more subjects should be incorporated. This result needs to be interpreted as a **preliminary** one. If more studies find the same trend as this one, then it is likely that a teacher's anxiety over math can affect her female students.

1. According to the passage, the main finding of the research is that _____.
   (A) teachers' anxiety over math can affect both genders.
   (B) female students have more anxiety over math than male students.
   (C) female teachers' anxiety over math greatly affects female students' attitude toward math.
   (D) female teachers' anxiety has little to do with how confident students are in learning math.

2. The word "preliminary" is closest in meaning to
   _____.

   (A) mature   (B) optional
   (C) complete   (D) preparatory

3. What does the author suggest future researchers do?

   (A) Compare and contrast cross-cultural differences.
   (B) Include more samples of teachers and students.
   (C) Study the relationship between anxiety and other subjects.
   (D) Observe how teachers actually teach math in classrooms.

4. According to the findings of the research, what can be inferred about teaching math?

   (A) Teachers need to be confident about math and comfortable with teaching it, especially to female students.
   (B) Teachers need to make math more interesting by making use of visual aids.
   (C) Teachers should encourage slow learners by giving them fewer tests.
   (D) Teachers are advised to take new approaches rather than conventional ones to motivate student learning.

TEST 7 詳解

Going to school means learning new skills *and* facts *in subjects*

*such as math, reading, science, history **or** geography.*

　　上學的意思就是學習在數學、閱讀、科學、歷史或地理等的科目中新的技巧及事實。

* mean[1] 〔 min 〕 *v.* 意思是　　skill[1] 〔 skɪl 〕 *n.* 技巧；技能
subject[2] 〔'sʌbdʒɪkt 〕 *n.* 科目；接受實驗者
math[3] 〔 mæθ 〕 *n.* 數學 (= *mathematics*[3])
science[2] 〔'saɪəns 〕 *n.* 科學　　geography[2] 〔 dʒɪ'ɑgrəfɪ 〕 *n.* 地理學

Many scientists have been interested in *how teacher behaviors are*

related to student learning.

許多科學家感興趣的是，老師的行為與學生的學習狀況之間的關係。

* scientist[2] 〔'saɪəntɪst 〕 *n.* 科學家　　**be interested in** 對…感興趣
behavior[4] 〔 bɪ'hevjə 〕 *n.* 行為；態度　　**be related to** 和…有關
learning[4] 〔'lɜnɪŋ 〕 *n.* 學習；學問

*In a new study about **how** children learn math in elementary schools,*

Beilock and Levine, *psychologists at the University of Chicago,*

found a surprising relationship *between **what** female teachers think*

***and what** female students learn in terms of math learning.*

在一個探討小學生如何學習數學的新研究中，貝拉克跟萊文這兩位芝加哥大學的心理學家，發現一個驚人的事實：女教師對學習數學的想法與女學生學習數學有著令人驚訝的關係。

* study[1] 〔'stʌdɪ〕 *n.* 研究　***elementary school*** 小學
  Beilock〔be'lak〕 *n.* 貝拉克　　Levine〔lə'vaɪn〕 *n.* 萊文
  psychologist[4] 〔saɪ'kalədʒɪstɪ〕 *n.* 心理學家
  university[4] 〔ˌjunə'vɝsətɪ〕 *n.* 大學
  Chicago〔ʃə'kago〕 *n.* 芝加哥
  surprising[1] 〔sə'praɪzɪŋ〕 *adj.* 令人驚訝的
  relationship[2] 〔rɪ'leʃənʃɪp〕 *n.* 關係
  female[2] 〔'fimel〕 *adj.* 女性的　　***in terms of*** 就…而言

The subjects *of the study* included 65 girls, 52 boys ***and*** 17 first-

and second-grade teachers *in elementary schools in the American*

Midwest.

此研究的實驗對象，包括來自美國中西部一間小學的六十五名女學生、五十二名男學生，以及十七名一、二年級的老師。

* grade[2] 〔gred〕 *n.* 年級
  Midwest〔'mɪdˌwɛst〕 *n.*（美國）中西部

The students were asked to take math achievement tests *at the*

*beginning **and** also the end of the school year.*

這些學生被要求在學年之初與結束參加數學能力測驗。

* ***take a test*** 參加考試　　achievement[3] 〔ə'tʃivmənt〕 *n.* 成就
  school year 學年

The researchers *then* asked teachers *how they felt **when** they came across math such as **when** reading a sales receipt.*

研究人員則詢問老師，當他們遇到數學時的感覺，像是閱讀一張銷售收據時。

* researcher[4] 〔 rɪ'sɝtʃɚ 〕 *n.* 研究人員
  come across 偶然遇見
  sales 〔 selz 〕 *adj.* 銷售的
  receipt[3] 〔 rɪ'sit 〕 *n.* 收據

> come across 偶然遇見
> = run into
> = bump into
> = encounter[4]

A teacher *who got nervous **when** looking at the numbers on a sales receipt* was *probably* anxious about math.

一個老師若是看著銷售收據上的數字會感到緊張，那他可能會對數學感到焦慮。

* nervous[3] 〔 'nɝvəs 〕 *adj.* 緊張的　　anxious[4] 〔 'æŋkʃəs 〕 *adj.* 焦慮的

The test scores were *later* compared *by the researchers.*

測驗成績隨後就被研究人員拿來做比較。

* score[2] 〔 skor 〕 *n.* 分數；成績　　later[1] 〔 'letɚ 〕 *adv.* 後來
  compare[2] 〔 kəm'pɛr 〕 *v.* 比較

The result suggests ***that when** female teachers feel anxious about math **or** uncomfortable with their own math skills,* their female students tend to believe ***that** boys are better at math **than** girls.*

結果顯示，當女老師對於數學感到焦慮，或對自己的數學能力感到不安時，她們的女學生就比較容易相信，男生在數學方面就是比女生強。

> * result[2] 〔rɪ'zʌlt〕 *n.* 結果；成果
> suggest[3] 〔sə'dʒɛst〕 *v.* 顯示
> uncomfortable[2] 〔ʌn'kʌmfətəbḷ〕 *adj.* 不舒服的；不安的
> ***tend to V.*** 易於；傾向於（ = *be inclined to V.* ）
> ***be better at*** 比較精通【***be good at*** 精通】

Consequently, ***if this kind of belief persists***, these girls may not do as well ***as they would have done if they were more confident.***

因此，如果這樣的看法持續存在，這些失去信心的女學生可能就無法表現得很好。

> * consequently[4] 〔'kɑnsə,kwɛntlɪ〕 *adv.* 因此
> belief[2] 〔bɪ'lif〕 *n.* 信念；看法
> persist[5] 〔pɚ'zɪst,-'sɪst〕 *v.* 持續存在　　***do well*** 表現好
> confident[3] 〔'kɑnfədənt〕 *adj.* 有信心的

On the contrary, boys, *on average*, seem to be *less* affected *by a teacher's anxiety.*

相反地，平均而言，男學生似乎比較不受老師焦慮的態度所影響。

> * ***on the contrary*** 相反地　　***on average*** 平均而言；一般而言
> affect[3] 〔ə'fɛkt〕 *v.* 影響　　anxiety[4] 〔æŋ'zaɪətɪ〕 *n.* 焦慮

The scale *of the study*, *however*, is *too* small to see large patterns. *For later research*, more subjects should be included.

　　然而，這個研究的規模太小，我們無法看出大的模式。往後的研究
應該囊括更多的實驗對象。

　　* scale[3] 〔skel〕 *n.* 規模　　pattern[2] 〔'pætən〕 *n.* 模式
　　research[4] 〔rɪ'sɝtʃ〕 *n.* 研究

This result needs to be interpreted *as a <u>preliminary</u> one*.
這次的研究結果必須被解讀為初步結論。

　　* interpret[4] 〔ɪn'tɝprɪt〕 *v.* 解釋；口譯
　　preliminary[6] 〔prɪ'lɪmə,nɛrɪ〕 *adj.* 初步的

If more studies find the same trend as this one, then it is likely *that a*

teacher's anxiety over math can affect her female students.
如果更多的研究顯示出同樣的趨勢，那麼老師對於數學的焦慮，可能會
影響到她的女學生。

　　* trend[3] 〔trɛnd〕 *n.* 趨勢

1. (**C**) 根據本文，此研究主要的發現是 ＿＿＿＿＿＿＿＿ 。
    (A) 老師對數學的焦慮可能會影響男女學生
    (B) 女學生對數學的焦慮多於男學生
    (C) <u>女老師對數學的焦慮大大地影響了女學生對數學的態度</u>
    (D) 女老師的焦慮和學生學習數學的信心沒有太大的關聯

　　* main[2] 〔men〕 *adj.* 主要的
　　finding[1] 〔'faɪndɪŋ〕 *n.* 發現；研究的結果
　　gender[5] 〔'dʒɛndə〕 *n.* 性別　　male[5] 〔mel〕 *adj.* 男性的
　　attitude[3] 〔'ætə,tjud〕 *n.* 態度
　　toward[1] 〔tə'wɔrd〕 *prep.* 朝向…
　　have little to do with 和…沒什麼關聯

2.(**D**) "**preliminary**" 這個字的意思和 _____ 最接近。

    (A) mature[3] 〔 məˈtʃʊr 〕 adj. 成熟的

    (B) optional[6] 〔ˈɑpʃənḷ 〕 adj. 可選擇的

    (C) complete[2] 〔 kəmˈplit 〕 adj. 完整的；全部的

    (D) *preparatory* 〔 prɪˈpærə‚torɪ 〕 adj. 預備的；籌備的

3.(**B**) 作者建議未來的研究人員應該做什麼？

    (A) 對比和對照跨文化的差異。

    (B) <u>包含更多師生的樣本。</u>

    (C) 研究焦慮和其他學科之間的關聯。

    (D) 觀察老師實際上在課堂如何教數學。

    * contrast[4] 〔 kənˈtræst 〕 v. (為使差異明顯) 使 (兩物) 對照、對比
    cross-cultural adj. 不同文化間的；跨文化的
    sample[2] 〔ˈsæmpḷ 〕 n. 樣本

4.(**A**) 根據研究的結果，關於教數學可以推論出什麼？

    (A) <u>老師需要對數學有信心，而且自在地教學，特別是在教女</u>
    <u>學生。</u>

    (B) 老師需要藉由使用一些視覺教具讓數學更有趣。

    (C) 老師應該藉由舉行較少的測驗來鼓勵理解慢的學習者。

    (D) 老師被建議採用新的而不是傳統的方法激勵學生學習。

    * infer[6] 〔 ɪnˈfɝ 〕 v. 推論
    comfortable[2] 〔ˈkʌmfətəbḷ 〕 adj. 舒服的；自在的
    especially[2] 〔 əˈspɛʃəlɪ 〕 adv. 尤其；特別是
    make use of 利用   visual[4] 〔ˈvɪʒʊəl 〕 adj. 視覺的
    aid[2] 〔 ed 〕 n. 幫助；(pl.) 補助器具   *visual aids* 視覺教具
    encourage[2] 〔 ɪnˈkɝɪdʒ 〕 v. 鼓勵   slow[1] 〔 slo 〕 adj. 遲鈍的
    give a test 舉行考試   advise[3] 〔 ədˈvaɪz 〕 v. 勸告；建議
    approach[3] 〔 əˈprotʃ 〕 n. 方法   *rather than* 而不是
    conventional[4] 〔 kənˈvɛnʃənḷ 〕 adj. 傳統的
    motivate[4] 〔ˈmotə‚vet 〕 v. 激勵

TEST 8

Read the following passage and choose the best answer for each question.

A very important world problem is the increasing number of people on this planet. In an early survey conducted in 1888, there were only a billion and a half people. Now the population exceeds six billion and is growing fast. Even though the rate of growth has begun to slow down, most experts believe the population will exceed nine billion within the next 40 years.

So why is this huge increase in population taking place? Through various technological innovations that include farming methods and sanitation, as well as the control of deadly diseases, we have found ways to reduce the rate at which we die—creating a population explosion. We used to think that reaching seventy years old was a remarkable achievement, but now eighty or even ninety is considered the normal lifespan for humans. Biologically **this is the very definition of success** and we have become the dominant animal on the planet.

If we examine the amount of land available for this ever-increasing population, we begin to see a problem. If everyone on the planet had an equal share of land, we would each have about 50,000 square meters. This figure seems to be quite encouraging until we examine the type of land we would have. Not all land is useful to humans as it cannot produce food. We can cut out about one fifth of it because it is permanently covered by snow and ice. Then we can cut out another fifth because it is desert. Another fifth is too mountainous or is too great a height above sea-level. A tenth doesn't have enough soil for crops to grow—it is bare rock. Obviously, with so little land to support us, we should be taking great care not to reduce it further.

1. What is the main purpose of the first paragraph?
   (A) To stress how quickly the world population is rising.
   (B) To argue that world population has to be reduced.
   (C) To put emphasis on the need for a large world population.
   (D) To introduce the reasons for the growth in world population.

2. According to the passage, all of the following bring about a reduction in death rates except
   _____.

   (A) better control of fatal diseases
   (B) democratic society
   (C) clean surroundings
   (D) improved food production

3. "**This is the very definition of success**" refers to
   _____.

   (A) new inventions
   (B) becoming 70 years old
   (C) having an average lifespan
   (D) having a lifespan of 80 to 90 years

4. How much per person of the earth's surface can be used to grow food?
   (A) 25,000 square meters.
   (B) 15,000 square meters.
   (C) 5,000 square meters.
   (D) 2,500 square meters.

TEST 8 詳解

A *very* important world problem is the increasing number *of people on this planet*.

一個很重要的全球問題就是，世界上的人越來越多了。

* increasing[2] 〔ɪnˈkrisɪŋ〕*adj.* 越來越多的；日益增加的
  planet[2] 〔ˈplænɪt〕*n.* 行星【在此指「地球」】

In an early survey conducted in 1888, there were only a billion *and* a half people. *Now* the population exceeds six billion *and* is *growing fast*.

在早期 1888 年所做的一份調查中，全世界只有十五億人。現在，人口總數已經超過六十億，而且正在快速成長中。

* survey[3] 〔ˈsɝve〕*n.* 調查　　conduct[5] 〔kənˈdʌkt〕*v.* 進行
  billion[3] 〔ˈbɪljən〕*n.* 十億
  population[2] 〔͵pɑpjəˈleʃən〕*n.* 人口總數
  exceed[5] 〔ɪkˈsid〕*v.* 超過　　grow[1] 〔gro〕*v.* 成長；生長

Even though the rate of growth has begun to slow down, most experts believe *the population will exceed nine billion within the next 40 years*.

即使增加的速度已經開始減慢，但是大多數的專家認為，在接下來的四十年內，人口會超過九十億。

* *even though* 即使　　rate[3] 〔ret〕*n.* 速度；比率

slow down 減慢　　expert[2] 〔ˈɛkspɝt〕*n.* 專家
within[2] 〔wɪðˈɪn〕*prep.* 在⋯之內

So why is this huge increase *in population* taking place?
所以為什麼人口總數會如此大量地增加呢？

* **huge**[1] 〔hjudʒ〕*adj.* 巨大的　　**increase**[2] 〔ˈɪnkris〕*n.* 增加
take place 發生

Through *various technological innovations* ***that*** *include farming*

methods ***and*** *sanitation,* ***as well as*** *the control of deadly diseases,* we

have found ways *to reduce the rate at* ***which*** *we die*—*creating a*

population explosion.

透過各種不同的科技創新，包括農耕方法還有環境衛生，以及對致命疾
病的控制，我們已經找到方法降低死亡率——創造人口總數的劇增。

* **through**[1] 〔θru〕*prep.* 透過　　**various**[3] 〔ˈvɛrɪəs〕*adj.* 各種不同的
technological[4] 〔ˌtɛknəˈlɑdʒɪkḷ〕*adj.* 科技的
innovation[6] 〔ˌɪnəˈveʃən〕*n.* 創新
include[2] 〔ɪnˈklud〕*v.* 包括
farming 〔ˈfɑrmɪŋ〕*n.* 農業　*adj.* 農業的；用來耕種的
method[2] 〔ˈmɛθəd〕*n.* 方法
sanitation[6] 〔ˌsænəˈteʃən〕*n.* 環境衛生
control[2] 〔kənˈtrol〕*n.* 控制　　**deadly**[6] 〔ˈdɛdlɪ〕*adj.* 致命的
disease[3] 〔dɪˈziz〕*n.* 疾病　　**reduce**[3] 〔rɪˈdjus〕*v.* 減少
create[2] 〔krɪˈet〕*v.* 創造
explosion[4] 〔ɪkˈsploʒən〕*n.* 爆炸；擴張；劇增

We used to think ***that*** *reaching seventy years old was a remarkable*

achievement, ***but*** *now* eighty ***or*** *even* ninety is considered the normal

lifespan *for humans.*

我們以前總認爲，活到七十歲是一項非常卓越的成就，但現在八十歲或
甚至九十歲，都被認爲是正常的人類壽命。

> * ***used to*** + ***V.*** 以前… reach[1] 〔 ritʃ 〕 v. 抵到
> remarkable[4] 〔 rɪ'mɑrkəbḷ 〕 adj. 卓越的；出色的
> achievement[3] 〔 ə'tʃivmənt 〕 n. 成就
> consider[3] 〔 kən'sɪdɚ 〕 v. 認爲　　***be considered*** (***to be***) 被認爲是
> normal[3] 〔'nɔrmḷ 〕 adj. 正常的　　lifespan 〔'laɪf,spæn 〕 n. 壽命

Biologically this is the *very* definition *of success* ***and*** we have

become the dominant animal *on the planet.*

在生物學上，這就是成功的定義，而我們已經成爲地球上最有勢力的動
物。

> * biologically[6] 〔,baɪə'lɑdʒɪkḷɪ 〕 adv. 生物學地
> very[1] 〔'vɛrɪ 〕 adv. 正是；就是
> definition[3] 〔,dɛfə'nɪʃən 〕 n. 定義　　success[2] 〔 sək'sɛs 〕 n. 成功
> dominant[4] 〔'dɑmənənt 〕 adj. 最有勢力的；佔優勢的

If *we examine the amount of land available for this ever-increasing*

population, we begin to see a problem.

　　如果我們查看可供這些不斷增加的人口可使用的土地數量，我們就
會開始看到一個問題。

* examine[1] 〔 ɪg'zæmɪn 〕 *v.* 檢查；仔細研究
amount[2] 〔 ə'maʊnt 〕 *n.* 數量
available[3] 〔 ə'veləbḷ 〕 *adj.* 可獲得的；可使用的
ever-increasing 〔 ə'veləbḷ 〕 *adj.* 不斷增加的

If everyone on the planet had an equal share of land, we would each have about 50,000 square meters.

如果地球上的每個人都能擁有相同大小的土地，我們每個人就會有大約五萬平方公尺的土地。

* equal[1] 〔 'ikwəl 〕 *adj.* 相等的　　share[2] 〔 ʃɛr 〕 *n.* 一份
square[2] 〔 skwɛr 〕 *adj.* 平方的　　meter[2] 〔 mitɚ 〕 *n.* 公尺

This figure seems to be *quite* encouraging ***until** we examine the type of land we would have.*

這個數字看來還蠻令人開心的，直到我們檢視我們擁有的土地類型。

* figure[2] 〔 'fɪgjɚ 〕 *n.* 數字
encouraging[2] 〔 ɪn'kɝɪdʒɪŋ 〕 *adj.* 鼓舞人心的　　type[2] 〔 taɪp 〕 *n.* 類型

Not all land is useful *to humans **as** it cannot produce food.* We can cut out about one fifth of it ***because** it is permanently covered by snow **and** ice.*

當土地不能生產食物時，那就不是全部的土地都對人類有用。我們可能要去除大約五分之一的土地，因為這些的土地長年被冰雪所覆蓋。

* useful[1] (ˈjusfəl) *adj.* 有用的　　produce[2] (prəˈdjus) *v.* 生產
cut out 除去　　***one fifth*** 五分之一
permanently[4] (ˈpɝmənəntlɪ) *adv.* 永久地　　cover[1] (ˈkʌvɚ) *v.* 覆蓋

Then we can cut out another fifth ***because*** *it is desert.* Another fifth

is *too* mountainous *or* is *too* great a height *above sea-level.*
然後我們可以再除去另外的五分之一，因為是沙漠。另外五分之一是太
多山，或是海拔太高的土地。

* desert[2] (ˈdɛzɚt) *n.* 沙漠　　mountainous[4] (ˈmauntn̩əs) *adj.* 多山的
too[1] (tu) *adv.* 過於…；太…　　height[2] (haɪt) *n.* 高度
too great a height 高度太高（ = a too great height ）
【 ***too large a room*** 房間太大（ = a too large room ）】
sea-level (ˈsiˈlɛvl̩) *n.* 海平面

A tenth doesn't have enough soil *for crops to grow*—it is bare rock.
十分之一的土地沒有足夠的土壤讓農作物生長──只有光禿禿的岩石。

* ***a tenth*** 十分之一　　soil[1] (sɔɪl) *n.* 土壤
crop[2] (krɑp) *n.* 農作物　　bare[3] (bɛr) *adj.* 光禿的

Obviously, *with so little land to support us,* we should be taking great

care *not to reduce it further.*

顯然，只有這麼少的土地能養活我們，我們應該要很小心，不要讓能使
用的土地再減少下去。

* obviously[3] (ˈɑbvɪəslɪ) *adv.* 明顯地；顯然
support[2] (səˈport) *v.* 支持；養活　　***take care*** 小心；注意
further[2] (ˈfɝðɚ) *adv.* 更進一步地

1. (**A**) 第一段的主要目的是什麼？

(A) 強調世界人口總數增加得有多快。

(B) 主張世界人口總數必須減少。

(C) 強調需要大量的世界人口總數。

(D) 介紹世界人口總數成長的原因。

*stress[2] 〔strɛs〕v. 強調　　rise[1] 〔raɪz〕v. 上升；增加
argue[2] 〔'ɑrgju〕v. 主張；認為　　emphasis[4] 〔'ɛmfəsɪs〕n. 強調
***put emphasis on** 強調 (= emphasize[3])
introduce[2] 〔ˌɪntrə'djus〕v. 介紹；提出
growth[2] 〔groθ〕n. 成長；增加

2. (**B**) 根據本文，以下都會造成死亡率的減少，除了＿＿＿＿＿＿。

(A) 對致命疾病較好的控制　　(B) 民主社會

(C) 乾淨的環境　　　　　　　(D) 改良的糧食生產方式

****bring about** 導致；造成　　reduction[4] 〔rɪ'dʌkʃən〕n. 減少
death rate 死亡率　　except[1] 〔ɪk'spɛt〕prep. 除了
democratic[5] 〔ˌdɛmə'krætɪk〕adj. 民主的
society[2] 〔sə'saɪətɪ〕n. 社會
surroundings[4] 〔sə'raʊndɪŋz〕n. pl. 環境
improved[2] 〔ɪm'pruvd〕adj. 改進過的；改良的
production[4] 〔prə'dʌkʃən〕n. 生產

3. (**D**) "**This is the very definition of success**" 是指＿＿＿＿＿。

(A) 新發明　　　　　　　(B) 變成七十歲

(C) 有平均的壽命　　　　(D) 有八十到九十歲的壽命

****refer to** 是指　　invention[4] 〔ɪn'vɛnʃənt〕n. 發明
average[3] 〔'ævərɪdʒ〕adj. 平均的

4. (**B**) 每個人在地表上可以種植食物的土地有多少？

(A) 25,000 平方公尺。　　(B) 15,000 平方公尺。

(C) 5,000 平方公尺。　　　(D) 2,500 平方公尺。

*per[2] 〔pɚ〕prep. 每…　　surface[2] 〔'sɝfɪs〕n. 表面
$50,000 \times (1 - 1/5 - 1/5 - 1/5 - 1/10) = 50,000 \times 0.3 = 15,000$

TEST 9

Read the following passage and choose the best answer for each question.

One of the most dangerous drugs for pregnant women to consume is alcohol. Because alcohol is delivered quickly into the blood and passes quickly into the tissues and membranes, the human fetus is particularly vulnerable to its effects. In fact, the negative effects on a fetus are so obvious that babies born after exposure to alcohol are said to be suffering from fetal alcohol syndrome.

As a pregnant woman drinks alcohol, the alcohol is passed into her bloodstream almost simultaneously. Moreover, because the bloodstream of the fetus is tied to that of the mother, the alcohol passes directly into the bloodstream of the fetus as well. Furthermore, the concentration of alcohol in the fetus is exactly the same as in the mother. For the mother, this concentration is not a problem because her liver can remove one ounce of alcohol from her system per hour. However, the fetus's liver is not completely developed. The rate at which it is able to take the alcohol from the blood of the fetus is much slower.

Eventually, the alcohol will be returned to the mother's system by passing across the placenta, but this process is slow. By the time this takes place, major neurological damage may have already occurred. Research has shown that as little as one drink of alcohol can produce significant, irreversible damage to the fetus. Babies born after exposure to alcohol generally exhibit facial distortion, inability to concentrate, and difficulty in remembering. Simply speaking, it is a must that pregnant women avoid alcohol.

1. What is the passage mainly about?
   (A) Women and drugs.
   (B) The dangers of pregnancy.
   (C) The dangers of drinking while pregnant.
   (D) Drinking and the human body.

2. How much time does it take alcohol to enter a woman's bloodstream after she takes a drink?
   (A) About one hour.
   (B) A few seconds.
   (C) Several minutes.
   (D) At least 24 hours.

3. What can be inferred from the passage?

   (A) Drugs have a greater effect on a fetus than they do on its mother.

   (B) It takes only one alcoholic drink to kill a fetus.

   (C) Large fetuses are not adversely affected by alcohol.

   (D) Fathers should also avoid alcohol when expecting a child.

4. According to the passage, how is alcohol finally returned to the mother's system?

   (A) It is carried through the bloodstream.

   (B) It is transferred across the placenta.

   (C) It is expelled by the fetus's liver.

   (D) It is not completely returned.

【劉毅老師的話】

　　做「7000 字閱讀測驗」，裡面沒有超出 7000 字範圍的單字，可以當課本一樣朗讀，等於複習「高中常用 7000 字」。

TEST 9 詳解

One *of the most dangerous drugs for pregnant women to consume*
is alcohol.

對孕婦來說，所服用的藥物中，最危險的就是酒精。

* dangerous[2] (ˈdendʒərəs) *adj.* 危險的
 drug[2] (drʌg) *n.* 藥；毒品　　pregnant[4] (ˈprɛgnənt) *adj.* 懷孕的
 consume[4] (kənˈsum) *v.* 吃；喝　　alcohol[4] (ˈælkəˌhɔl) *n.* 酒精

Because alcohol is delivered quickly into the blood *and* passes quickly

into the tissues and membranes, the human fetus is *particularly*

vulnerable *to its effects.*

因爲酒精會被迅速輸送到血液裡，並很快地通過組織和細胞膜，所以人
類的胎兒特別容易受到酒精的影響。

* deliver[2] (dɪˈlɪvɚ) *v.* 傳送　　blood[1] (blʌd) *n.* 血液
 tissue[3] (ˈtɪʃʊ) *n.* 組織　　membrane (ˈmɛmbren) *n.* (薄) 膜
 human[1] (ˈhjumən) *n.* 人類　　fetus (ˈfitəs) *n.* 胎兒
 particularly[2] (pɚˈtɪkjələˌlɪ) *adv.* 尤其；特別地
 vulnerable[6] (ˈvʌlnərəbl) *adj.* 易受傷害的；易受影響的
 effect[2] (ɪˈfɛkt) *n.* 影響

In fact, the negative effects *on a fetus* are *so* obvious *that babies*

born after exposure to alcohol are said to be suffering from fetal

alcohol syndrome.

事實上，這種對胎兒的負面影響非常明顯，以致於接觸過酒精的嬰兒出生後，據說會罹患胎兒酒精症候群。

* negative[2] 〔'nɛɡətɪv〕 *adj.* 負面的（↔ positive[2] *adj.* 正面的）
obvious[3] 〔'ɑbvɪəs〕 *adj.* 明顯的
exposure[4] 〔ɪk'spoʒɚ〕 *n.* 接觸 < to >
be said to V. 據說⋯ ***suffer from*** 罹患（疾病）
fetal 〔'fitḷ〕 *adj.* 胎兒的 syndrome 〔'sɪn‚drom〕 *n.* 症候群
fetal alcohol syndrome 胎兒酒精症候群【簡稱 FAS，懷孕期間喝酒的婦女可能產下罹患 FAS 的嬰兒，酒精可能會使胎兒生長遲緩、腦部跟神經系統受損，這些都是永久的傷害，醫生建議懷孕期間最好完全不要喝酒】

As a pregnant woman drinks alcohol, the alcohol is passed *into*

her bloodstream almost simultaneously.

當孕婦飲酒時，酒精幾乎會同時進入她的血液。

* bloodstream 〔'blʌd‚strim〕 *n.* （循環體內的）血流
simultaneously[6] 〔‚saɪmḷ'tenɪəslɪ〕 *adv.* 同時地

Moreover, ***because** the bloodstream of the fetus is tied to **that** of the*

mother, the alcohol passes *directly into the bloodstream of the fetus*

as well.

而且，因為胎兒的血液流動與母親的相連，所以酒精也會直接進入胎兒的血液。

* moreover[4] 〔mor'ovɚ〕 *adv.* 此外；而且 ***be tied to*** 和～連結
directly[1] 〔də'rɛktlɪ〕 *adv.* 直接地；立即地 ***as well*** 也（= *too*）

Furthermore, the concentration *of alcohol in the fetus* is *exactly* the

same *as in the mother*.

此外，在胎兒體內的酒精濃度和母親體內的酒精濃度是完全相同的。

* furthermore[4]〔'fɝðə,mor〕*adv.* 此外；而且
  concentration[4]〔,kɑnsn̩'treʃən〕*n.* 濃度
  exactly[2]〔ɪg'zæktlɪ〕*adv.* 確切地；完全地
  exactly the same as 和…完全相同

For the mother, this concentration is not a problem *because* her liver

can remove one ounce of alcohol from her system per hour.

對母親來說，這種濃度不會是問題，因為母親的肝臟每小時可以從她的
身體中移除掉一盎司的酒精。

* liver[3]〔'lɪvə〕*n.* 肝臟　　remove[3]〔rɪ'muv〕*v.* 移除
  ounce[5]〔auns〕*n.* 盎司【重量單位，簡寫作 oz.，等於 1/16 磅】
  system[3]〔'sɪstəm〕*n.* 系統；身體　　per[2]〔pə〕*prep.* 每～

However, the fetus's liver is not *completely* developed. The rate *at*

which it is able to take the alcohol from the blood of the fetus is *much*

slower.

然而，胎兒的肝臟還沒發育完全，能從血液中除去酒精的速率也緩慢得
多。

* completely[2]〔kəm'plitlɪ〕*adv.* 完全地
  develop[2]〔dɪ'vɛləp〕*v.* 發展；發育　　rate[3]〔ret〕*n.* 速率
  be able to V. 能夠…

Eventually, the alcohol will be returned *to the mother's system by passing across the placenta*, *but* this process is slow. *By the time this takes place*, major neurological damage may have *already* occurred.

最後，酒精會通過胎盤，回到母親的身體，但這個過程很慢。等到這個過程發生的時候，可能已經造成胎兒重大的神經損傷。

* eventually[4] (ɪˋvɛntʃʊəlɪ) *adv.* 最後   return[1] (rɪˋtɝn) *v.* 返回
placenta (pləˋsɛntə) *n.* 胎盤   process[3] (ˋprɑsɛs) *n.* 過程
by the time 到了…的時候   *take place* 發生
major[3] (ˋmedʒɚ) *adj.* 重大的
neurological (ˏnjʊrəˋlɑdʒɪkəl) *adj.* 神經的
damage[2] (ˋdæmɪdʒ) *n.* 損害   occur[2] (əˋkɝ) *v.* 發生

Research has shown *that as little as one drink of alcohol can produce significant, irreversible damage to the fetus.*

研究顯示，只要喝一口酒，就會對胎兒造成顯著且無法復原的傷害。

* research[4] (ˋrisɝtʃ) *n.* 研究
drink[1] (drɪŋk) *n.* (酒的) 一杯；一口
produce[2] (prəˋdus) *v.* 產生
significant[3] (sɪgˋnɪfəkənt) *adj.* 顯著的；相當大的
irreversible (ˏɪrɪˋvɝsəbl̩) *adj.* 不可逆轉的

Babies *born after exposure to alcohol generally* exhibit facial distortion, inability *to concentrate*, *and* difficulty *in remembering*.

接觸過酒精後出生的嬰兒，通常會出現臉部扭曲、注意力無法集中，和記憶困難的現象。

* generally[2] ('dʒɛnərəlɪ) *adv.* 通常　　exhibit[4] (ɪg'zɪbɪt) *v.* 顯示
facial[4] ('feʃəl) *adj.* 臉部的　　distortion[6] (dɪs'tɔrʃən) *n.* 扭曲
inability[2] (,ɪnə'bɪlətɪ) *n.* 無能力
concentrate[4] ('kɑnsn̩,tret) *v.* 專心

Simply speaking, it is a must *that pregnant women avoid alcohol.*
簡單來說，孕婦絕對要避免喝酒。

* simply[2] ('sɪmplɪ) *adv.* 簡單地　　*simply speaking* 簡單來說
must[1] (mʌst) *n.* 必須要做的事　　avoid[2] (ə'vɔɪd) *v.* 避免

1. (**C**) 本文主要是關於什麼？
(A) 女人和藥。　　　　　　　　(B) 懷孕的危險。
(C) 懷孕時喝酒的危險。　　　　(D) 喝酒和人體。
* danger[5] ('dʒendɚ) *n.* 危險　　pregnancy[4] ('prɛgnənsɪ) *n.* 懷孕
drinking[1] ('drɪŋkɪŋ) *n.* 喝酒

2. (**B**) 在女人喝一杯酒後，酒精會需要多久的時間進入她的血液中？
(A) 大約一個小時。　　　　　　(B) 幾秒鐘。
(C) 幾分鐘。　　　　　　　　　(D) 至少 24 小時。
* take[1] (tek) *v.* 需要　　*take a drink* 喝一杯 (= *have a drink*)

3. (**A**) 從本文可以推論什麼？
(A) 藥對胎兒的影響比對母親的影響大。
(B) 只要一杯含酒精的飲料就可以殺害一個胎兒。
(C) 酒精對大的胎兒沒有不利影響。
(D) 在懷孕期間，父親應該也要避免喝酒。
* infer[6] (ɪn'fɝ) *v.* 推論　　*have an effect on* 對…有影響
adversely (æd'vɝslɪ) *adv.* 不利地　　affect[3] (ə'fɛkt) *v.* 影響
expect[2] (ɪk'spɛkt) *v.* (用進行式) 懷孕；懷胎

4. (**B**) 根據本文，酒精最後是如何回到母親的身體？
(A) 經由血液流動帶回。　　　　(B) 轉移遍及至胎盤各處。
(C) 經由胎兒的肝臟排出。　　　(D) 沒有完全回歸。
* transfer[4] (træns'fɝ) *v.* 轉移　　expel[6] (ɪk'spɛl) *v.* 驅逐；排出

TEST 10

Read the following passage and choose the best answer for each question.

Now let us look at how we read. When we read a printed text, our eyes move across a page in short, jerky movements. We usually recognize words when our eyes are still. Each time they fixate, we see a group of words. This is known as the recognition span or the visual span. The length of time for which the eyes stop—the duration of the fixation—varies considerably from person to person. It also varies within any one person according to his purpose in reading and his familiarity with the text. Furthermore, it can be affected by such factors as lighting and tiredness.

Unfortunately, in the past, many reading improvement courses have paid too much attention to how our eyes move across the printed page, so numerous exercises have been devised to train the eyes to see more words at one fixation. For example, in some exercises, words are flashed on to a screen for a tenth or a twentieth of a second. One of the exercises has required students to fix their eyes on some central point, taking in the words on either side. Such word patterns are often constructed in the shape of rather steep pyramids so the reader takes in more and more words at each successive fixation. All these exercises are very clever, but it's one thing to improve a person's ability to see words and quite another thing to improve his ability to read a text efficiently. Reading requires the ability to understand the relationship between words. As a consequence, many experts have now begun to question the usefulness of eye training, especially since any approach which trains a person to read isolated words and phrases would seem unlikely to help him in reading a continuous text.

1. The time of the recognition span may not be influenced by _____.
   - (A) one's familiarity with the content
   - (B) one's intention in reading
   - (C) exhaustion and brightness
   - (D) the length of a group of words

2. What can be inferred from the passage?

(A) A good reader needs to receive more eye training.

(B) It is essential for a reader to see words more quickly.

(C) A deeply involved mind is beneficial to reading.

(D) Reading requires a reader to recognize more words at each fixation.

3. Which of the following is NOT true?

(A) The duration of the visual span varies from person to person.

(B) Eye training helps readers understand articles efficiently.

(C) The effectiveness of eye training is doubted.

(D) The ability to see as many words as possible during the visual span is not necessarily indispensable to readers.

4. What is the tone of the author in writing this article?

(A) Optimistic.

(B) Pessimistic.

(C) Critical.

(D) Indifferent.

TEST 10 詳解

Now let us look at ***how*** we read.　***When*** we read a printed text, our eyes move *across a page in short, jerky movements.*

現在讓我們看一下我們如何閱讀。當我們讀印刷文字時，我們的眼睛會以短暫又急促的方式，在頁面上移動。

* printed[1] ('prɪntɪd) *adj.* 印刷的　　text[3] (tɛkst) *n.* 內文
move[1] (muv) *v.* 移動　　across[1] (ə'krɔs) *prep.* 在…到處
page[1] (pedʒ) *v.* 頁　　jerky ('dʒɜˋkɪ) *adj.* 急促的
movement[1] ('muvmənt) *n.* 移動；活動
jerky movement 急促的動作

We *usually* recognize words ***when*** our eyes are still.　***Each time*** they *fixate*, we see a group of words.　This is known ***as** the recognition span **or** the visual span.*

通常是當我們的眼睛靜止不動時，我們才認出字。每次眼睛不動時，我們會看到一組字。這被稱為識別期間，或者稱為視覺期間。

* recognize[3] ('rɛkəg͵naɪz) *v.* 認出　　still[1] (stɪl) *adj.* 靜止不動的
fixate ('fɪkset) *v.* 固定【fix[2] (fɪks) *v.* 固定】
be known as 被稱為　　recognition[4] (͵rɛkəg'nɪʃən) *n.* 認出；識別
span[6] (spæn) *n.* 持續時間段　　***recognition span*** 識別期間
visual[4] ('vɪʒuəl) *adj.* 視覺的　　***visual span*** 視覺期間

The length *of time for **which** the eyes stop—the duration of the fixation*—varies *considerably from person to person.*

眼睛停下來的時間長度——注視期間——每個人都不同。

* length[2] 〔 lɛŋθ 〕 *n.* 長度　　duration[5] 〔 dju'reʃən 〕 *n.* 持續期間
fixation 〔 fɪks'eʃən 〕 *n.* 固定；注視　　vary[3] 〔'vɛrɪ 〕 *v.* 不同
considerably[3] 〔 kən'sɪdərəbl̩ɪ 〕 *adv.* 相當大地
vary from person to person 每個人都不同

It *also* varies *within any one person according to his purpose in*

*reading **and** his familiarity with the text. Furthermore*, it can be

affected *by such factors as lighting **and** tiredness.*

它還會依據每個人閱讀的目的以及對內文的熟悉度，而有所不同。此
外，它可能會受到照明或疲倦等因素的影響。

* within[2] 〔 wɪ'ðɪn 〕 *prep.* 在…之內　　purpose[1] 〔'pɝpəs 〕 *n.* 目的
familiarity[6] 〔 fə‚mɪlɪ'ærətɪ 〕 *n.* 熟悉
furthermore[4] 〔'fɝðə‚mor 〕 *adv.* 此外（ = *moreover*[4] ）
affect[3] 〔 ə'fɛkt 〕 *v.* 影響　　factor[3] 〔'fæktə 〕 *n.* 因素
lighting[2] 〔'laɪtɪŋ 〕 *n.* 照明；燈光　　tiredness 〔'taɪrdnɪs 〕 *n.* 疲倦

Unfortunately, *in the past*, many reading improvement courses

have paid *too* much attention *to **how** our eyes move across the printed*

page, **so** numerous exercises have been devised *to train the eyes to*

see more words at one fixation.

遺憾的是，過去很多改善閱讀的課程，太注重我們的眼睛如何在紙面上移動，所以設計出許多的練習，以訓練眼睛一次就看到更多的字。

* unfortunately[4] (ʌnˈfɔrtʃənɪtlɪ) *adv.* 不幸地；遺憾地
  in the past 在過去　　improvement[2] (ɪmˈpruvmənt) *n.* 改善
  course[1] (kors) *n.* 課程
  attention[2] (əˈtɛnʃən) *n.* 注意；注意力　　***pay attention to*** 注意
  numerous[4] (ˈnjumərəs) *adj.* 許多的
  exercise[2] (ˈɛksəˌsaɪz) *n.* 練習
  devise[4] (dɪˈvaɪz) *v.* 想出；設計
  train[1] (tren) *v.* 訓練

For example, in some exercises, words are flashed *on to a screen for a tenth **or** a twentieth of a second.*

例如，在某些練習中，字很快地閃過螢幕，時間可能是十分之一或二十分之一秒。

* flash[2] (flæʃ) *v.* 閃過　　screen[2] (skrin) *n.* 螢幕
  a tenth of 十分之一　　***a twentieth of*** 二十分之一

One *of the exercises* has required students to fix their eyes *on some central point, taking in the words on either side.*

其中一項練習要求學生將眼睛固定在某個中心點上，也要看兩旁出現的字。

* require[2] (rɪˈkwaɪr) *v.* 要求　　fix[2] (fɪks) *v.* 使固定
  some[1] (sʌm) *adj.* 某個
  central[2] (ˈsɛntrəl) *adj.* 中心的；中央的
  take in 觀看；看到　　either[1] (ˈiðə) *prep.* 兩者之一的

Such word patterns are *often* constructed *in the shape of rather steep*

pyramids **so** the reader takes in more **and** more words *at each*

successive fixation.

這樣的文字模式通常會以相當斜的金字塔形狀所組成，讓閱讀的人可以
在每次連續的注視中，看到愈來愈多的字。

> * pattern[2] 〔ˋpætən〕 *n.* 模式
> construct[4] 〔kənˋstrʌkt〕 *v.* 建造；構成　　shape[1] 〔ʃep〕 *n.* 形狀
> ***in the shape of*** 以…形式　　rather[2] 〔ˋræðɚ〕 *adv.* 相當地
> steep[3] 〔stip〕 *adj.* 陡的；斜的　　pyramid[5] 〔ˋpɪrəmɪd〕 *n.* 金字塔
> successive[6] 〔səkˋsɛsɪv〕 *adj.* 連續的

All these exercises are *very* clever, ***but*** it's one thing to improve a

person's ability *to see words* **and** *quite* another thing to improve his

ability *to read a text efficiently*.　Reading requires the ability *to*

understand the relationship between words.

這些練習都非常巧妙，但是，增進一個人看字的能力是一回事，而增進
他有效率地閱讀文章的能力，又是另一回事。閱讀需要了解文字關係的
能力。

> * clever[2] 〔ˋklɛvɚ〕 *adj.* 聰明的；巧妙的
> ***…is one thing…is (quite) another thing*** …是一回事…又是另一
> 　　回事
> improve[2] 〔ɪmˋpruv〕 *v.* 改善；增進　　ability[4] 〔əˋbɪlətɪ〕 *n.* 能力
> efficiently[3] 〔ɪˋfɪʃəntlɪ〕 *adv.* 有效率地
> relationship[2] 〔rɪˋleʃənˋʃɪp〕 *n.* 關係；關聯

As a consequence, many experts have *now* begun to question the usefulness *of eye training,* *especially **since** any approach **which*** *trains a person to read isolated words **and** phrases* would seem unlikely to help him *in reading a continuous text.*

因此，現在很多專家開始質疑眼睛訓練是否有用，尤其因為訓練一個人閱讀單獨出現的單字和片語，似乎不太可能幫助他閱讀一篇連貫的文章。

* consequence[4] 〔'kɑnsə,kwɛns 〕 n. 後果
  as a consequence 因此 (= *consequently*[4])
  expert[2] 〔'ɛkspɝt 〕 n. 專家　　question[1] 〔'kwɛstʃən 〕 v. 質疑
  usefulness[1] 〔'jusfəlnɪs 〕 n. 有用；有益
  especially[2] 〔ə'spɛʃəlɪ 〕 adv. 尤其　　approach[3] 〔ə'protʃ 〕 n. 方法
  isolated[4] 〔'aisḷ,etɪd 〕 adj. 單獨的　　phrase[4] 〔frez 〕 n. 片語
  unlikely[1] 〔ʌn'laɪklɪ 〕 adj. 不可能的
  continuous[4] 〔kən'tɪnjuəs 〕 adj. 連續的

1. (**D**) 識別期間可能不會被 ＿＿＿＿＿＿ 影響。

   (A) 一個人對於內容的熟悉程度

   (B) 一個人閱讀的目的

   (C) 筋疲力竭和光線亮度

   (D) 一組字詞的長度

   * influence[2] 〔'ɪnfluəns 〕 v. 影響 (= *affect*[3])
     content[4] 〔'kɑntɛnt 〕 n. 內容
     intention[4] 〔ɪn'tɛnʃən 〕 n. 意圖；目的
     exhaustion[4] 〔ɪg'zɔstʃən 〕 n. 筋疲力竭
     brightness[1] 〔'braɪtnɪs 〕 n. 亮度

2. (**C**) 從本文可以推論什麼？

(A) 一個好的讀者必須接受更多的眼睛訓練。

(B) 對一個讀者來說，看字更快速是必要的。

(C) 全心投入對閱讀有益。

(D) 閱讀需要讀者每次注視都能夠辨識更多的字。

* infer[6] ﹝ ɪnˋfɝ ﹞ v. 推論　　receive[1] ﹝ rɪˋsiv ﹞ v. 收到；受到

essential[4] ﹝ əˋsɛnʃəl ﹞ adj. 必須的；非常重要的

deeply[1] ﹝ diplɪ ﹞ adv. 深深地

involved[4] ﹝ ɪnˋvɑlvd ﹞ adj. 全心投入的【involve[4] 使牽涉在內】

beneficial[5] ﹝ˌbɛnəˋfɪʃəl ﹞ adj. 有益的

3. (**B**) 以下何者為非？

(A) 每個人的視覺持續期間都各不相同。

(B) 眼睛訓練幫助讀者更有效率地了解文章。

(C) 眼睛訓練的有效性備受質疑。

(D) 在視覺期間盡可能看越多字，不一定是讀者不可或缺的能力。

* duration[5] ﹝ djʊˋreʃən ﹞ n. 持續期間

article[2] ﹝ ˋɑrtɪkl̩ ﹞ n. 文章

effectiveness[2] ﹝ əˋfɛktɪvnɪs ﹞ n. 有效　　doubt[2] ﹝ daʊt ﹞ v. 懷疑

necessarily[2] ﹝ ˋnɛsəˌsɛrɪlɪ ﹞ adv. 必定

not necessarily 未必；不一定 (= *not always*)

indispensable ﹝ˌɪndɪsˋpɛnsəbl̩ ﹞ adj. 不可或缺的

4. (**C**) 作者寫這篇文章的語氣如何？

(A) optimistic[3] ﹝ˌɑptəˋmɪstɪk ﹞ adj. 樂觀的

(B) pessimistic[4] ﹝ˌpɛsəˋmɪstɪk ﹞ adj. 悲觀的

(C) ***critical***[4] ﹝ ˋkrɪtɪkl̩ ﹞ adj. 批判的

(D) indifferent[5] ﹝ ɪnˋdɪfrənt ﹞ adj. 漠不關心的

* tone[1] ﹝ ton ﹞ n. 語氣　　author[3] ﹝ ˋɔðɚ ﹞ n. 作者

TEST 11

Read the following passage and choose the best answer for each question.

Perhaps the most familiar plant movement belongs to one species of mimosa called the sensitive plant. Within seconds, it can lower its leaves and make its tiny leaflets close up like folding chairs. This movement is thought to be initiated by electrical impulses remarkably similar to nerve signals in animals. But without a complex motion mechanism, the mimosa has to be creative in devising a way to move.

For motion, the plant depends on tiny bulb-shaped organs located at the base of each leaf stalk and leaflet. Called pulvini, these organs hold the plant parts in place. When the mimosa is stimulated, say, by a crawling insect or a sudden change in temperature, an electrical impulse sweeps through the plant. This causes potassium and then water to be shifted from certain cells in the pulvini to others, quickly turning one side of the organs limp. Because the pulvini can no longer support the leaves and leaflets, this shift results in a corresponding change in their position.

1. This passage is mainly concerned with the
   _____.

   (A) geographical distribution of plant and animal
       species
   (B) location and purpose of the pulvini
   (C) appearance of the mimosa
   (D) process that causes movement in mimosa

2. The author mentions folding chairs in the first
   paragraph in order to _____.

   (A) settle a dispute   (B) evaluate a claim
   (C) provide an illustration   (D) point out a difference

3. We can infer from the passage that the mimosa is called
   the sensitive plant because it _____.

   (A) reacts to outside stimulation
   (B) has smaller leaves than most other plants
   (C) depends on organs called pulvini
   (D) contains potassium and water

4. According to the passage, what is the function of the
   pulvini?

   (A) To stimulate movement.
   (B) To send electrical impulses.
   (C) To support leaves and leaflets.
   (D) To produce potassium and water.

TEST 11 詳解

Perhaps the *most* familiar plant movement belongs to one

species *of mimosa called the sensitive plant.*

或許大家最熟悉的植物運動，就是屬於被稱爲敏感植物的含羞草。

* familiar[3] 〔 fə'mɪljə 〕 *adj.* 熟悉的　　plant[1] 〔 plænt 〕 *n.* 植物
  movement[1] 〔'muvmənt 〕 *n.* 運動；移動；活動
  belong to 屬於
  species[4] 〔'spiʃiz 〕 *n.* 物種
  mimosa 〔 mɪ'mosə 〕 *n.* 含羞草
  sensitive[3] 〔'sɛnsətɪv 〕 *adj.* 敏感的
  sensitive plant 敏感植物

mimosa

Within seconds, it can lower its leaves *and* make its tiny leaflets

close up *like folding chairs.* This movement is thought to be

initiated *by electrical impulses remarkably similar to nerve signals*

in animals.

在幾秒鐘內，它可以低垂葉子，使微小的葉子像折疊椅一樣合攏起來。
這樣的動作，被認爲是由非常類似動物神經訊號的電脈衝所啓動。

* lower[2] 〔'loə 〕 *v.* 降低　　leaves[1] 〔 livz 〕 *n. pl.* 葉子
  tiny[1] 〔'taɪnɪ 〕 *adj.* 微小的　　leaflet 〔'liflɪt 〕 *n.* 嫩葉；小葉
  close up 合攏　　fold[3] 〔 fold 〕 *v.* 摺疊
  folding chair 摺疊椅　　initiate[5] 〔 ɪ'nɪʃɪ,et 〕 *v.* 開始；引起
  electrical[3] 〔 ɪ'lɛktrɪkḷ 〕 *adj.* 電的　　impulse[5] 〔'ɪmpʌls 〕 *n.* 脈衝

remarkably[4] 〔rɪ'mɑrkəblɪ〕 *adv.* 非常地
similar[2] 〔'sɪmələ 〕 *adj.* 相似的 < *to* >
nerve[3] 〔nɝv〕 *n.* 神經　　signal[3] 〔'sɪgnl̩〕 *n.* 訊號

But *without a complex motion mechanism*, the mimosa has to be

creative *in devising a way to move*.

但是沒有複雜的運動機制，含羞草必須有創意地設計出一種運動方式。

* complex[3] 〔'kɑmplɛks〕 *adj.* 複雜的
motion[2] 〔'moʃən〕 *n.* 運動；動作
mechanism[6] 〔'mɛkə͵nɪzəm〕 *n.* 機制
creative[3] 〔krɪ'etɪv〕 *adj.* 有創造力的
devise[4] 〔dɪ'vaɪz〕 *v.* 設計 (= *design*[2])

For motion, the plant depends on tiny bulb-shaped organs

located at the base of each leaf stalk **and** *leaflet*. *Called pulvini*, these

organs hold the plant parts *in place*.

含羞草依靠著微小球莖狀的器官來運動，它們位於每個葉柄和嫩葉
的底部。這些被稱爲葉枕的器官，使植物的每個部分都在正確的位置。

* **depend on** 依靠　　bulb[3] 〔bʌlb〕 *n.* 球莖
shaped[1] 〔ʃept〕 *adj.* 形狀的【常形成複合字】
organ[2] 〔'ɔrgən〕 *n.* 器官　　locate[2] 〔lo'ket〕 *v.* 使位於
be located at 位於 (= *be situated at*)
base[1] 〔bes〕 *n.* 根基；底部　　stalk[5,6] 〔stɔk〕 *n.* 莖；葉柄
pulvini 〔pʌl'vaɪnaɪ〕 *n. pl.* 葉枕【單數 pulvinus 〔pʌl'vaɪnəs〕 *n.*】
hold[1] 〔hold〕 *v.* 使保持　　**in place** 在正確的位置

When the mimosa is stimulated, say, by a crawling insect **or** a sudden

change in temperature, an electrical impulse sweeps *through the plant.*

例如，當含羞草受到爬行的昆蟲，或突然改變的溫度的刺激，電脈衝就
會急速流過整株植物。

* stimulate[6] ('stɪmjə,let) v. 刺激　　say[1] (se) v. 例如
  crawling[3] ('krɔlɪŋ) adj. 爬行的　　insect[2] ('ɪnsɛkt) n. 昆蟲
  sudden[2] ('sʌdn̩) adj. 突然的　　temperature[2] ('tɛmprətʃə) n. 溫度
  sweep[2] (swip) v. 橫掃；快速移動

This causes potassium **and** then water to be shifted from certain cells

in the pulvini to others, *quickly turning one side of the organs limp.*

這會讓在葉枕中特定細胞的鉀和水轉換到其他細胞，迅速使器官的其中
一邊變得軟弱無力。

* potassium (pə'tæsɪəm) n. 鉀　　shift[4] (ʃɪft) v. 轉移　n. 轉變
  certain[1] ('sɝtn̩) adj. 某些　　cell[2] (sɛl) n. 細胞
  turn[1] (tɝn) adj. 使變得；使成為
  limp[5] (lɪmp) adj. 軟的；無力的；沒有精神的

Because the pulvini can no longer support the leaves **and** leaflets, this

shift results in a corresponding change *in their position.*

因為葉枕無法再支撐葉子和嫩葉，這樣的轉變導致它們的姿勢有對應的
變化。

* *no longer* 不再　　support[2] (sə'port) v. 支持；支撐
  results in 導致；造成
  corresponding[4] (,kɔrɪ'spandɪŋ) adj. 相對應的
  position[1] (pə'zɪʃən) n. 姿勢

1. (**D**) 本文主要是關於 _____ 。

    (A) 植物和動物的地理分布　　(B) 葉枕的位置和用途

    (C) 含羞草的外觀　　　　　　(D) <u>造成含羞草運動的過程</u>

    * mainly^2 〔'menlɪ〕*adv.* 主要地　　***be concerned with*** 關於
    geographical^5〔,dʒɪə'græfɪkḷ〕*adj.* 地理的
    distribution^4〔,dɪstrə'bjuʃən〕*n.* 分布（區域）
    appearance^2〔ə'pɪrəns〕*n.* 外表
    purpose^1〔'pɜpəs〕*n.* 目的；用途
    process^3〔'prɑsɛs〕*n.* 過程　　cause^1〔kɔz〕*v.* 造成；導致

2. (**C**) 作者在第一段提到折疊椅是為了 _____ 。

    (A) 解決爭論　　　　　　　　(B) 評估要求

    (C) <u>提供說明</u>　　　　　　　　(D) 指出不同點

    * settle^2〔'sɛtḷ〕*v.* 解決（= *solve*^{2}）
    dispute^4〔dɪ'spjut〕*n.* 爭論　　evaluate^4〔ɪ'væljʊ,et〕*v.* 評估
    claim^2〔klem〕*n.* 要求　　provide^2〔prə'vaɪd〕*v.* 提供
    illustration^4〔ɪ,lʌs'treʃən〕*n.* 說明　　***point out*** 指出

3. (**A**) 我們可以從本文推論，含羞草被稱為敏感植物，因為它
    _____ 。

    (A) <u>會對外界的刺激做出反應</u>

    (B) 有比其他大部份植物更小的葉子

    (C) 依靠名叫葉枕的器官　　(D) 包含鉀和水

    * react^3〔rɪ'ækt〕*v.* 做出反應 < *to* >
    outside^1〔'aʊt'saɪd〕*adj.* 外面的
    stimulation^6〔,stɪmjə'leʃən〕*n.* 刺激
    contain^2〔kən'ten〕*v.* 包含

4. (**C**) 根據本文，葉枕的功能是什麼？

    (A) 刺激運動。　　　　　　　(B) 發送電脈衝。

    (C) <u>支撐葉子和嫩葉。</u>　　　　(D) 產生鉀和水。

    * function^2〔'fʌŋkʃən〕*n.* 功能　　produce^2〔prə'djus〕*v.* 產生

TEST 12

Read the following passage and choose the best answer for each question.

Depression may be a serious condition that requires a doctor's treatment. But through a healthy lifestyle, you can prevent depression or give yourself a boost if you're feeling down. First, look for mood-boosting fruit, such as kiwi, bananas, and pineapples. They are all naturally high in serotonin, a natural mood booster. In addition to these fruits, you can also eat foods high in tryptophan, an essential amino acid that your body converts to serotonin. Tryptophan is found in proteins such as fish, nuts, eggs, and beans. Eating these foods also has another benefit, as they contain omega-3s, which help people avoid depression. A Dutch study found that people who consume diets rich in omega-3 fatty acids, commonly found in cold-water fish such as salmon and mackerel, were less likely to suffer from depression than people whose diets were low in this important fat. Another study in England found that pregnant women who didn't eat fish had twice the rate of depression as women who ate 10 ounces of fish a day. Omega-3 fatty acids can also be found in flaxseeds, walnuts, soybeans, kidney beans, and black beans.

Secondly, exercise. Numerous studies have revealed that exercise increases both the production and the release of serotonin. Types of exercise from the more dynamic aerobic exercise to calming ones like yoga are all beneficial. Some vigorous outdoor recreations, like hiking, canoeing, or biking can weave their magic on your mood, too. If you are too tired to move, getting a 12-minute massage three times a week is also a good choice. Various studies have found that massage boosts serotonin levels 17% higher and reduces levels of the stress hormone cortisol. Try these simple methods through diet and physical exercise, and you will find it easy to stay up-lifted.

1. What is the main idea of the passage?
   (A) Some foods and exercise can help us avoid depression.
   (B) Some natural foods are good for our mental health.
   (C) Doing exercise can help lift our spirits.
   (D) Getting a massage is useful in combating depression.

2. According to the passage, which of the following statements about serotonin is true?

   (A) It can be converted to tryptophan.

   (B) It can be found in some fruits.

   (C) It is a natural substance found in proteins.

   (D) It cannot be produced by a human body.

3. According to the passage, how can people stay happy?

   (A) They can eat more warm-water fish.

   (B) They can eat flaxseeds or some types of beans sometimes.

   (C) They can choose sports that require more energy and strain.

   (D) They can massage family and friends to become stronger.

4. In which of the following is the passage most likely to be found?

   (A) A newspaper.

   (B) A biology textbook.

   (C) A new-parent pamphlet.

   (D) A doctor's prescription.

TEST 12 詳解

Depression may be a serious condition *that requires a doctor's treatment.*

憂鬱症可能是很嚴重的疾病，需要醫生治療。

* depression[4] 〔dɪ'prɛʃən〕 *n.* 沮喪；憂鬱症
  serious[2] 〔'sɪrɪəs〕 *adj.* 嚴重的
  condition[3] 〔kən'dɪʃən〕 *n.* 情況；（健康等）狀態；疾病
  require[2] 〔rɪ'kwaɪr〕 *v.* 需要　　treatment[5] 〔'tritmənt〕 *n.* 治療

But through a healthy lifestyle, you can prevent depression *or* give yourself a boost *if you're feeling down.*

但是憑藉健康的生活方式，你可以預防憂鬱症，或如果你感到情緒低落時，激勵自己。

* through[2] 〔θru〕 *prep.* 憑藉　　healthy[2] 〔'hɛlθɪ〕 *adj.* 健康的
  lifestyle 〔'laɪf,staɪl〕 *n.* 生活方式　　prevent[3] 〔prɪ'vɛnt〕 *v.* 預防
  boost[6] 〔bust〕 *n.* 提高；激勵
  down[1] 〔daʊn〕 *adj.* 情緒低落的；消沉的

First, look for mood-boosting fruit, *such as kiwi, bananas, and pineapples.*

首先，尋找可以提升情緒的水果，像是奇異果、香蕉，和鳳梨。

* *look for* 尋找　　mood[3] 〔mud〕 *n.* 心情
  kiwi 〔'kiwɪ〕 *n.* 奇異果　　pineapple[2] 〔'paɪn,æpḷ〕 *n.* 鳳梨

They are all *naturally* high in serotonin, *a natural mood booster.*

它們天生就富含血清素，這是一種天然的情緒助推器。

* naturally² 〔'nætʃərəlɪ 〕 *adv.* 生來；天生地
  serotonin 〔 sɛrə'tonɪn 〕 *n.* 血清素
  natural² 〔'nætʃərəl 〕 *adj.* 天然的
  booster⁶ 〔'bustɚ 〕 *n.* 推進器；令人振奮的事物

In addition to these fruits, you can *also* eat foods *high in tryptophan,*

*an essential amino acid **that** your body converts to serotonin.*

除了這些水果之外，你還可以吃富含色胺酸的食物，色胺酸是一種必要的氨基酸，你的身體可以把它轉換成血清素。

* ***in addition to*** 除了⋯之外
  tryptophan 〔'trɪptəfæn 〕 *n.* 色胺酸
  essential⁴ 〔 ɪ'sɛnʃəl 〕 *adj.* 必要的　　acid⁴ 〔'æsɪd 〕 *n.* 酸
  amino acid 〔 ə'mino 'æsɪd 〕 *n.* 氨基酸
  convert⁵ 〔 kən'vɝt 〕 *v.* 使轉變；轉換

Tryptophan is found *in proteins such as fish, nuts, eggs, **and** beans.*

色胺酸可以在像是魚類、堅果、蛋和豆，這類的蛋白質中發現。

* protein⁴ 〔'protiɪn 〕 *n.* 蛋白質　　nut² 〔 nʌt 〕 *n.* 堅果
  bean² 〔 bin 〕 *n.* 豆子

Eating these foods *also* has another benefit, ***as** they contain*

*omega-3s, **which** help people avoid depression.*

吃這些食物也有另一種益處，因為它們富含omega-3 脂肪酸，可以幫助
人類避免憂鬱症。

> benefit[3] 〔'bɛnəfɪt〕 *n.* 利益；好處
> contain[2] 〔kən'ten〕 *v.* 包含
> Omega-3 〔o'mɛgə'θri〕是一種不飽和脂肪酸，是人體很重要的且
> 　　必要的「好脂肪」，只能從食物中攝取。
> avoid[2] 〔ə'vɔɪd〕 *v.* 避免

A Dutch study found *that* people who consume diets rich in omega-3

fatty acids, *commonly found in cold-water fish such as salmon and*

mackerel, were *less* likely to suffer from depression *than people*

whose diets were low in this important fat.

一項荷蘭的研究發現，吃富含omega-3 脂肪酸的飲食的人，比起那些在
飲食中這項重要脂肪吃得少的人，較不易罹患憂鬱症，而omega-3 脂肪
酸常見於深海魚中，例如鮭魚和鯖魚。

> * Dutch 〔dʌtʃ〕 *adj.* 荷蘭的　　study[1] 〔'stʌdɪ〕 *n.* 研究
> consume[4] 〔kəm'sjum〕 *v.* 消耗；吃
> diet[3] 〔'daɪət〕 *n.* 飲食　　*be riich in* 富含
> fatty[1] 〔'fætɪ〕 *adj.* 脂肪的　　*fatty acid* 脂肪酸
> commonly[1] 〔'kɑmənlɪ〕 *adv.* 通常
> *cold-water fish* 深海魚；冷水性魚
> salmon[5] 〔'sæmən〕 *n.* 鮭魚　　mackerel 〔'mækərəl〕 *n.* 鯖魚
> likely[1] 〔'laɪklɪ〕 *adj.* 很可能的　　*suffer from* 罹患
> low[1] 〔lo〕 *adj.* 不夠的；缺乏的　　fat[1] 〔fæt〕 *n.* 脂肪

Another study *in England* found *that pregnant women **who** didn't eat*

*fish had twice the rate of depression **as** women **who** ate 10 ounces of*

fish a day.

另一項英國的研究發現，不吃魚的孕婦罹患憂鬱症的比例，是一天吃
10 盎司魚的孕婦的兩倍。

* pregnant[4] 〔'prɛgnənt 〕 *adj.* 懷孕的
twice[1] 〔 twaɪs 〕 *adv.* 兩倍　　rate[3] 〔 ret 〕 *n.* 比例
ounce[5] 〔 aʊns 〕 *n.* 盎司【盎司等於 1/16 磅】

Omega-3 fatty acids can *also* be found *in flaxseeds, walnuts,*

*soybeans, kidney beans, **and** black beans.*

Omega-3 脂肪酸也可以在亞麻籽、核桃、大豆、菜豆，以及黑豆中發
現。

* flaxseed 〔'flæks,sid 〕 *n.* 亞麻籽　　walnut[4] 〔'wɔlnət 〕 *n.* 核桃
soybean[2] 〔'sɔɪ,bin 〕 *n.* 大豆；黃豆　　kidney[3] 〔'kɪdnɪ 〕 *n.* 腎臟
kidney bean 菜豆

Secondly, exercise.　Numerous studies have revealed *that*

*exercise increases both the production **and** the release of serotonin.*

其次是運動。許多研究顯示，運動會增加血清素的產生和釋放。

* exercise[2] 〔'ɛksɚ,saɪz 〕 *n.* 運動
numerous[4] 〔'njumərəs 〕 *adj.* 許多的
reveal[3] 〔 rɪ'vil 〕 *v.* 顯示　　increase[2] 〔 ɪn'kris 〕 *v.* 增加
production[4] 〔 prə'dʌkʃən 〕 *n.* 產生　　release[3] 〔 rɪ'lis 〕 *n.* 釋放

Types | *of exercise from the more dynamic aerobic exercise to calming*

ones like yoga | are all beneficial.

運動的類型，從動態的有氧運動，到使人平靜的運動，像是瑜珈，都是有益的。

* type[2] 〔 taɪp 〕 *n.* 類型　　dynamic[4] 〔 daɪˈnæmɪk 〕 *adj.* 動態的
  aerobic 〔 eəˈrobɪk 〕 *adj.* 有氧的
  calming[2] 〔ˈkɑmɪŋ 〕 *adj.* 使人平靜的　　yoga[5] 〔ˈjogə 〕 *n.* 瑜珈
  beneficial[5] 〔ˌbɛnəˈfɪʃəl 〕 *adj.* 有益的

Some vigorous outdoor recreations, *like hiking, canoeing,* **or biking**

can weave their magic *on your mood, too.*

有些激烈的戶外休閒活動，像是健行、划獨木舟，或騎腳踏車，也可以在你的心情上施展魔法。

* vigorous[5] 〔ˈvɪgərəs 〕 *adj.* 精力充沛的；激烈的
  outdoor[3] 〔ˈaʊt͵dor 〕 *adj.* 戶外的
  recreation[4] 〔ˌrɛkrɪˈeʃən 〕 *n.* 休閒娛樂
  hiking[3] 〔ˈhaɪkɪŋ 〕 *n.* 健行　　canoeing[3] 〔 kəˈnuɪŋ 〕 *n.* 划獨木舟
  biking[3] 〔ˈbaɪkɪŋ 〕 *n.* 騎腳踏車
  weave[3] 〔 wiv 〕 *v.* 編織；編入　　magic[2] 〔ˈmædʒɪk 〕 *n.* 魔法
  weave one's **magic** 施展魔法 (= *cast one's magic*)

***If* you are too tired to move,** getting a 12-minute massage *three times*

a week is *also* a good choice.

如果你太累不想動，一個禮拜做三次 12 分鐘的按摩，也是一個好選擇。

    * move¹ (muv) *v.* 動；移動   massage⁵ (mə'sɑʒ) *n.* 按摩

Various studies have found ***that** massage boosts serotonin levels 17%*

*higher **and** reduces levels of the stress hormone cortisol.*

各式各樣的研究發現，按摩可以使血清素的含量提升 17%，並減低壓力激素。

    * various³ ('vɛrɪəs) *adj.* 各式各樣的
    level¹ ('lɛvḷ) *n.* 程度；水平；含量   reduce³ (rɪ'djus) *v.* 減少
    stress² (strɛs) *n.* 壓力   hormone⁶ ('hɔrmon) *n.* 荷爾蒙
    cortisol ('kɔrtɪsɑl) *n.* 皮質醇
    stress hormone cortisol 壓力激素

Try these simple methods *through diet **and** physical exercise, **and***

you will find it easy *to stay up-lifted.*

如果你能嘗試這些透過飲食和身體運動的簡單方法，你就會發現保持開心是很容易的。

    * simple¹ ('sɪmpḷ) *adj.* 簡單的   method² ('mɛθəd) *n.* 方法
    physical⁴ ('fɪzɪkḷ) *adj.* 身體的   stay¹ (ste) *v.* 保持
    up-lifted ('ʌp,lɪftɪd) *adj.* 受鼓舞的

1. (**A**) 本文的主旨為何？
    (A) 有些食物和運動可以幫助我們避免憂鬱症。
    (B) 有些天然的食物對我們的心理健康有好處。
    (C) 做運動可以幫助我們振作精神。
    (D) 按摩能用來對抗憂鬱症。

* mental³〔ˋmɛntl〕*adj.* 心理的　　health¹〔hɛlθ〕*n.* 健康
lift¹〔lɪft〕*v.* 振作（精神）　　spirits²〔ˋspɪrɪts〕*n. pl.* 精神
useful¹〔ˋjusfəl〕*adj.* 有用的
combat⁵〔ˋkɑmbæt〕*v.* 戰鬥；對抗

2.（**B**）根據本文，下列關於血清素的敘述何者為眞？

　　(A) 它可以轉變成色胺酸。

　　(B) <u>它可以在一些水果中被發現。</u>

　　(C) 它是一種可在蛋白質中發現的天然物質。

　　(D) 它不能被人體所製造。

　　* substance³〔ˋsʌbstəns〕*n.* 物質
　　produce²〔prəˋdjus〕*v.* 生產；製造

3.（**B**）根據本文，人要如何才能一直都很快樂？

　　(A) 他們可以吃更多的溫水魚。

　　(B) <u>他們有時可以吃亞麻籽或一些豆類。</u>

　　(C) 他們可以選擇比較費力的運動。

　　(D) 他們可以替家人和朋友按摩，以變得更強壯。

　　* ***warm-water fish*** 溫水魚　　reuqire²〔rɪˋkwaɪr〕*v.* 需要
　　sport¹〔sport〕*n.* 運動　　energy²〔ˋɛnədʒɪ〕*n.* 活力
　　strain⁵〔stren〕*n.* 拉力；努力；盡力
　　massage⁵〔məˋsɑʒ〕*v.* 對…按摩

4.（**A**）本文最有可能在下列哪裡被發現？

　　(A) <u>報紙。</u>　　　　　　　　(B) 生物課本。

　　(C) 新手父母手册。　　　　　(D) 醫生的處方。

　　* biology⁴〔baɪˋɑlədʒɪ〕*n.* 生物
　　textbook²〔ˋtɛkst͵bʊk〕*n.* 教科書
　　pamphlet⁵〔ˋpæmflɪt〕*n.* 小册子
　　prescription⁶〔prɪˋskrɪpʃən〕*n.* 處方

TEST 13

Read the following passage and choose the best answer for each question.

In an effort to discourage the keeping of dangerous dogs, the British government is supposedly drafting a law that would require every dog owner to take a costly "competence test" to prove they can handle their pets. Owners of all breeds would also have to buy third-party insurance in case their pet attacked someone, and pay for the insertion of a microchip in their animal recording their name and address. The proposals are among a range of measures to mend dog laws in England and Wales being considered by senior ministers, who are expected to announce a public consultation within weeks.

However, critics said yet more red tape and higher bills—one expert estimated the extra costs at £60 or more—would be an imposition on responsible dog owners while irresponsible owners of dangerous dogs would just ignore the measures. They added that genuine dog lovers could end up paying for efforts to control a small number of "devil dogs" that terrorized socially deprived areas.

The Royal Society for the Prevention of Cruelty to Animals (RSPCA) said it would welcome a review of legislation which has failed to curb the numbers of dangerous dogs that can attack, and sometimes kill, children and adults. But a spokesman for the charity added, "We would not support anything that would hit sensible owners while failing to police those who are a danger."

A government source said the proposal follows mounting public concern about the serious injuries and deaths inflicted by dogs. Under the proposal, would-be owners would have to show they had a basic understanding of their dogs before being allowed to keep one.

1. What is the proposal designed to do?
   (A) Ensure that dog owners are competent to care for their pets.
   (B) Control a small number of "devil dogs" known for causing trouble.
   (C) Force dog owners to give up dangerous animals.
   (D) Mend legislation that encourages dog ownership.

2. What is the passage mainly about?

   (A) Dangerous dogs.

   (B) A proposed law.

   (C) Public concern over the cost of owning a dog.

   (D) Government red tape.

3. Why does the RSPCA object to the proposal?

   (A) Not all dogs are dangerous.

   (B) Microchips are too expensive.

   (C) It may negatively affect sensible dog owners.

   (D) There is no proof that dogs are a threat.

4. Which of the following statements is NOT true?

   (A) The British government wants to control the keeping of dangerous dogs.

   (B) The RSPCA welcomes a review of current legislation.

   (C) The new proposal would outlaw the keeping of dangerous dogs.

   (D) The new proposal would require dog owners to take a competency test.

TEST 13 詳解

In an effort to discourage the keeping of dangerous dogs, the

British government is *supposedly* drafting a law *that would require*

every dog owner to take a costly "competence test" to prove they can

handle their pets.

　　爲了努力勸阻大衆飼養危險的狗，根據推測，英國政府正在擬定法規，將要求每位狗主人都要參加昂貴的「能力測驗」，以證明他們能管好自己的寵物。

* effort² 〔ˈɛfət〕 *n.* 努力　　*in an effort to V.* 努力～
  discourage⁴ 〔dɪsˈkɝɪdʒ〕 *v.* 勸阻　　keeping¹ 〔ˈkipɪŋ〕 *n.* 飼養
  British² 〔ˈbrɪtɪʃ〕 *adj.* 英國的
  government² 〔ˈgʌvənmənt〕 *n.* 政府
  supposedly³ 〔səˈpozɪdlɪ〕 *adv.* 根據推測；據稱
  draft⁴ 〔dræft〕 *v.* 草擬　　require² 〔rɪˈkwaɪr〕 *v.* 要求
  owner³ 〔ˈonə〕 *n.* 擁有者　　costly² 〔ˈkɔstlɪ〕 *adj.* 昂貴的
  competence⁶ 〔ˈkɑmpətəns〕 *n.* 能力　　prove¹ 〔pruv〕 *v.* 證明
  handle² 〔ˈhændl〕 *v.* 管理；指揮；處理　　pet¹ 〔pɛt〕 *n.* 寵物

Owners *of all breeds* would *also* have to buy third-party insurance

in case their pet attacked someone, **and** pay for the insertion *of a*

microchip in their animal recording their name **and** *address.*

所有品種的飼主也將必須購買第三方保險，以防自己的寵物攻擊其他人，並且爲寵物植入記錄著飼主名字和住址的微晶片付費。

* breed[4] 〔 brid 〕 *n.* 品種　　third-party 〔 'θɜd'pɑrtɪ 〕 *n.* 第三方
insurance[4] 〔 ɪn'ʃʊrəns 〕 *n.* 保險

third-party insurance 第三方保險【指承擔第三方損失的保險，
而該損失是因受保人的行為而產生的。受損範圍通常包括人體受傷
（Bodily Injury）及財物損失（Property Damage），或第三方的
個人傷害（Personal Injury）】

in case 以防萬一　　attack[2] 〔 ə'tæk 〕 *v.* 攻擊
pay for 支付…的錢　　insertion[4] 〔 ɪn's ɜ ʃ ən 〕 *n.* 插入
microchip 〔 'maɪkro͵tʃɪp 〕 *n.* 微晶片　　record[2] 〔 rɪ'kɔrd 〕 *v.* 記錄

The proposals are among a range of measures *to mend dog laws in*

England and Wales being considered by senior Ministers, who are

expected to announce a public consultation within weeks.

這些提案是由國務資政所構思，一系列措施要修正英格蘭及威爾斯與狗
有關的法規，他們預計將在幾週內發布一場公眾諮詢會。

* proposal[3] 〔 prə'pozl̩ 〕 *n.* 提案；建議
among[1] 〔 ə'mʌŋ 〕 *prep.* 在…當中；為…中之一
range[2] 〔 rendʒ 〕 *n.* 一系列；範圍　　measure[4] 〔 'mɛʒɚ 〕 *n.* 措施
mend[3] 〔 mɛnd 〕 *v.* 修正　　England 〔 'ɪŋglənd 〕 *n.* 英格蘭；英國
Wales 〔 welz 〕 *n.* 威爾斯【英國西南部的地區】
consider[2] 〔 kən'sɪdɚ 〕 *v.* 考慮
senior[4] 〔 'sinjɚ 〕 *adj.* 資深的；地位較高的
minister[4] 〔 'mɪnɪstɚ 〕 *n.* 部長　　*senior minister* 國務資政
expect[2] 〔 ɪk'spɛkt 〕 *v.* 期待；預計　　announce[3] 〔 ə'naʊns 〕 *v.* 宣布
public[1] 〔 'pʌblɪk 〕 *adj.* 公開的；公眾的
consultation[6] 〔 ͵kɑnsl̩'teʃən 〕 *n.* 諮詢
public consultation 諮詢公眾意見
within[2] 〔 wɪð'ɪn 〕 *prep.* 在…之內

However, critics said *yet more red tape **and** higher bills—one expert estimated the extra costs at £60 **or** more*—would be an imposition *on responsible dog owners **while*** irresponsible owners *of dangerous dogs* would *just* ignore the measures.

然而，評論家說這只是更多的官僚作風還有更高的帳單金額——有位專家估計，會有六十磅或更多的額外花費——會是個強加在負責任的狗主人身上的負擔，而危險狗兒的不負責任飼主，可能就只會忽視這些措施。

* critic[4] 〔ˈkrɪtɪk〕 *n.* 評論家　　tape[2] 〔tep〕 *n.* 帶子
  red tape 官僚作風【來自以前官方文件都是由紅色帶子捆起來的做法，據相信，Charles Dickens（狄更斯）在文章中就有以 red tape 表示官僚作為。因此引申爲人們在和政府或官方機構打交道時，經常遇到的拖延、混亂等令人煩惱的障礙】
  bill[2] 〔bɪl〕 *n.* 帳單；帳款　　expert[2] 〔ˈɛkspɝt〕 *n.* 專家
  estimate[4] 〔ˈɛstəˌmet〕 *v.* 估計　　extra[2] 〔ˈɛkstrə〕 *adj.* 額外的
  imposition 〔ˌɪmpəˈzɪʃən〕 *n.* 不公平的負擔；強加 < *on* >
  responsible[2] 〔rɪˈspɑnsəbḷ〕 *adj.* 負責任的（↔ *irresponsible*）
  while[1] 〔hwaɪl〕 *conj.* 然而　　ignore[2] 〔ɪgˈnor〕 *v.* 忽視（= *neglect*[4]）

They added ***that*** *genuine dog lovers could end up paying for efforts to control a small number of* "*devil dogs*" ***that*** *terrorized socially deprived areas.*

他們又說，眞正的愛狗人士，可能最後會花更多的錢，努力管制那些威脅著較貧困地區的少數「惡犬」。

* add[3] 〔æd〕 *v.* 補充說 < *that* >　　genuine[4] 〔ˈdʒɛnjuɪn〕 *adj.* 眞正的
  lover[2] 〔ˈlʌvɚ〕 *n.* 愛好者；熱愛者　　***end up** + **V-ing*** 最後～

control³〔kən'trol〕*v.* 控制；管理
a small number of 少數的　　devil³〔'dɛvḷ〕*n.* 魔鬼
terrorize⁴〔'tɛrə,raɪz〕*v.* 脅迫；恐嚇
socially²〔'soʃəlɪ〕*adv.* 在社會（地位）上
deprived⁶〔dɪ'praɪvd〕*adj.* 被剝奪的；貧困的【deprived⁶ *v.* 剝奪】
socially deprived 缺乏社會資源的　　area¹〔'ɛrɪə〕*n.* 地區

The Royal Society for the Prevention of Cruelty to Animals

(RSPCA) said it would welcome a review *of legislation **which** has*

*failed to curb the numbers of dangerous dogs **that** can attack, **and***

*sometimes kill, children **and** adults.*

　「皇家防止虐待動物協會」（RSPCA）說，歡迎任何對此立法的
批評指教，這項法案無法遏止會攻擊，而且有時會咬死大人和小孩的危
險惡犬數量。

　　* royal²〔'rɔɪəl〕*adj.* 皇家的　　society²〔sə'saɪətɪ〕*n.* 社會；協會
　　prevention²〔prɪ'vɛnʃən〕*n.* 防止　　cruelty⁴〔'kruəltɪ〕*n.* 殘忍
　　Royal Society for the Prevention of Cruelty to Animals 皇家防止
　　　虐待動物協會【最古老也最知名的動物福利組織，於 1824 年創立】
　　review²〔rɪ'vju〕*n.* 評論；批評
　　legislation⁵〔,lɛdʒɪs'leʃən〕*n.* 立法；法規
　　fail to V. 未能～　　curb⁵〔kɝb〕*v.* 控制；遏止

But a spokesman *for the charity* added, "We would not support

anything ***that** would hit sensible owners **while** failing to police those*

***who** are a danger.*"

但該慈善機構的發言人又說：「我們不支持任何會打擊到明智的飼主，而無法管制那些危險飼主的事。」

* spokesman[6]〔'spoksmən〕*n.* 發言人
charity[4]〔'tʃærətɪ〕*n.* 慈善機構　　support[2]〔sə'port〕*v.* 支持
hit[1]〔hɪt〕*v.* 打擊　　sensible[3]〔'sɛnsəbḷ〕*adj.* 明智的
police[1]〔pə'lis〕*v.* 維持治安；管制
danger[1]〔'dendʒɚ〕*n.* 危險；危險事物

A government source said *the proposal follows mounting public concern about the serious injuries **and** deaths inflicted by dogs.*

政府的消息來源說，因為大眾對於狗造成的嚴重死傷案件日益增加的關注，才會有這個提案。

* source[2]〔sors〕*n.* 消息來源；提供消息者
follow[1]〔'falo〕*v.* 跟隨；因⋯而起
mounting[5]〔'mauntɪŋ〕*adj.* 增加的
concern[3]〔kən'sɜn〕*n.* 關心　　serious[2]〔'sɪrɪəs〕*adj.* 嚴重的
injury[3]〔'ɪndʒərɪ〕*n.* 傷害
inflict[3]〔ɪn'flɪkt〕*v.* 使遭受；使承受；強加

Under the proposal, would-be owners would have to show *they had a basic understanding of their dogs before being allowed to keep one.*

依據這個提案，未來的飼主將必須表現對自己的狗有基本的了解後，才可以養狗。

* under[1]〔'ʌndɚ〕*prep.* 按照；依據
would-be〔'wud,bi〕*adj.* 即將成為的；未來的
show[1]〔ʃo〕*v.* 顯示；表現　　basic[1]〔'besɪk〕*adj.* 基本的
allow[1]〔ə'lau〕*v.* 允許　　keep[1]〔kip〕*v.* 飼養

1. (**A**) 這項提案的目的是要做什麼？

(A) 確保狗飼主有能力照顧他們的寵物。

(B) 管制少數以造成麻煩出名的「惡犬」。

(C) 強迫狗飼主放棄危險的動物。　(D) 修正鼓勵養狗的法規。

* design² ﹝dɪˋzaɪn﹞ v. 設計

be designed to V. 目的是為了… (= be meant to V.)

ensure ﹝ɪnˋʃʊr﹞ v. 確保

competent⁶ ﹝ˋkɑmpətənt﹞ adj. 有能力的　　**care for** 照顧

be known for 以…（特點）而有名　　force¹ ﹝fors﹞ v. 強迫

give up 放棄　　encourage² ﹝ɪnˋkɝɪdʒ﹞ v. 鼓勵

ownership³ ﹝ˋonɚˌʃɪp﹞ n. 所有權；擁有

2. (**B**) 本文主要是關於什麼？

(A) 危險的狗。　　　　　　　　(B) 一項被提議的法案。

(C) 大家對於養狗花費的關注。　(D) 政府的官僚作風。

* propose² ﹝prəˋpoz﹞ v. 提議

3. (**C**) 皇家防止虐待動物協會為什麼反對這項提案？

(A) 不是所有的狗都是危險的。　(B) 微晶片太貴。

(C) 這可能會對明智的狗飼主有負面的影響。

(D) 沒有證據可以證明狗會構成威脅。

* object² ﹝ˋɑbdʒɪkt﹞ v. 反對 < to >　　affect³ ﹝əˋfɛkt﹞ v. 影響

negatively² ﹝ˋnɛgətɪvlɪ﹞ adj. 負面的　　proof³ ﹝pruf﹞ n. 證據

threat³ ﹝θrɛt﹞ n. 威脅；構成威脅的人或物

4. (**C**) 下列陳述何者為非？

(A) 英國政府想要管制危險犬隻的飼養。

(B) 皇家動物保護協會歡迎對目前立法的評論。

(C) 新的提案將會禁止危險犬隻的飼養。

(D) 新的提案將會要求狗飼主做能力測驗。

* current³ ﹝ˋkɝənt﹞ adj. 目前的；現行的

outlaw⁶ ﹝ˋautˌlɔ﹞ v. 宣布…為不合法；禁止 (= forbid⁴)

competency⁶ ﹝ˋkɑmpətənsɪ﹞ n. 能力

TEST 14

Read the following passage and choose the best answer for each question.

Dancing has been around for thousands of years. Ballroom dancing can be fun and challenging. Among the many different types of ballroom dances, the most popular and well-known is the waltz. It is probably the first dance you will ever learn; anyone, at any age, can do the waltz. This style of dancing used to be popular in Europe during the days of Louis the XIII. The dance is fast and has a smooth flow to it. Dancers touch each other the entire time and move in a three-beat rhythm. It is a dancing style that is full of twists and turns.

Another popular dancing style is the tango. Historically, it is connected to dances from Spain, Africa, and Argentina. It's a very passionate dance, full of tight embraces. Females often flick their heads. Short and sharp movements **characterize** this emotional dance. Men are crouched down during this dance. The sexy moves give the female dancer a chance to show off.

The foxtrot actually has nothing to do with animals. It was named after the man who performed the dance in shows in New York. This dance is unique and is danced to jazz music. When a couple is dancing, they simply appear to be walking gracefully. This dancing style has inspired many other dances. It was seen as being very original when it hit the dancing scene in the early 1900s.

The last style of ballroom dancing is the quickstep, which is by all means quick. It's a very fast dance that has even been described as someone dancing on hot coals. Because the music for the quickstep is so fast, dancers adapted their dancing style and added small runs and hops. This is one dance that is sure to tire out a dancer. The quickstep, like any of the other dances mentioned, is challenging and fun to learn.

1. Which kind of dancing inspired many other dances?
    (A) Waltz.
    (B) Tango.
    (C) Foxtrot.
    (D) Quickstep.

2. Which of the following statements is true?

(A) The quickstep dancers have to dance on hot coals.

(B) The foxtrot dance is an imitation of a fox walking.

(C) Tango dancers usually hold each other tightly in their arms.

(D) The waltz was very popular in New York in the early 1900s.

3. What can we infer from the passage?

(A) The quickstep is not suitable for people with joint problems.

(B) Foxtrot dancers have to learn how to walk elegantly first.

(C) Outgoing girls should not learn the tango.

(D) Dancers usually twist their feet when waltzing.

4. The best definition for the underlined word **characterize** is _____.

(A) be typical of

(B) be exceptional to

(C) be capable of

(D) be related to

TEST 14 詳解

Dancing has been around *for thousands of years*. Ballroom dancing can be fun **and** challenging.

舞蹈已經有好幾千年的歷史了。國標舞是相當有趣而且很有挑戰性的。

* around[1] 〔ə'raʊnd〕*adj.* 存在的　ballroom〔'bɔl,rʊm〕*n.* 舞廳
  ballroom dancing 國標舞　fun[1]〔fʌn〕*adj.* 有趣的
  challenging[3]〔'tʃælɪndʒɪŋ〕*adj.* 有挑戰性的

Among the many different types of ballroom dances, the *most* popular **and** well-known is the waltz. It is *probably* the first dance *you will ever learn*; anyone, *at any age*, can do the waltz.

在許多不同類型的國標舞中，最受歡迎而且也最廣爲人知的，就是華爾滋。它可能就是你學會的第一支舞；任何人，不論年紀大小，都可以學華爾滋。

* among[1]〔ə'mʌŋ〕*prep.* 在…當中　type[2]〔taɪp〕*n.* 類型
  popular[2,3]〔'pɑpjələ〕*adj.* 流行的；受歡迎的
  well-known〔'wɛl'non〕*adj.* 有名的（=*famous*[2]）
  waltz〔wɔlts〕*n.* 華爾滋舞　ever[1]〔'ɛvə〕*adv.* 曾經
  do[1]〔du〕*v.* 學習

This style *of dancing* used to be popular *in Europe during the days of Louis the XIII*. The dance is fast **and** has a smooth flow *to it*.

在法王路易十三的時代，這種風格的舞蹈在歐洲相當流行。這種舞蹈速度很快，而且舞步流暢。

* style[3] 〔staɪl〕*n.* 風格；型式　　Europe〔'jʊrəp〕*n.* 歐洲
days[1] 〔dez〕*n.* 時代
Louis the XIII 〔'luɪ ðə 'θɜtinθ〕*n.* 路易十三【法國國王】
smooth[3] 〔smuð〕*adj.* 平順的；流暢的　　flow[2] 〔flo〕*n.* 流暢
to[1] 〔tə〕*prep.* 屬於；歸於【（如 the key to the house（房子的鑰匙）、the door to the office（辦公室的門）】

Dancers touch each other *the entire time **and** move in a three-beat rhythm*. It is a dancing style ***that** is full of twists **and** turns.*

整個跳舞的期間，舞者會互相碰觸，以三拍子的節奏舞動。這是充滿旋轉的舞蹈風格。

* dancer[1] 〔'dænsɚ〕*n.* 舞者　　***each other*** 互相
entire[2] 〔ɪn'taɪr〕*adj.* 整個的（= *whole*[1]）
move[1] 〔muv〕*v.* 移動　　beat[1] 〔bit〕*n.* 拍子
rhythm[4] 〔'rɪðəm〕*n.* 節奏；韻律　　***be full of*** 充滿了
twist[3] 〔twɪst〕*n.* 旋轉；扭轉　　turn[1] 〔tɜn〕*n.* 轉動；旋轉

Another popular dancing style is the tango. *Historically*, it is connected to dances *from Spain, Africa, **and** Argentina.*

另一種流行的舞蹈風格是探戈。根據歷史的記載，它和來自西班牙、非洲，和阿根廷的舞蹈有關。

* tango 〔'tæŋgo〕*n.* 探戈舞
historically[3] 〔hɪs'tɔrɪkl̩ɪ〕*adv.* 在歷史上
connect[3] 〔kə'nɛkt〕*v.* 連結　　***be connected to*** 和…有關
Spain 〔spen〕*n.* 西班牙　　Africa 〔'æfrɪkə〕*n.* 非洲
Argentina 〔ˌɑrdʒən'tinə〕*n.* 阿根廷

It's a *very* passionate dance, *full of tight embraces*. Females *often*

flick their heads. Short *and* sharp movements **characterize** this

emotional dance.

它是一種很熱情的舞蹈，舞者必須緊緊相擁。女舞者常會快速甩頭。急
促且突然的動作，是這種充滿感情舞蹈的特色。

* passionate⁵〔'pæʃənɪt〕*adj.* 熱情的　　tight³〔taɪt〕*adj.* 緊的
  embrace⁵〔ɪm'bres〕*n.* 擁抱
  female²〔'fɪmel〕*n.* 女人　*adj.* 女性的
  flick⁵〔flɪk〕*v.* 輕彈；（急速地）輕輕轉動
  short¹〔ʃɔrt〕*adj.* 短促的；急速的　　sharp¹〔ʃɑrp〕*adj.* 突然的
  movement¹〔'muvmənt〕*n.* 動作
  characterize⁶〔'kærəktə,raɪz〕*v.* 是⋯的特色
  emotional⁴〔ɪ'moʃənl〕*adj.* 表現強烈情感的

Men are crouched down *during this dance*. The sexy moves give the

female dancer a chance *to show off.*

男舞者在跳舞時，必須要蹲低。性感的舞步讓女舞者有機會展現自己。

* crouch⁵〔krautʃ〕*v.* 蹲伏；彎身 < *down* >
  sexy³〔'sɛksɪ〕*adj.* 性感的　　*show off* 炫耀；賣弄；表現自己

The foxtrot *actually* has nothing *to do with animals*. It was

named *after the man **who** performed the dance in shows in New York.*

This dance is unique *and* is danced *to jazz music*.

　　狐步舞其實和動物沒有什麼關係。它是因為一個在紐約的節目中表
演舞蹈的男人而得名。這種舞蹈很獨特，是配合著爵士樂而舞動。

* foxtrot〔'faks,trat〕*n.* 狐步舞　　actually[3]〔'æktʃʊəlɪ〕*adj.* 實際上
have nothing to do with 和…無關
be named after 以…的名字命名　　perform[3]〔pɚ'fɔrm〕*v.* 表演
show[1]〔ʃo〕*n.* 演出；節目　　unique[4]〔ju'nik〕*adj.* 獨特的
jazz[2]〔dʒæz〕*n.* 爵士樂

When *a couple is dancing*, they *simply* appear to be walking

gracefully. This dancing style has inspired many other dances. It

was seen as being *very* original ***when*** *it hit the dancing scene in the*

early 1900s.

當一對舞者在跳狐步舞時，他們看起來好像是很優雅地走路。這種舞蹈
啓發許多其他的舞步。當狐步舞在 20 世紀初期打進舞蹈界時，被認爲
是極具原創性的。

* couple[2]〔'kʌpḷ〕*n.* 一對男女；（跳舞的）一對舞伴
simply[2]〔'sɪmplɪ〕*adv.* 完全地　　appear[1]〔ə'pɪr〕*v.* 看起來；好像
gracefully[4]〔'gresfəlɪ〕*adv.* 優雅地
inspire[4]〔ɪn'spaɪr〕*v.* 啓發；激勵　　***be seen as*** 被認爲是
original[3]〔ə'rɪdʒənḷ〕*adj.* 原創性的；有創意的
hit[1]〔hɪt〕*v.* 達到；到達　　scene[1]〔sin〕*n.* …的舞台；…界
in the early 1900s 在二十世紀初

The last style *of ballroom dancing* is the quickstep, ***which is by***

all means quick. It's a *very* fast dance ***that*** *has even been described*

as someone dancing on hot coals.

　　最後一種國標舞是快步舞，這種舞蹈當然是跳得很快。這是一種很快的舞蹈，甚至被形容爲是在熱炭上跳舞。

* quickstep〔'kwɪkˌstɛp〕*n.* 快步舞
  by all means 當然（ = *of course* ）
  describe[2]〔dɪ'skraɪb〕*v.* 描述；形容
  be described as 被形容成　　coal[2]〔kol〕*n.* 煤炭

Because the music for the quickstep is so fast, dancers adapted their

dancing style ***and*** added small runs ***and*** hops. This is one dance

that is sure to tire out a dancer.

因爲快步舞的音樂非常快，所以舞者就改變他們的舞蹈風格，加入小跑步和小跳躍。這是一種絕對會累垮舞者的舞蹈。

* adapt[4]〔ə'dæpt〕*v.* 使適應；使適合；改編　　add[1]〔æd〕*v.* 增加
  hop[2]〔hɑp〕*n.* 跳躍　　sure[1]〔ʃur〕*adj.* 必定的
  tire out 使…十分疲累；把…累垮

The quickstep, *like any of the other dances mentioned*, is challenging

and fun to learn.

就像其他提到過的舞蹈一樣，快步舞很有挑戰性，而且學起來很有趣。

* mention[3]〔'mɛnʃən〕*v.* 提到

1. (**C**) 哪一種舞蹈啓發許多其他的舞步？
   (A) 華爾滋。　　　　　　(B) 探戈。
   (C) <u>狐步舞。</u>　　　　　　(D) 快步舞。

2. (**C**) 下列敘述何者爲眞？

(A) 快步舞的舞者必須在熱炭上跳舞。

(B) 狐步舞是一種模仿狐狸走路的舞蹈。

(C) <u>探戈舞者通常會把舞伴緊緊擁抱在懷中。</u>

(D) 二十世紀初華爾滋在紐約非常流行。

* imitation[4] 〔͵ɪmə'teʃən〕 n. 模仿
fox[2] 〔faks〕 n. 狐狸　　hold[1] 〔hold〕 v. 擁抱
tightly[3] 〔'taɪtlɪ〕 adv. 緊緊地　　*in one's arms* 在懷中

3. (**A**) 我們可從本文推論出什麼？

(A) <u>快步舞不適合關節有問題的人。</u>

(B) 狐步舞的舞者必須先學習如何優雅地走路。

(C) 外向的女孩不應該學探戈。

(D) 舞者通常在跳華爾滋時會扭到腳。

* infer[6] 〔ɪn'fɝ〕 v. 推論　　suitable[3] 〔'sutəbḷ〕 adj. 適合的
joint[2] 〔dʒɔɪnt〕 n. 關節　　elegantly[4] 〔'ɛləgəntlɪ〕 adv. 優雅地
outgoing[5] 〔'aʊt͵goɪŋ〕 adj. 外向的
twist[1] 〔twɪst〕 v. 扭傷　　waltz 〔wɔlz〕 v. 跳華爾滋舞

4. (**A**) 畫底線的字 **characterize** 的最佳定義是 ＿＿＿＿＿＿。

(A) *be typical of* 是…的特色

(B) be exceptional to 是…的例外

(C) be capable of 能夠

(D) be related to 和…相關

* definition[3] 〔͵dɛfə'nɪʃən〕 n. 定義
underline[5] 〔͵ʌndə'laɪn〕 v. 在…下面畫線
typical[3] 〔'tɪpɪkḷ〕 adj. 有代表性的
exceptional[5] 〔ɪk'sɛpʃənḷ〕 adj. 例外的
capable[3] 〔'kepəbḷ〕 adj. 有能力的
related[3] 〔rɪ'letɪd〕 adj. 相關的

TEST 15

Read the following passage and choose the best answer for each question.

Nowadays, people love to keep pets as their companions. The most commonly seen pets are dogs and cats. Interestingly, when there is interaction among dog owners and cat owners, just as dogs and cats bear distinct behaviors from heritage prior to domestication, the two categories of pet owner display clearly different characters, according to a survey conducted in Austin, Texas.

Dogs and cats have drastically different natural characters. In the wild, canines are diurnal, more sociable and enjoy working in packs, while cats are usually nocturnal and usually hunt alone. After they are domesticated, they retain these traits. This well explains why dogs like to intrude upon people's ongoing activities, for example, by waking their owners up in the early morning or begging for attention during a family reunion. Dogs may be unhappy or lost if there are no human family members around. Cats, by contrast, often hide during the day, appearing at night to do their own things. They sometimes engage in social activities, but their attention span is very limited. They usually drift away from a game while their masters are still very enthusiastic. On the other hand, dogs are more zealous in playing and it's usually the masters that give up first.

The different behavior modes of the two species can reflect the underlying human personality differences of the people who choose one kind over the other as a pet. As predicted in the survey, dog lovers are 20% more extroverted and 15% more amiable than cat lovers. In addition, dog people are 12% more conscientious than cat people, which means dog people may be more self-disciplined and display less spontaneous behavior. However, as for the openness trait, cat people are 12% more open than dog people, which means cat people are more able to appreciate art, more imaginative, curious, and adventurous. Thus, they tend to accept unconventional beliefs more readily than dog people, who, on the contrary, are more comfortable with traditional ideas.

Though the survey may suggest the general traits of dog owners and cat owners, life is not just black and white and there is no need to have prejudice against people based on their type of pet. No matter what kind of pet people keep, what matters is the company both the owner and the pet enjoy.

1. According to the passage, what is the author's attitude toward the result of the survey?

   (A) Outraged.   (B) Thrilled.

   (C) Approving.   (D) Neutral.

2. According to the passage, which of the following statements is true?

   (A) Dog people like to interrupt others' activities.

   (B) Cat people's attention span is very short.

   (C) Dog people are less likely to act impulsively.

   (D) Cat people tend to embrace conventional thoughts.

3. The passage mainly _____.

   (A) illustrates how cats and dogs are different

   (B) explains human personality traits from the angle of pet ownership

   (C) tells people how to deal with dog people and cat people

   (D) shows what a dog or a cat may do when it is around its master

4. Which of the following can best define the word nocturnal?

   (A) Active at night.   (B) Living in seclusion.

   (C) Fearful of crowds.   (D) Arrogant.

TEST 15 詳解

Nowadays, people love to keep pets *as their companions*. The

most commonly seen pets are dogs *and* cats.

現今，人們喜歡養寵物做伴。最普遍的寵物就是貓跟狗。

* nowadays[4] ('nauə,dez) *adv.* 現今　　pet[1] (pɛt) *n.* 寵物
keep a pet 養寵物　　companion[4] (kəm'pænjən) *n.* 同伴
commonly[1] ('kamənlı) *adv.* 常見地；普遍地

Interestingly, **when** *there is interaction among dog owners* **and** *cat*

owners, *just* **as** *dogs* **and** *cats bear distinct behaviors from heritage*

prior to domestication, the two categories *of pet owner* display *clearly*

different characters, *according to a survey conducted in Austin, Texas.*

有趣的是，根據一份在德州奧斯丁所做的研究指出，當狗主人和貓主人
互動的時候，就像狗和貓在被人類馴養前所具有的天性一樣，這兩種寵
物的主人呈現出截然不同的性格。

* interaction[4] (,ıntə'ækʃən) *n.* 互動
among[3] (ə'mʌŋ) *prep.* 在…之間　　owner[2] ('onə) *n.* 擁有者
bear[2,1] (bɛr) *v.* 具有 (= carry[1] = possess[4])
distinct[4] (dı'stıŋkt) *adj.* 不同的 (= different[1])
behavior[4] (bı'hevjə) *n.* 行為
heritage[6] ('hɛrətıdʒ) *n.* 遺產；繼承物；遺留物 (= legacy)
prior to 在～之前 (= before[1])

domestication〔də͵mɛstəˈkeʃən〕*n.* 馴養

　【domestic[3] *adj.* 家庭的；馴服的】

category[5]〔ˈkætə͵gorɪ〕*n.* 種類（= *classification*[4]）

display[2]〔dɪˈsple〕*v.* 展現

character[2]〔ˈkærəktɚ〕*n.* 性格（= *personality*[3]）

survey[3]〔ˈsɝve〕*n.* 調查（= *research*[4] = *investigation*[4]）

conduct[5]〔kənˈdʌkt〕*v.* 進行；做（= *do*[1] = *carry out*）

Dogs *and* cats have *drastically different* natural characters.

貓和狗天生有著徹底不同的個性。

　* drastically[6]〔ˈdræstɪkəlɪ〕*adv.* 徹底地

　natural[2]〔ˈnætʃərəl〕*adj.* 天生的；自然的

In the wild, canines are diurnal, more sociable *and* enjoy working

in packs, *while* cats are *usually* **nocturnal** *and* usually hunt *alone*.

在野外，犬科動物是白天活動的，比較善於交際，並且喜歡成群結隊地
活動；而貓通常是在夜間活動，並且會獨自狩獵。

　* *the wild* 野外　　canine〔ˈkenaɪn〕*n.* 犬科動物

　diurnal〔daɪˈɝnl̩〕*adj.* 白天活動的

　sociable[6]〔ˈsoʃəbl̩〕*adj.* 善於交際的

　enjoy[2]〔ɪnˈdʒɔɪ〕*v.* 喜歡　　pack[2]〔pæk〕*n.*（狼、犬）一群

　nocturnal〔nɑkˈtɝnl̩〕*adj.* 夜間活動的

　hunt[2]〔hʌnt〕*v.* 打獵　　alone[1]〔əˈlon〕*adv.* 單獨地

After they are domesticated, they retain these traits.

在被馴養之後，牠們還是保有這些特性。

　* domesticate〔dəˈmɛstə͵ket〕*v.* 馴養

　retain[4]〔rɪˈten〕*v.* 保持　　trait[6]〔tret〕*n.* 特性

This *well* explains *why* *dogs like to intrude upon people's ongoing*

activities, for example, by waking their owners up in the early morning

or begging for attention during a family reunion.

這就充分說明了為什麼狗會喜歡干擾人類正在進行的活動，例如在一大早去叫醒主人，或是在家人團聚時，乞求主人的注意。

* well[1] [wɛl] *adv.* 充分地；十分地　　explain[2] [ɪk'splen] *v.* 解釋
intrude[6] [ɪn'trud] *v.* 入侵；闖入；干涉；干擾 < on/upon >
ongoing [ɑn'goɪŋ] *adj.* 進行中的　　activity[3] [æk'tɪvətɪ] *n.* 活動
for example 例如　　*wak sb. up* 叫醒某人
beg[2] [bɛg] *v.* 乞求　　attention[2] [ə'tɛnʃən] *n.* 注意力
reunion[4] [rɪ'junjən] *n.* 重聚；團圓

Dogs may be unhappy *or* lost *if there are no human family members*

around.

如果沒有主人家庭中的成員在牠們身邊，狗的心情會不好或有悵然若失的感覺。

* human[1] ['hjumən] *adj.* 人的；人類的
around[1] [ə'raʊnd] *adv.* 在周圍；在附近

Cats, *by contrast, often* hide *during the day, appearing at night to do*

their own things.

對比之下，貓白天常常會躲起來，晚上才出現做牠們的事。

* *by contrast* 對照之下　　hide[2] [haɪd] *v.* 躲藏
during the day 在白天　　appear[1] [ə'pɪr] *v.* 出現

They *sometimes* engage in social activities, ***but*** their attention span
is *very* limited.

牠們有時會參與社交活動，但牠們專注力持續的時間相當有限。

* engage³〔ɪnˈgedʒ〕*v.* 從事 < *in* >　　social²〔ˈsoʃəl〕*adj.* 社交的
span⁶〔spæn〕*n.* 期間　　***attention span*** 注意力持續的時間
limited²〔ˈlɪmɪtɪd〕*adj.* 有限的

They *usually* drift away from a game *while their masters are still very*
enthusiastic.

牠們經常在主人還很興致勃勃地想繼續玩遊戲的時候悄悄離場。

* drift⁴〔drɪft〕*v.* 漂流；漸漸散去　　***drift away*** 慢慢離開
master¹〔ˈmæstɚ〕*n.* 主人
enthusiastic⁵〔ɪnˌθuzɪˈæstɪk〕*adj.* 熱情的 (= *passionate*⁵)

On the other hand, dogs are *more* zealous *in playing* ***and*** it's *usually*
the masters ***that*** *give up first.*

相對而言，狗就會更熱情參與玩耍，通常是主人先不想玩。

* ***on the other hand*** 另一方面　　zealous⁶〔ˈzɛləs〕*adj.* 狂熱的
give up 放棄

The different behavior modes *of the two species* can reflect the
underlying human personality differences *of the people **who** choose*
one kind over the other as a pet.

這兩種動物不同的行爲模式，可以反映出選擇其中一種當寵物，而不選另一種的飼主，其潛在人格特質的差異。

* mode[5]〔mod〕*n.* 模式　　species[4]〔'spiʃiz〕*n.* 物種
  reflect[4]〔rɪ'flɛkt〕*v.* 反映
  underlying〔ˌʌndə'laɪɪŋ〕*adj.* 潛在的 (= *potential*[5])
  personality[3]〔ˌpɝsn̩'ælətɪ〕*n.* 個性
  choose A over B 選 A 不選 B　　kind[1]〔kaɪnd〕*n.* 種類

As predicted in the survey, dog lovers are 20% *more* extroverted *and*

15% *more* amiable *than* cat lovers.

如同調查中所預測的，愛狗的人外向的比例比愛貓的人多出百分之二十，而親切友善的部分則是多出百分之十五。

* predict[4]〔prɪ'dɪkt〕*v.* 預測
  extroverted〔'ɛkstroˌvɝtɪd〕*adj.* 外向的 (= *extrovert*)
  amiable[6]〔'emɪəbl̩〕*adj.* 親切友善的

In addition, dog people are 12% *more* conscientious *than* cat people,

which means dog people may be more self-disciplined *and* display

less spontaneous behavior.

此外，愛狗的人負責盡職的程度，比愛貓的人多出百分之十二，這就表示愛狗的人可能比較自律，也比較不會有不由自主的行爲。

* conscientious[6]〔ˌkɑnʃɪ'ɛnʃəs〕*adj.* 負責盡職的
  self-disciplined〔sɛlf'dɪsəplɪnd〕*adj.* 嚴以律己的
  spontaneous[6]〔spɑn'tenɪəs〕*adj.* 自動自發的；(動作等)無意識的；
  　不由自主的

However, as for the openness trait, cat people are 12% *more* open

than dog people, *which means cat people are more able to appreciate*

art, more imaginative, curious, and adventurous.

然而，至於心胸寬大的特點，愛貓的人比愛狗的人開放的程度多百分之
十二，這表示愛貓的人比較會欣賞藝術，比較有想像力、比較好奇，也
更勇於冒險。

* *as for* 至於　　openness〔'opənnɪs〕*n.*（心胸）寬大
  open[1]〔'opən〕*adj.* 開放的；寬大的　　*be able to V.* 能夠…
  appreciate[3]〔ə'priʃɪ,et〕*v.* 欣賞　　art[1]〔ɑrt〕*n.* 藝術
  imaginative[4]〔ɪ'mædʒə,netɪv〕*adj.* 有想像力的
  curious[2]〔'kjʊrɪəs〕*adj.* 好奇的
  adventurous[3]〔æd'vɛntʃərəs〕*adj.* 愛冒險的

Thus, they tend to accept unconventional beliefs *more readily than*

dog people, who, on the contrary, are more comfortable with

traditional ideas.

因此，他們比愛狗的人更易於接受非傳統的看法，相反地，愛狗的人則
比較安於傳統的想法。

* *tend to V.* 易於；傾向於
  accept[2]〔ək'sɛpt〕*v.* 接受
  unconventional[4]〔,ʌnkən'vɛnʃənl〕*adj.* 不依慣例的；不落俗套的
  belief[2]〔bɪ'lif〕*n.* 信念；看法
  readily[1]〔'rɛdɪlɪ〕*adv.* 輕易地；迅速地；樂意地
  contrary[4]〔'kɑntrɛrɪ〕*adj.* 相反的　　*on the contrary* 相反地

comfortable[2] ('kʌmfətəbl̩) *adj.* 舒服的;滿意的 < *with* >
traditional[2] (trə'dɪʃənl̩) *adj.* 傳統的　　idea[1] (aɪ'diə) *n.* 想法

Though the survey may suggest the general traits of dog owners

and cat owners, life is not *just* black *and* white *and* there is no need

to have prejudice *against people based on their type of pet.*

　　雖然研究可能指出了養狗和養貓人士普遍的特質,但是人生不是那麼絕對的,而且不需要根據他們養的寵物類型而對他們有偏見。

　　* suggest[3] (səg'dʒɛst) *v.* 暗示;指出
　　general[1,2] ('dʒɛnərəl) *adj.* 普遍的
　　black and white 黑白分明;絕對化
　　there is no need 沒有必要;不需要
　　prejudice[6] ('prɛdʒədɪs) *n.* 偏見 (= *bias*[6]) < *against* >
　　based on 根據　　type[2] (taɪp) *n.* 類型

No matter what kind of pet people keep, *what* matters is the company

both the owner and the pet enjoy.

無論養什麼寵物,真正重要的是人類與寵物之間的陪伴。

　　* matter[1] ('mætɚ) *v.* 重要;有關係　　*no matter* 無論
　　company[2] ('kʌmpənɪ) *n.* 陪伴

1. (**D**) 根據本文,作者對於調查結果的態度為何?
　　(A) outraged[6] ('aʊt,redʒd) *adj.* 氣憤的
　　(B) thrilled[5] (θrɪld) *adj.* 興奮的
　　(C) approving[3] (ə'pruvɪŋ) *adj.* 認同的
　　(D) *neutral*[6] ('nutrəl) *adj.* 中立的

* author[3] 〔 'ɔθə 〕 *n.* 作者
attitude[3] 〔 'ætə,tjud 〕 *n.* 態度；看法 < *toward* >
result[2] 〔 rɪ'zʌlt 〕 *n.* 結果

2. (**C**) 根據本文，下列敘述爲眞？

(A) 愛狗人士喜歡打斷他人的活動。

(B) 愛貓人士的注意力持續的時間非常短。

(C) 愛狗人士較不可能衝動行事。

(D) 愛貓人士比較欣然接受傳統的想法。

* statement[1] 〔 'stetmənt 〕 *n.* 敘述
interrupt[3] 〔 ,ɪntə'rʌpt 〕 *v.* 打斷　　act[1] 〔 ækt 〕 *v.* 行爲表現
impulsively[5] 〔 ɪm'pʌlsɪvlɪ 〕 *adv.* 衝動地
embrace[5] 〔 ɪm'bres 〕 *v.* 擁抱；欣然接受
conventional[4] 〔 kən'vɛnʃənḷ 〕 *adj.* 傳統的
thought[1] 〔 θɔt 〕 *n.* 思想

3. (**B**) 本文主要是要 ＿＿＿＿＿＿＿＿ 。

(A) 描述貓和狗是如何不同

(B) 從寵物主人的角度來解釋人類的性格特質

(C) 告訴人們如何與愛狗人士和愛貓人士相處

(D) 說明當在主人身邊時，狗或貓可能會做什麼

* illustrate[4] 〔 'ɪləstret 〕 *v.* 說明　　angle[3] 〔 'æŋgḷ 〕 *n.* 角度
ownership[3] 〔 'onə,ʃɪp 〕 *n.* 所有權；物主身份
deal with 處理；對待

4. (**A**) 下列何者最能定義 "nocturnal" 這個字？

(A) 在夜間很活躍。　　　　(B) 過隱居的生活。

(C) 害怕人群。　　　　　　(D) 自大的。

* define[3] 〔 dɪ'faɪn 〕 *v.* 爲…下定義
active[2] 〔 'æktɪv 〕 *adj.* 活躍的
seclusion 〔 sɪ'kluʒən 〕 *n.* 隔離；隔絕；退隱
fearful[2] 〔 'fɪrfəl 〕 *adj.* 害怕的 < *of* >
crowd[2] 〔 kraʊd 〕 *n.* 群衆；人群
arrogant[6] 〔 'zrəgənt 〕 *adj.* 自大的

TEST 16

Read the following passage and choose the best answer for each question.

Academy Award nominees who go home empty-handed may not have a shiny Oscar to show off, but they may turn out to be the bigger winners in the game of life.

According to a study published in British Medical Journal in December, Oscar-winning screenwriters are more successful and more respected than losing nominees; however, they die sooner by about four years. Although success is usually linked to better health, "this is the first occupation ever that success is not associated with improved longevity," says Donald Reddish, lead author of the study.

Researchers tracked down information about every person who was ever nominated for an Oscar since the awards were first handed out 73 years ago. To explain the puzzling findings, he offers two theories. The first is the "work-to-death hypothesis." According to Reddish, screenwriters are more apt to lead unhealthy lifestyles, meaning they smoke more, exercise less, and work a lot of late-night hours, which translates into not enough sleep.

Screenwriters don't have a boss to report to, which
accounts for Reddish's second explanation, the "party-hearty
hypothesis." "When you become a successful screenwriter,
you gain status without daily accountability, and as a
consequence your success may lead you to more alcohol,
more parties, and more obesity," he says.

Reddish hopes his study will stress how important it is
to lead a healthy lifestyle. "The bottom line," he says, "is
that greater success may sometimes lead to worse health if
people fail to look after themselves."

1. What is the passage mainly about?
   (A) The reason why many screenwriters died young.
   (B) Why some Oscar winners didn't enjoy longevity.
   (C) The importance of living a healthy life for
       successful people.
   (D) Success and health of celebrities in the film
       industry.

2. Which of the following is NOT a reason for Oscar
   winners to live unhealthily?
   (A) Working late hours.   (B) Lack of exercise.
   (C) Effects of heredity.   (D) Excessive partying.

3. What was Donald Reddish's purpose in conducting this study?

   (A) To tell people health is more important than being successful.
   (B) To advise people against the pursuit of success.
   (C) To inform people of the benefits of choosing a health-related occupation.
   (D) To compare the longevity of successful screenwriters and less successful screenwriters.

4. What does Donald Reddish imply about most professions?

   (A) Success in most professions often brings about stress.
   (B) Success in most professions leads people to early death.
   (C) Successful people in most professions don't pay attention to their health.
   (D) Successful people in most professions tend to enjoy longer lives.

TEST 16 詳解

Academy Award nominees *who go home empty-handed* may not have a shiny Oscar *to show off*, *but* they may turn out to be the bigger winners *in the game of life*.

空手而回的奧斯卡入圍者，也許沒有閃亮的奧斯卡獎座可以炫耀，但是他們可能成為人生這場遊戲中較大的贏家。

* academy[5] ﹝ə'kædəmɪ﹞ *n.* 學院   award[3] ﹝ə'wɔrd﹞ *n.* 獎
  Academy Award 奧斯卡金像獎
  nominee[6] ﹝ˌnɑmə'ni﹞ *n.* 被提名人
  empty-handed ﹝'ɛmptɪ'hændɪd﹞ *adj.* 空手的
  shiny[3] ﹝'ʃaɪnɪ﹞ *adj.* 閃耀的   Oscar ﹝'ɔskɚ﹞ *n.* 奧斯卡金像獎
  show off 炫耀   *turn out* 結果（成為）
  winner[2] ﹝'wɪnɚ﹞ *n.* 贏家

According to a study published in British Medical Journal in December, Oscar-winning screenwriters are *more* successful *and more* respected *than losing nominees*; *however*, they die *sooner by about four years*.

根據一篇發表在十二月《英國醫學期刊》的研究指出，獲得奧斯卡獎的編劇比起落選的入圍者，是較成功，且較受人尊敬，但卻早死了四年左右。

* *according to* 根據   study[1] ﹝'stʌdɪ﹞ *n.* 研究

publish[4] ('pʌblɪʃ) v. 出版；刊登
medical[3] ('mɛdɪk!) adj. 醫學的　　journal[3] ('dʒɜn!) n. 期刊
British Medical Journal 英國醫學期刊
screenwriter ('skrin,raɪtɚ) n. 編劇
successful[2] (sək'sɛsfəl) adj. 成功的
respect[2] (rɪ'spɛkt) v. 尊敬　　losing[2] ('luzɪŋ) adj. 失敗的

Although *success is usually linked to better health,* "this is the first

occupation *ever* **that** *success is not associated with improved*

longevity," says Donald Reddish, *lead author of the study.*

雖然成功通常和較好的健康狀況有關連，但是該研究的主要作者唐納
德・雷迪許說：「這是有史以來的第一份，成功和長壽無關的職業。」

* success[2] (sək'sɛs) n. 成功　　link[2] (lɪŋk) v. 連結
  be linked to 和…有關　　health[1] (hɛlθ) n. 健康
  occupation[4] (,ɑkjə'peʃən) n. 職業
  ever[1] ('ɛvɚ) adv. 至今【在比較級、最高級之後，用以強調】
  associate[4] (ə'soʃɪ,et) v. 聯想；使有關連
  be associated with 和…有關
  improved[2] (ɪm'pruvd) adj. 比以前好的；已改善的
  longevity[6] (lɑn'dʒɛvətɪ) n. 長壽
  Donald Reddish ('dɑnəld 'rɛdɪʃ) n. 唐納德・雷迪許
  lead[4] (lid) adj. 主要的　　author[3] ('ɔθɚ) n. 作者

Researchers tracked down information *about every person* **who**

was ever nominated for an Oscar **since** *the awards were first handed*

out 73 years ago.

研究人員追蹤從七十三年前，自奧斯卡獎第一次頒發後的每一位入圍者的資訊。

* researcher[4] 〔 rɪ'sɝtʃɚ 〕 *n.* 研究人員　　***track down*** 經追蹤而發現
nominate[5] 〔'nɑmə,net 〕 *v.* 提名　　***hand out*** 分發

To explain the puzzling findings, he offers two theories.　The first is the "work-to-death hypothesis."

爲了解釋這個令人困惑的發現，他提供兩種理論。第一種是「工作到死的假設」。

* explain[2] 〔 ɪk'splen 〕 *v.* 解釋
puzzling[2] 〔'pʌzlɪŋ 〕 *adj.* 令人困惑的
finding[1] 〔'faɪndɪŋ 〕 *n.* 發現；研究結果
offer[2] 〔'ɔfɚ 〕 *v.* 提供　　theory[3] 〔'θɪərɪ 〕 *n.* 理論
hypothesis 〔 haɪ'pɑθəsɪs 〕 *n.* 假說

According to Reddish, screenwriters are *more* apt to lead unhealthy lifestyles, *meaning they smoke more, exercise less,* ***and*** *work a lot of* late-night hours, ***which*** *translates into not enough sleep.*

根據雷迪許的說法，編劇較容易過著不健康的生活，也就是說他們比較常抽菸、較少運動，而且工作到很晚，這說明了不足的睡眠時間。

* apt[5] 〔 æpt 〕 *adj.* 偏好…的　　***be apt to*** 易於；傾向於
lead[1,4] 〔 lid 〕 *v.* 過（某種生活）
unhealthy[2] 〔 ʌn'hɛlθɪ 〕 *adj.* 不健康的
lifestyle 〔'laɪf,staɪl 〕 *n.* 生活方式　　mean[1] 〔 min 〕 *v.* 意思是
exercise[2] 〔'ɛksɚ,saɪz 〕 *n.* 運動　　late-night 〔'let,naɪt 〕 *adj.* 夜間的
translate[4] 〔 træns'let 〕 *v.* 說明；表達 < *into* >

Screenwriters don't have a boss *to report to*, **which** *accounts for*

Reddish's second explanation, the "party-hearty hypothesis."

編劇沒有老闆要報告進度，這就解釋了雷迪許第二項說明的原因，「盡情狂歡的假說」。

* boss[1] 〔bɔs〕 *n.* 老闆   report[1] 〔rɪ'port〕 *v.* 報告
  report to 向…負責；向…報告；是…的屬下
  account[3] 〔ə'kaʊnt〕 *v.* 說明
  account for 解釋…的原因
  explanation[4] 〔͵ɛksplə'neʃən〕 *n.* 說明
  hearty[5] 〔'hɑrtɪ〕 *adj.* 盡情的
  party-hearty *adj.* 盡情狂歡的

*"**When** you become a successful screenwriter, you gain status without*

*daily accountability, **and** as a consequence your success may lead*

you *to more alcohol, more parties, **and** more obesity*," he says.

「當你變成一位成功的編劇，獲得社會地位，而且沒有每天應盡的責任，因此你的成功可能使你喝更多多酒、參加更多的派對，以及變得更肥胖，」他說。

* gain[2] 〔gen〕 *v.* 獲得   status[4] 〔'stetəs〕 *n.* 地位
  daily[2] 〔'delɪ〕 *adj.* 每天的
  accountability[6] 〔ə͵kaʊntə'bɪlətɪ〕 *n.* 負有責任
  consequence[4] 〔'kɑnsə͵kwɛns〕 *n.* 後果
  as a consequence 因此（= *consequently*[4]）
  lead[1] 〔lid〕 *v.* 引導（某人）
  alcohol[4] 〔'ælkə͵hɔl〕 *n.* 酒
  obesity 〔o'bisətɪ〕 *n.* 肥胖

Reddish hopes *his study will stress **how** important it is to lead a healthy lifestyle.* "The bottom line," he says, "is **that** *greater success may sometimes lead to worse health* **if** *people fail to look after themselves.*"

雷迪許希望他的研究可以強調，健康的生活方式是多麼重要。他說：「基本上來說就是，如果人們無法照顧自己，更好的成就可能導致更糟的健康狀況。」

* stress² 〔strɛs〕 v. 強調 (= *emphasize*³)
  important¹ 〔ɪm'pɔrtn̩t〕 *adj.* 重要的
  healthy² 〔'hɛlθɪ〕 *adj.* 健康的
  bottom¹ 〔'batəm〕 *n.* 底部　　line¹ 〔laɪn〕 *n.* 線；行
  the bottom line 最低限度；最根本的事實
  lead to 導致　　worse¹ 〔wɝs〕 *adj.* 更壞的
  fail to *V.* 未能　　**look after** 照顧

1. (**B**) 本文主要是關於什麼？
   (A) 許多編劇爲什麼早夭的原因。
   (B) 有些奧斯卡得獎者爲什麼不能長壽。
   (C) 成功人士過健康生活的重要性。
   (D) 電影業名人的成功與健康。

   * reason¹ 〔'rizn̩〕 *n.* 原因
     enjoy² 〔ɪn'dʒɔɪ〕 *v.* 享受；享有
     importance² 〔ɪm'pɔrtn̩s〕 *n.* 重要性
     celebrity⁵ 〔sɪ'lɛbrətɪ〕 *n.* 名人
     film² 〔fɪlm〕 *n.* 電影
     industry² 〔'ɪndəstrɪ〕 *n.* …業

2.(**C**) 以下何者不是奧斯卡得獎人過著不健康生活的原因？

        (A) 工作時間晚。   (B) 缺乏運動。

        (C) <u>遺傳的影響。</u>   (D) 過度的盡情狂歡。

        * unhealthily[2] 〔ʌnˈhɛlθɪlɪ〕*adv.* 不健康地
        effect[2] 〔ɪˈfɛkt〕*n.* 影響   lack[1] 〔læk〕*n.* 影響
        heredity 〔həˈrɛdətɪ〕*n.* 遺傳
        excessive[6] 〔ɪkˈsɛsɪv〕*adj.* 過度的

3.(**D**) 唐納德・雷迪許做此研究的目的是什麼？

        (A) 告訴人們健康比成功更重要。

        (B) 勸告人們不要追求成功。

        (C) 告知人們選擇和健康相關的職業的好處。

        (D) <u>比較成功的編劇和不成功的編劇的壽命。</u>

        * conduct[5] 〔kənˈdʌkt〕*v.* 進行；做
        advise[3] 〔ədˈvaɪz〕*v.* 勸告   against[1] 〔əˈgɛnst〕*prep.* 反對
        pursuit[4] 〔pɚˈsut〕*n.* 追求
        inform[3] 〔ɪnˈfɔrm〕*v.* 告知 < *of* >
        benefit[3] 〔ˈbɛnəfɪt〕*n.* 好處
        health-related *adj.* 和健康相關的
        compare[2] 〔kəmˈpɛr〕*v.* 比較

4.(**D**) 關於大多數的職業，唐納德・雷迪許暗示什麼？

        (A) 多數職業的成功常常帶來壓力。

        (B) 多數職業的成功會使人早死。

        (C) 多數職業的成功人士都不注意他們的健康。

        (D) <u>多數職業的成功人士傾向享有較長的壽命。</u>

        * imply[4] 〔ɪmˈplaɪ〕*v.* 暗示
        profession[4] 〔prəˈfɛʃən〕*n.* 職業   ***bring about*** 導致
        attention[2] 〔əˈtɛnʃən〕*n.* 注意力   ***pay attention to*** 注意
        tend to V . 易於；傾向於

TEST 17

Read the following passage and choose the best answer for each question.

Secure, authenticated identity is the birthright of every Estonian: before a newborn even arrives home, the hospital will have issued a digital birth certificate and his health insurance will have been started automatically. All residents of the small Baltic state aged 15 or over have electronic ID cards, which are used in health care, electronic banking and shopping, and e-mail, to sign contracts, to buy tram tickets, and much more besides— even to vote.

Estonia's approach makes life efficient: taxes take less than an hour to file, and refunds are paid within 48 hours. By law, the state may not ask for any piece of information more than once, people have the right to know what data are held on them and all government databases must be compatible, a system known as the X-road. In all, the Estonian state offers over 600 e-services to its citizens and 2,400 to businesses.

Some good ideas never take off because too few people embrace them, and with just 1.3m residents, Estonia is a small player. To fill the gap in the global market, Estonia will issue ID cards to non-resident "satellite Estonians", thereby creating a global, government-standard digital identity. Applicants will pay a small fee, probably around $41-68, and provide the same biometric data and documents as Estonian residents. If all is in order, a card will be issued, or its virtual equivalent on a smartphone. What may provide a bigger market is a European Union rule soon to come into force that will require member states to accept each others' digital IDs. That means non-resident holders of Estonian IDs, wherever they are, will be able not only to send each other email and to prove their identity but to do business with governments anywhere in the EU. Soon multiple satellite citizenship may even become the norm.

1. What is the best title for the passage?
   (A) Estonia Leads in Implementing Digital Identity Cards
   (B) Innovative Technology in Estonia
   (C) Benefits and Risks of Digital Identity Cards
   (D) Global Citizenship in Technology

2. What is true about the X-road?

   (A) Information about every citizen across the government systems is consistent.
   (B) It connects the Estonian system to those of other EU countries.
   (C) It is dedicated to ensuring a fair election can take place in Estonia.
   (D) It contains a lot of confidential data about citizens.

3. What is the organization of the passage?

   (A) introduction—the benefits of digital ID—the drawbacks of digital ID
   (B) definition—example in Estonia—example in EU
   (C) introduction—practice in Estonia—future plan for wider circulation
   (D) cxample in Estonia—problems—possible solutions

4. What can we infer about the "satellite citizenship" ID?

   (A) It requires a big budget to launch a global digital ID.
   (B) Users are required to provide data regularly for security checks.
   (C) It can facilitate global e-commerce.
   (D) It aims to enhance Estonia's influence in the EU.

TEST 17 詳解

Secure, authenticated identity is the birthright *of every Estonian*: *before a newborn even arrives home*, the hospital will have issued a digital birth certificate *and* his health insurance will have been started *automatically*.

確實經過驗證的身分，是每一個愛沙尼亞人與生俱來的權利：甚至在新生兒到家之前，醫院就會核發數位出生證明，並且他的健康保險也會自動啓動。

* secure[5] 〔sɪ'kjʊr〕 *adj.* 完全的；確定的
　authenticate 〔ɔ'θɛntɪ,ket〕 *v.* 證實；鑑定；認證
　【authentic[6] *adj.* 眞正的】
　identity[3] 〔aɪ'dɛntətɪ〕 *n.* 身分
　birthright 〔'bɝθ,raɪt〕 *n.* 與生俱來的權利
　Estonian 〔ɛs'tonɪən〕 *n.* 愛沙尼亞人　*adj.* 愛沙尼亞的
　newborn 〔'nju,bɔrn〕 *n.* 新生兒　　issue[5] 〔'ɪʃju〕 *v.* 核發
　digital[4] 〔'dɪdʒɪtl̩〕 *adj.* 數位的
　certificate[5] 〔sə'tɪfəkɪt〕 *n.* 證明書　　*birth certificate* 出生證明
　health[1] 〔hɛlθ〕 *n.* 健康　　insurance[4] 〔ɪn'ʃʊrəns〕 *n.* 保險
　automatically[3] 〔,ɔtə'mætɪkl̩ɪ〕 *adv.* 自動地

All residents *of the small Baltic state aged 15 or over* have electronic ID cards, *which are used in health care, electronic banking and shopping, and e-mail, to sign contracts, to buy tram tickets, and much more besides—even to vote.*

這個波羅的海的小國，所有15歲或超過15歲的居民，都有電子身分證，可以用於醫療保健、電子銀行業務、購物，以及電子郵件、簽合約、購買電車票，還有其他更多用途——甚至是投票。

* resident[5] (ˈrɛzədənt) *n.* 居民　　Baltic (ˈbɔltɪk) *adj.* 波羅的海的
  state[1] (stet) *n.* 國家　　electronic[3] (ɪˌlɛkˈtrɑnɪk) *adj.* 電子的
  ID 身份證明 (= *identification*[4])　　*ID card* 身份證
  health care 醫療保健　　banking (ˈbæŋkɪŋ) *n.* 銀行業務
  sign[2] (saɪn) *v.* 簽署　　contract[3] (ˈkɑntrækt) *n.* 合約
  tram (træm) *n.* 電車　　besides[2] (bɪˈsaɪdz) *adv.* 加上；還有
  vote[5] (vot) *v.* 投票

Estonia's approach makes life efficient: taxes take less than an hour *to file*, and refunds are paid *within 48 hours*.

　　愛沙尼亞的方法使得生活更有效率：報稅用不到一小時，而且48小時內就會退稅。

* Estonia (ɛsˈtonɪə) *n.* 愛沙尼亞【位於歐洲東北部，是波羅的海三國之一】
  approach[3] (əˈprotʃ) *n.* 方法　　efficient[3] (ɪˈfɪʃənt) *adj.* 有效率的
  tax[3] (tæks) *n.* 稅
  file[3] (faɪl) *v.* 提出；提送（報告等正式文件）
  refund[6] (ˈriˌfʌnd) *n.* 退款；退稅

By law, the state may not ask for any piece of information *more than once*, people have the right *to know **what** data are held on them **and** all government databases must be compatible, *a system known as the X-road*.

根據法規，國家最多只能要求任何資料一次，民眾有權知道政府擁有關於他們的什麼資料，而且所有政府的資料庫必須要能相容，這個系統被稱爲X-road。

* law[1]〔lɔ〕 *n.* 法律　　***by law*** 依法　　***ask for*** 要求
a piece of information 一項資料　　right[1]〔raɪt〕 *n.* 權利
data[2]〔'detə〕 *n. pl.* 資料　　hold[1]〔hold〕 *v.* 擁有
on[1]〔ɑn〕*prep.* 關於　　database〔'detə,bes〕 *n.* 資料庫
compatible[6]〔kəm'pætəbļ〕 *adj.* 相容的；一致的
system[3]〔'sɪstəm〕 *n.* 系統　　***be known as*** 被稱爲

In all, the Estonian state offers over 600 e-services *to its citizens and 2,400 to businesses.*

總計，愛沙尼亞政府提供超過600項電子服務給它的公民，2,400項給企業。

* ***in all*** 總計；共計　　offer[2]〔'ɔfɚ〕 *v.* 提供
e-service *n.* 電子服務（ = *electronic service* ）
citizen[2]〔'sɪtəzn〕 *n.* 市民；公民
business[2]〔'bɪznɪs〕 *n.* 企業

Some good ideas *never* take off *because too few people embrace them, and with just 1.3m residents*, Estonia is a small player.

因爲欣然接受的人少，一些很好的想法並未大受歡迎，而且只有130萬居民的愛沙尼亞是個小國家。

* idea[1]〔aɪ'diə〕 *n.* 想法　　***take off*** 大受歡迎
embrace[5]〔ɪm'bres〕 *v.* 欣然接受（提議等）
player[1]〔'pleɚ〕 *n.* 選手；玩家【is a small player 在此引伸爲「是個小國家」】

To fill the gap in the global market, Estonia will issue ID cards *to*

non-resident "satellite Estonians", ***thereby*** *creating a global*,

government-standard digital identity.

為了要填補與國際市場的差距，愛沙尼亞會發行身分證給非當地居民的
「衛星國家的愛沙尼亞人」，藉此創造出一個全球性、符合國家標準的
數位身分。

    * fill[1] 〔 fɪl 〕 v. 填補；使充滿   gap[3] 〔 gæp 〕 n. 差距；裂縫
    global[3] 〔'globḷ 〕 adj. 全球的   non-resident adj. 非居民的
    satellite[4] 〔'sætḷˌaɪt 〕 adj. 衛星的；處於衛星般關係的；鄰近的
        【如 satellite city「衛星城市」，satellite Estonians 在此是指「移入
        愛沙尼亞的移民」】
    thereby[6] 〔 ðɛr'baɪ 〕 adv. 藉以   create[2] 〔 krɪ'et 〕 v. 創造
    government-standard adj. 符合國家標準的

Applicants will pay a small fee, *probably around $41-68*, ***and*** provide

the same biometric data ***and*** documents *as Estonian residents*.

申請人要支付大約41-68元美金的小額費用，並像愛沙尼亞居民一樣，
提供生物測量資料和文件。

    * applicant[4] 〔'æpləkənt 〕 n. 申請人   fee[2] 〔 fi 〕 n. 費用
    probably[3] 〔'prɑbəblɪ 〕 adv. 或許   provide[2] 〔 prə'vaɪd 〕 v. 提供
    biometric 〔ˌbaɪə'mɛtrɪks 〕 adj. 生物測量的
    biometric data 生物特徵資料【如人臉辨識、指紋識別和虹膜掃瞄】
    document[5] 〔'dɑkjəmənt 〕 n. 文件

If *all is in order*, a card will be issued, ***or*** its virtual equivalent *on a*

smartphone.

如果一切就緒，卡片就會核發，或是核發智慧型手機上虛擬的身份證。

* order[1] 〔'ɔrdə〕 *n.* 順序　　***in order*** 井然有序；適當的；妥當的
virtual[6] 〔'vɜtʃuəl〕 *adj.* 實際上的；【電腦】虛擬的
equivalent[6] 〔ɪ'kwɪvələnt〕 *n.* 相等物
smartphone 〔,smɑrt'fon〕 *n.* 智慧型手機

What *may provide a bigger market is a European Union rule soon to*

*come into force **that** will require member states to accept each others'*

digital IDs.

有一項歐盟條款很快就會開始生效，將要求會員國接受彼此的數位身分證，這可能會提供較大的市場。

* European 〔,jurə'piən〕 *adj.* 歐洲的　　union[3] 〔'junjən〕 *n.* 聯盟
rule[1] 〔rul〕 *n.* 規定；條例　　***European Union rule*** 歐盟條款
force[1] 〔fors〕 *n.* 力量　　***come into force*** 生效；開始執行
require[2] 〔rɪ'kwaɪr〕 *v.* 要求　　***member state*** 會員國
accept[2] 〔ək'spɛt〕 *v.* 接受

That means *non-resident holders of Estonian IDs,* ***wherever*** *they are,*

*will be able **not only** to send each other email **and** to prove their*

*identity **but** to do business with governments anywhere in the EU.*

Soon multiple satellite citizenship may *even* become the norm.

這就表示，非本地居民的愛沙尼亞身分證持有者，不論他們在哪裡，不僅可以發送電子郵件給彼此、證明自己的身分，還可以和歐盟的各國政府做生意。不久之後，多重衛星公民身分可能甚至會成為常態。

* mean[1]〔 min 〕 *v.* 意思是　　holder[2]〔'holdə 〕 *n.* 持有者
wherever[2]〔 hwɛr'ɛvə 〕 *conj.* 無論何處　***be able to V.*** 能夠…
prove[1]〔 pruv 〕 *v.* 證明　　***do business*** 做生意
multiple[4]〔'mʌltəpḷ 〕 *adj.* 多重的
citizenship〔'sɪtəzn,ʃɪp 〕 *n.* 公民身份
norm[6]〔 nɔrm 〕 *n.* 常態；規範

1. (**A**) 本文最好的標題爲何？

　　(A) 愛沙尼亞率先推行數位身份證
　　(B) 愛沙尼亞的創新科技
　　(C) 數位身份證的利益和風險
　　(D) 全球公民身份的科技

　　* title[2]〔'taɪtḷ 〕 *n.* 標題　　lead[4]〔 lid 〕 *v.* 領先；居首位
　　　implement[6]〔'ɪmplə,mɛnt 〕 *v.* 實施
　　　innovative[6]〔'ɪno,vetɪv 〕 *adj.* 創新的
　　　technology[3]〔 tɛk'nalədʒɪ 〕 *n.* 科技
　　　benefit[3]〔'bɛnəfɪt 〕 *n.* 利益；好處　　risk[3]〔 rɪsk 〕 *n.* 風險

2. (**A**) 關於 X-road，何者爲眞？

　　(A) 每位公民的資訊在政府系統中是一致的。
　　(B) 它連接愛沙尼亞的系統和其他歐盟國家的系統。
　　(C) 它用於確保愛沙尼亞有一場公平的選舉。
　　(D) 它包含許多關於公民的機密資料。

　　* consistent[4]〔 kən'sɪstənt 〕 *adj.* 一致的
　　　connect[3]〔 kə'nɛkt 〕 *v.* 連接
　　　dedicated[6]〔'dɛdə,ketɪd 〕 *adj.* 專用的
　　　be dedicated to 被用在…上；致力於
　　　ensure〔 ɪn'ʃur 〕 *v.* 確保　　election[3]〔 ɪ'lɛkʃən 〕 *n.* 選舉
　　　contain[2]〔 kən'ten 〕 *v.* 包含　　***take place*** 舉行
　　　confidential[6]〔,kanfə'dɛnʃəl 〕 *adj.* 機密的

3. (**C**) 本文的文章組織架構爲何？

(A) 引言——數位身份證的好處——數位身份證的缺點

(B) 定義——愛沙尼亞的例子——歐盟的例子

(C) <u>引言——愛沙尼亞的做法——未來更廣泛流通的計劃</u>

(D) 愛沙尼亞的例子——問題——可能的解決辦法

* organization[2] 〔ˌɔrgənəˈzeʃən〕 *n.* 組織；構造
introduction[3] 〔ˌɪntrəˈdʌkʃən〕 *n.* 介紹；引言；序言
drawback[6] 〔ˈdrɔˌbæk〕 *n.* 缺點
definition[3] 〔ˌdɛfəˈnɪʃən〕 *n.* 定義
practice[1] 〔ˈpræktɪs〕 *n.* 實行；做法
circulation[4] 〔ˌsɝkjəˈleʃən〕 *n.* 流通；循環
solution[2] 〔səˈluʃən〕 *n.* 解決之道

4. (**C**) 關於「衛星公民」身分證，我們可以推論出什麼？

(A) 發行全球數位身份證需要一大筆預算。

(B) 爲了安全檢查，使用者必須定期提供資料。

(C) <u>可以促進全球的電子商務。</u>

(D) 它的目標是增加愛沙尼亞在歐盟的影響力。

* infer[6] 〔ɪnˈfɝ〕 *v.* 推論   budget[3] 〔ˈbʌdʒɪt〕 *n.* 預算
launch[4] 〔lɔntʃ〕 *v.* 開辦；創辦
user[2] 〔ˈjuzɚ〕 *n.* 使用者
regularly[2] 〔ˈrɛgjələˌlɪ〕 *adv.* 定期地
security[3] 〔sɪˈkjurətɪ〕 *n.* 安全
facilitate[6] 〔fəˈsɪləˌtet〕 *v.* 促進
commerce[4] 〔ˈkɑmɝs〕 *n.* 商業
e-commerce 〔ˌiˈkɑmɝs〕 *n.* 電子商務
aim[2] 〔em〕 *v.* 打算；企圖
aim to V. 目標是…；目的是…
enhance[6] 〔ɪnˈhæns〕 *v.* 提高；增加
influence[2] 〔ˈɪnfluəns〕 *n.* 影響力

TEST 18

Read the following passage and choose the best answer for each question.

Large office buildings can be as big as a small village; they have their own trains, buses and shops. Such buildings can be found in most cities of the world. When the Pentagon was built in the early 1940s, however, it was the world's largest office complex, and it is still among the largest today.

The Pentagon is different from all other office buildings because it is used by only one organization—the American Defense Department. This means it is the headquarters of the three arms of the United States military—the army, navy and air force. When people think of the military strength of the United States of America, they usually think of the Pentagon.

The Pentagon was built next to the Potomac River in Washington, D.C. during the Second World War. It took only two years to build in spite of its massive size. Built in the shape of a pentagon, which is a five-sided figure, the building consists of five concentric pentagons that are divided into ten sections. Each side of the outer pentagon is about 300 meters long, and there is a large space open to the sky in the center. Six stories high, the Pentagon has a total usable floor space of about 344,000 square meters. Around it, there are about 45 kilometers of roads that are part of the complex, and inside the building itself, there are more than 25 kilometers of passages. In spite of its great size, however, no office is more than a six-minute walk from any other office in the building.

About 13,000 people worked on building the Pentagon, and there are about 30,000 people working in it for the Defense Department today. It cost US$80 million dollars to build, and many Americans thought that was too much. If the Defense Department had to rent such a building today, however, it would cost it around US$30 million a day! The building was therefore a bargain.

1. What is this passage mainly about?
   (A) The United States military.
   (B) The headquarters of the United States military.
   (C) People working for the U.S. Defense Department.
   (D) Where and why the Pentagon was built.

2. According to the passage, the Pentagon is one of the largest _____.

(A) departments in the United States

(B) office buildings in the world

(C) non-profit organizations in the world

(D) metropolitan areas in the United States

3. According to the passage, the Pentagon was built _____.

(A) during the Second World War

(B) in the shape of a circle

(C) with ten sides

(D) to demonstrate the super power of the country

4. When it comes to the construction cost of the Pentagon, what is the attitude of the author?

(A) Disapproving.

(B) Neutral.

(C) Sarcastic.

(D) Supportive.

TEST 18 詳解

Large office buildings can be *as* big *as a small village*; they have their own trains, buses *and* shops. Such buildings can be found *in most cities of the world.*

大型辦公大樓可以和一個小村莊一樣大；他們有自己的列車、公車以及商店。這樣的大樓，在世界上大部分的城市中，都可以找得到。

* office[1]〔'ɔfɪs〕 *n.* 辦公室　　building[1]〔'bɪldɪŋ〕 *n.* 建築物
  office building 辦公大樓　　village[2]〔'vɪlɪdʒ〕 *n.* 村莊

When the Pentagon was built in the early 1940s, *however*, it was the world's largest office complex, *and* it is *still* among the largest *today*.

五角大廈建於1940年代初期，是當時世界上最大的辦公綜合大樓，而且它現在仍是全世界最大的大樓之一。

* pentagon〔'pɛntə,gɑn〕 *n.* 五邊形
  the Pentagon （美國國防部的）五角大廈
  complex[3]〔'kɑmplɛks〕 *n.* 綜合大樓
  among[1]〔ə'mʌŋ〕 *prep.* 為…中之一

The Pentagon is different from all other office buildings *because it is used by only one organization—the American Defense Department.*

　　五角大廈和其它所有的辦公大樓不同，因爲它僅由一個機構所使用
——美國國防部。

* organization[2] 〔͵ɔrgənə'zeʃən 〕 *n.* 組織；機構
defense[4] 〔 dɪ'fɛns 〕 *n.* 防禦　　department[2] 〔 dɪ'pɑrtmənt 〕 *n.* 部門
American Defense Department 美國國防部

This means *it is the headquarters of the three arms of the United*

States military—the army, navy and air force.

這就意味著，它是美國三軍的總部——陸軍、海軍，和空軍。

* mean[1] 〔 min 〕 *v.* 意味著
headquarters[3] 〔'hɛd'kwɔrtɚz 〕 *n. pl.* 總部
arm[2] 〔 ɑrm 〕 *n.* 軍種；兵種
military[2] 〔'mɪlə͵tɛrɪ 〕 *n.* 軍隊　*adj.* 軍事的
army[1] 〔'ɑrmɪ 〕 *n.* 陸軍　　navy[3] 〔'nevɪ 〕 *n.* 海軍　　***air force*** 空軍

When *people think of the military strength of the United States of*

America, they *usually* think of the Pentagon.

每當人們想到美國的軍事力量，通常都會想到五角大廈。

* strength[3] 〔 strɛŋθ 〕 *n.* 力量　　***military strength*** 軍事力量

The Pentagon was built *next to the Potomac River in*

Washington, D.C. during the Second World War.

五角大廈是在二戰時期建於華盛頓特區的波多馬克河旁。

* Potomac〔tə'tomæk〕*n.* 波多馬克
Washington〔'waʃɪŋtən〕*n.* 華盛頓
D.C. 華盛頓哥倫比亞特區（ = *District of Columbia* ）
Washinton, D.C. 美國首都華盛頓
Second World War 世界二次大戰

It took *only* two years *to build in spite of its massive size.*

儘管它的規模龐大，建造僅花兩年的時間。

* take[1]〔tek〕*v.* 花費　　***in spite of*** 僅管
massive[5]〔'mæsɪv〕*adj.* 大規模的；大的

Built in the shape of a pentagon, ***which*** *is a five-sided figure,* the

building consists of five concentric pentagons ***that*** *are divided into*

ten sections.

這棟建築物的外型是五角形的形狀，由五個同心五邊形所組成，劃分成
十個區域。

shape[1]〔ʃep〕*n.* 形狀　　figure[2]〔'fɪgjɚ〕*n.* 形狀
consist[4]〔kən'sɪst〕*v.* 組成　　***consist of*** 由⋯組成
concentric〔kən'sɛntrɪk〕*adj.* 同中心的
divide[2]〔də'vaɪd〕*v.* 劃分　　***be divided into*** 被分成
section[2]〔'sɛkʃən〕*n.* 部份；區域

Each side *of the outer pentagon* is about 300 meters long, ***and*** there

is a large space *open to the sky in the center.*

五角形外側的每一邊約三百公尺長，而且建物的中央有個大型露天的空間。

* outer[3] 〔'autɚ〕 *adj.* 外部的　　meter[2] 〔'mitɚ〕 *n.* 公尺
　space[1] 〔spes〕 *n.* 空間　　open[1] 〔'opən〕 *adj.* 開放的
　open to the sky 露天的　　center[1] 〔'sɛntɚ〕 *n.* 中心；中央

Six stories high, the Pentagon has a total usable floor space *of about*

344,000 square meters.

五角大廈有六層樓高，總計樓層可使用的空間約為三十四萬四千平方公尺。

* story[1] 〔'storɪ〕 *n.* 層；樓　　total[1] 〔'totl̩〕 *adj.* 總計的
　usable[5] 〔'juzəbl̩〕 *adj.* 可使用的
　floor[1] 〔flor〕 *n.* 樓層　　square[2] 〔skwɛr〕 *adj.* 平方的

Around it, there are about 45 kilometers of roads *that are part of the*

complex, **and** *inside the building itself*, there are more than 25

kilometers *of passages.*

大廈周圍有四十五公里長的道路，是這綜合建物的一部分，而在大樓裡面，它的通道則超過二十五公里長。

* kilometer[3] 〔'kɪlə,mitɚ〕 *n.* 公里
　inside[1] 〔'ɪn'saɪd〕 *prep.* 在…裡面
　passage[3] 〔'pæsɪdʒ〕 *n.* 走廊；通道

In spite of its great size, *however*, no office is more than a six-minute

walk *from any other office in the building.*

然而，儘管建物很大，但是建物內任何一間辦公室，都相距不超過六分鐘的路程。

　　* walk[1] ﹝wɔk﹞ *n.* 步行距離；路程

About 13,000 people worked on building the Pentagon, ***and*** there are about 30,000 people *working in it for the Defense Department today*. It cost US$80 million dollars *to build*, ***and*** many Americans thought ***that*** was *too* much.

　　約有13,000人建造五角大廈，現今約有30,000人在大廈裡為美國國防部工作。它花費美金八千萬元建造，而許多美國人認為金額太龐大。

　　* ***work on*** 從事　　　cost[1] ﹝kɔst﹞ *v.* 花費
　　　million[2] ﹝'mɪljən﹞ *n.* 百萬

If *the Defense Department had to rent such a building today*, *however*, it would cost it around US$30 million *a day*! The building was *therefore* a bargain.

然而，現在如果國防部要租一棟這樣的建物，可能每天要花費大約三千萬美元！因此，建造五角大廈是很划算的。

　　* rent[3] ﹝rɛnt﹞ *v.* 租　　therefore[2] ﹝'ðɛr,for﹞ *adv.* 因此
　　　bargain[4] ﹝'bɑrgɪn﹞ *n.* 划算的買賣；便宜貨

　1.(**B**) 本文主要是關於什麼？

　　(A) 美國軍隊。

　　(B) <u>美國軍隊的總部。</u>

(C) 爲美國國防部工作的人。

(D) 五角大廈在哪裡和爲什麼被建造。

* mainly[2]〔'menlɪ〕*adv.* 主要地

2. (**B**) 根據本文，五角大廈是最大的 _____ 之一。

(A) 美國部門　　　　　　(B) <u>全世界的辦公大樓</u>

(C) 全世界的非營利組織　(D) 美國的大都會區

* non-profit〔nɑn'prɑfɪt〕*adj.* 非營利的
metropolitan[6]〔ˌmɛtrə'pɑlətn〕*adj.* 大都市的
area[1]〔'ɛrɪə〕*n.* 區域

3. (**A**) 根據本文，五角大廈被建造 _____ 。

(A) <u>於二次大戰期間</u>

(B) 成圓形

(C) 有十個邊

(D) 是爲了要展示國家的超級實力

* demonstrate[4]〔'dɛmənˌstret〕*v.* 展示；證明
super[1]〔'supɚ〕*adj.* 超級的
power[1]〔'pauɚ〕*n.* 力量；國力；軍力

4. (**D**) 當提到五角大廈的建造費用時，作者的態度爲何？

(A) disapproving[6]〔ˌdɪsə'pruvɪŋ〕*adj.* 反對的

(B) neutral[6]〔'njutrəl〕*adj.* 中立的

(C) sarcastic〔sɑr'kæstɪk〕*adj.* 諷刺的

(D) *supportive*[2]〔sə'pɔrtɪv〕*adj.* 支持的

* *when it comes to* 一提到
construction[4]〔kən'strʌkʃən〕*n.* 建造
attitude[3]〔'ætəˌtjud〕*n.* 態度；看法
author[3]〔'ɔθɚ〕*n.* 作者

TEST 19

Read the following passage and choose the best answer for each question.

British physicist Alan Calverd thinks that giving up pork chops, lamb cutlets and chicken burgers would do more for the environment than burning less oil and gas. Calverd calculates that the animals we eat emit 21% of all the carbon dioxide that can be attributed to human activity. We could therefore slash man-made emissions of carbon dioxide simply by abolishing all livestock. Moreover, there would be no adverse effects to health and it would be an experiment that we could abandon at any stage. "Worldwide reduction of meat production in the pursuit of the targets set in the Kyoto treaty seems to carry fewer political unknowns than cutting our consumption of fossil fuels," he says.

The 2006 United Nations Food and Agriculture Organization (FAO) report "Livestock's Long Shadow" concluded that the livestock industry is responsible for 18 percent of greenhouse gas emissions. This figure is significant considering that global emissions from the transportation sector, the focus of many current government reduction programs, accounts for only 13 percent of greenhouse gases released worldwide.

Livestock's Long Shadow examined the end-to-end emissions attributable to the livestock industry, including those from producing fertilizer, growing food crops for livestock and raising, killing, processing, refrigerating and transporting animal products. The report found that livestock produce nine percent of human-caused carbon dioxide, 37 percent of methane and 67 percent of nitrous oxide emissions. The study also stated that over a hundred-year period methane has 23 times the global warming potential of carbon dioxide, while nitrous oxide has 296 times the global warming potential.

1. Which of the following statements is implied?
   (A) According to the Livestock's Long Shadow report, the transportation section emits more greenhouse gases worldwide than livestock.
   (B) Reducing meat production is less politically controversial than reducing the consumption of fossil fuels.
   (C) The Livestock's Long Shadow report concluded that livestock produce 18 percent of human-caused carbon dioxide.
   (D) Many countries are launching programs to reduce their livestock.

2. What is the main idea that this passage is trying to convey?

    (A) Livestock and transportation emissions overlap.

    (B) Livestock has nothing to do with climate change.

    (C) We can slow down global warming by becoming vegetarians.

    (D) Human gas emissions are destroying the earth.

3. Based on the passage, which of the following statements is NOT true?

    (A) Raising livestock makes a lot of methane and nitrous oxide gas.

    (B) The livestock sector causes serious environmental problems.

    (C) One way to save the planet is to stop animal breeding.

    (D) Carbon dioxide emissions are the number one factor of global warming.

4. All of the following statements are true EXCEPT _____

    (A) Methane is far more destructive than CO_2 as far as the process of global warming is concerned.

    (B) A diet without meat would have undesirable effects on health.

    (C) A plant-based diet would be more effective than reducing the consumption of oil in reducing the amount of pollutants in the atmosphere.

    (D) Emissions of nitrous oxide and methane are closely-related to global warming.

TEST 19 詳解

British physicist Alan Calverd thinks *that giving up pork chops,*
*lamb cutlets **and** chicken burgers would do more for the environment*
***than** burning less oil **and** gas.*

英國物理學家艾倫·卡爾佛德認為，放棄豬排、羊排和雞肉漢堡，對環境會比燃燒較少的石油跟天然氣更好。

* British〔'brɪtɪʃ〕*adj.* 英國的
  physicist[4]〔'fɪzəsɪst〕*n.* 物理學家
  Alan Calvers〔'ælən 'kælvəd〕*n.* 艾倫·卡爾佛德
  give up 放棄　　pork[2]〔pork〕*n.* 豬肉
  chop[3]〔tʃɑp〕*n.* 小肉片　***pork chop*** 豬排
  lamb[1]〔læm〕*n.* 小羊；羔羊　　cutlet〔'kʌtlɪt〕*n.* 薄肉片
  burger[2]〔'bɝgə〕*n.* 漢堡（= *hamburger*[2]）
  environment[2]〔ɪn'vaɪrənmənt〕*n.* 環境
  burn[2]〔'bɝn〕*v.* 燃燒　　oil[1]〔ɔɪl〕*n.* 油；石油
  gas[1]〔gæs〕*n.* 氣體；瓦斯

Calverd calculates *that the animals we eat emit 21% of all the carbon*
*dioxide **that** can be attributed to human activity.*

卡爾佛德計算出我們所吃的動物所釋放的二氧化碳，佔了人類活動所製造二氧化碳的百分之二十一。

* calculate[4]〔'kælkjə,let〕*v.* 計算；估計
  emit〔ɪ'mɪt〕*v.* 發射；發出　　carbon[5]〔'kɑrbən〕*n.* 碳
  dioxide〔daɪ'ɑksaɪd〕*n.* 二氧化物

carbon dioxide 二氧化碳   attribute〔ə'trɪbjut〕v. 歸因於
be attributed to⋯ 被歸因於   activity³〔æk'tɪvətɪ〕n. 活動

We could *therefore* slash man-made emissions *of carbon dioxide*

simply by abolishing all livestock.

因此,只要我們不再養家畜,就可以大幅減少人類的二氧化碳排放量。

* therefore²〔'ðɛr,for〕adv. 因此
  slash⁶〔slæʃ〕v. 大幅減少
  man-made〔'mæn'med〕adj. 人造的
  emission〔ɪ'mɪʃən〕n. 排放(量)
  simply²〔'sɪmplɪ〕adv. 僅僅
  abolish⁵〔ə'balɪʃ〕v. 廢除;廢止
  livestock⁵〔'laɪv,stak〕n. 家畜【集合名詞】

Livestock

Moreover, there would be no adverse effects *to health* *and* it would

be an experiment *that we could abandon at any stage.*

此外,這對健康不會有任何負面影響,而且這是我們在任何階段,都可
以終止的實驗。

* moreover⁴〔mor'ovə〕adv. 此外 (= *besides*² = *furthermore*⁴)
  adverse〔əd'vɝs〕adj. 不利的
  effect²〔ɪ'fɛkt〕n. 影響
  adverse effects 負面影響
  experiment³〔ɪk'spɛrəmənt〕n. 實驗
  abandon⁴〔ə'bændən〕v. 放棄;拋棄
  stage²〔stedʒ〕n. 階段

"Worldwide reduction *of meat production in the pursuit of the targets set in the Kyoto treaty* seems to carry fewer political unknowns ***than cutting our consumption of fossil fuels*,**" he says.

「追求京都議定書中所設立的目標，減少全球肉品產量所具有的政治不確定性，似乎比減少石化燃料的消耗量來得少，」他說。

* worldwide〔'wɜld'waɪd〕 *adj.* 全世界的　*adv.* 在全世界
  reduction[4]〔rɪ'dʌkʃən〕*n.* 減少　　meat[1]〔mit〕*n.* 肉
  production[4]〔prə'dʌkʃən〕*n.* 生產；製造
  pursuit[4]〔pə'sut〕*n.* 追求　　***in the pursuit of*** 追求
  target[2]〔'tɑrgɪt〕*n.* 目標　　set[1]〔sɛt〕*v.* 設定
  treaty[5]〔'tritɪ〕*n.* 條約

Kyoto treaty 京都議定書【又叫 Kyoto Protocol。1997 年聯合國氣候
  變化綱要公約（UN-FCCC）諦約國，於日本京都召開第三次大會時
  擬定，要求溫室氣體總排放量佔全球百分之五十五的工業國家，簽署
  控制造成全球暖化及溫室效應的氣體排放量之協議。此協議列入管制
  的氣體有二氧化碳、甲烷、氧化亞氮、氫氟氯碳化物、全氟碳化物及
  六氟化硫等六種氣體。第一階段目標是在 2008 年到 2012 年之間，讓
  這六種管制氣體的總排放量平均值，比 1990 年減少 5.2%。2001 年時，
  美國總統小布希宣布，全球溫室氣體排放量最高的美國，將永不簽署
  京都議定書，這對該公約是一大打擊。所以 2002 年在德國伯恩的會議
  中，新的議定書將管制量調降爲減少 2%，希望美國能簽署該條約，但
  目前爲止尚未得到美國回應。】

  carry[1]〔'kærɪ〕*v.* 具有　　political[3]〔pə'lɪtɪkl̩〕*adj.* 政治的
  unknown〔ʌn'non〕*n.* 未知數　　cut[1]〔kʌt〕*v.* 減少
  consumption[6]〔kən'sʌmpʃən〕*n.* 消耗
  fossil[4]〔'fɑsl̩〕*n.* 化石　　fuel[4]〔'fjuəl〕*n.* 燃料
  fossil fuel 石化燃料

The 2006 United Nations Food and Agriculture Organization (FAO) report "Livestock's Long Shadow" concluded *that the livestock industry is responsible for 18 percent of greenhouse gas emissions.*

根據2006年，「聯合國糧食及農業組織」的《畜牧業的巨大陰影》報告結論顯示，溫室氣體排放量的百分之十八是畜牧業造成的。

* ***the United Naitons*** 聯合國（ = *the U.N.* ）
  agriculture³〔'ægrɪ,kʌltʃɚ〕 *n.* 農業
  organization²〔,ɔrgənə'zeʃən〕 *n.* 組織
  United Nations Food and Agriculture Organization 聯合國糧食及農業組織（ = *U.N. FAO* ）
  report¹〔rɪ'port〕 *n.* 報告　　shadow³〔'ʃædo〕 *n.* 陰影；影子
  Livestock's Long Shadow 畜牧業的巨大陰影【「聯合國糧食及農業組織」在2006年所做的一項調查報告指出，畜牧業所產生的溫室氣體，佔總溫室氣體排放量的18%，而更新的報告指出，真實數據可能高達51%】
  conclude³〔kən'klud〕 *v.* 下結論；斷定
  industry²〔'ɪndəstrɪ〕 *n.* 產業
  responsible²〔rɪ'spɑnsəbḷ〕 *adj.* 作為原因的 < *for* >
  be responsible for 須為…負責；導致
  percent⁴〔pɚ'sɛnt〕 *n.* 百分之…
  greenhouse³〔'grin,haʊs〕 *n.* 溫室　　***greenhouse gas*** 溫室氣體

This figure is significant *considering **that** global emissions from the transportation sector, the focus of many current government reduction programs, accounts for only 13 percent of greenhouse gases released worldwide.*

這個數字很可觀，就全球交通運輸的排放量而論，也就是許多政府現在減量計畫的焦點，只佔全世界溫室氣體排放量的百分之十三。

* figure[2] 〔'fɪgjɚ〕 *n.* 數字
  significant[3] 〔sɪg'nɪfəkənt〕 *adj.* 顯著的；值得注意的
  consider[2] 〔kən'sɪdɚ〕 *v.* 考慮
  considering that… 鑒於…；就…而論
  global[3] 〔'globḷ〕 *adj.* 全球的
  transportation[4] 〔͵trænspɚ'teʃən〕 *n.* 交通運輸
  sector[6] 〔'sɛktɚ〕 *n.* 部門　　focus[2] 〔'fokəs〕 *n.* 焦點
  current[3] 〔'kɝənt〕 *adj.* 現在的；目前的
  program[3] 〔'progræm〕 *n.* 計畫
  account[3] 〔ə'kaʊnt〕 *v.* 說明；導致　***account for*** （在數量等上）佔…
  release[3] 〔rɪ'lis〕 *v.* 釋放

Livestock's Long Shadow examined the end-to-end emissions

attributable to the livestock industry, *including those from producing*

*fertilizer, growing food crops for livestock **and** raising, killing,*

*processing, refrigerating **and** transporting animal products.*

《畜牧業的巨大陰影》調查畜牧業每個環節所造成的排放量，包括製造肥料、種植給家畜的糧食作物、飼養、宰殺、加工、冷藏。以及運送動物產品等。

* examine[1] 〔ɪg'zæmɪn〕 *v.* 檢查；調查
  end-to-end 〔'ɛndtə'ɛnd〕 *adj.* 點對點的；頭尾相連的
  attributable 〔ə'trɪbjutəbḷ〕 *adj.* 可歸因於…的 < *to* >
  produce[2] 〔prə'djus〕 *v.* 製造
  fertilizer[5] 〔'fɝtḷ͵aɪzɚ〕 *n.* 肥料
  crop[2] 〔krɑp〕 *n.* 農作物　　raise[1] 〔rez〕 *v.* 飼養

process[3] 〔ˋprɑsɛs〕 *v.* 加工　 *n.* 過程
refrigerate 〔rɪˋfrɪdʒəˏret〕 *v.* 冷卻；冷藏【refrigerator[2] *n.* 冰箱】
transport[3] 〔trænˋsport〕 *v.* 運送
product[3] 〔ˋprɑdəkt〕 *n.* 產品

The report found *that* livestock produce nine percent of human-caused

carbon dioxide, 37 percent *of methane* *and* 67 percent *of nitrous oxide*

emissions.

報告發現，家畜所產生的排放量中，百分之九的人為二氧化碳，百分之
三十七的甲烷和百分之六十七的一氧化氮。

* methane 〔ˋmɛθen〕 *n.* 甲烷　　nitrous 〔ˋnaɪtrəs〕 *adj.* 含氮的
oxide 〔ˋɑksaɪd〕 *n.* 氧化物　 *nitrous oxide* 一氧化氮；笑氣

The study *also* stated *that* over a hundred-year period methane has 23

times the global warming potential of carbon dioxide, *while* nitrous

oxide has 296 times the global warming potential.

這項研究也說明了，在一百年期間，甲烷造成全球暖化的可能性，是二
氧化碳的二十三倍，而一氧化氮的可能性，則是兩百九十六倍。

* state[1] 〔stet〕 *v.* 說明　　period[2] 〔ˋpɪrɪəd〕 *n.* 期間
time[1] 〔taɪm〕 *n.* 倍　　 *global warming* 全球暖化
potential[5] 〔pəˋtɛnʃəl〕 *n.* 潛力；可能性
while[1] 〔hwaɪl〕 *conj.* 然而

1. (**B**) 下列敘述何者是本文所暗示的？

(A) 根據《畜牧業的巨大陰影》這份報告，全球交通運輸部份
比家畜排放出更多的溫室氣體。

(B) 和減少石化燃料的消耗相比，減少肉類生產的政治爭議較小。

(C) 《畜牧業的巨大陰影》這份報告的結論是，家畜製造了百分之十八人為的二氧化碳。

(D) 許多國家正發起減少家畜的計劃。

* politically³ 〔 pəˈlɪtɪk!ɪ 〕 *adv.* 在政治上
controversial⁶ 〔ˌkɑntrəˈvɝʃəl 〕 *adj.* 有爭議的
launch⁴ 〔 lɔntʃ 〕 *v.* 發起；開始

2. (**C**) 本文想要傳達的主旨為何？

(A) 家畜和交通運輸的排放量有所重疊。

(B) 家畜和氣候變遷無關。

(C) 我們可以藉由吃素減緩全球暖化。

(D) 人類瓦斯的排放正在摧毀地球。

* ***main idea*** 主旨　　convey⁴ 〔 kənˈve 〕 *v.* 傳達
overlap⁶ 〔ˌovɚˈlæp 〕 *v.* 重疊
climate² 〔ˈklaɪmɪt 〕 *n.* 氣候
have nothing to do with 和…無關　　***slow down*** 減緩
vegetarian⁴ 〔ˌvɛdʒəˈtɛrɪən 〕 *n.* 素食主義者
destroy³ 〔 dɪˈstrɔɪ 〕 *v.* 破壞　　earth¹ 〔 ɝθ 〕 *n.* 地球

3. (**D**) 根據本文，以下敘述何者為非？

(A) 飼養家畜製造很多甲烷和一氧化氮氣體。

(B) 畜牧業造成嚴重的環境問題。

(C) 拯救地球的方法之一就是停止飼養動物。

(D) 二氧化碳排放量是全球暖化的頭號因素。

* ***based on*** 根據
planet² 〔ˈplænɪt 〕 *n.* 行星【the planet 在此指「地球」】
breeding⁵ 〔ˈbridɪŋ 〕 *n.* (動物的) 飼養
factor³ 〔ˈfæktɚ 〕 *n.* 因素

4. (**B**) 以下的敘述都是真的，除了 _____

    (A) 就全球暖化的過程而言，甲烷遠比二氧化碳更具破壞性。

    (B) <u>無肉類的飲食可能對健康有不良的影響。</u>

    (C) 蔬食比減少消耗石油更能有效減少空氣中污染物的數量。

    (D) 一氧化氮和甲烷的排放和全球暖化密切相關。

* destructive[5] (dɪ'strʌktɪv) *adj.* 有破壞性的

as far as…is concerned 就…而言

diet[3] ('daɪət) *n.* 飲食

undesirable (ˌʌndɪ'zaɪrəbḷ) *adj.* 不受歡迎的；惹人厭的

amount[2] (ə'maʊnt) *n.* 數量

pollutant[6] (pə'lutṇt) *n.* 污染物

atmosphere[4] ('ætməsˌfɪr) *n.* 大氣（層）；氣氛

【補充資料】

    nitrous oxide「一氧化氮」，學名為一氧化二氮，無色有甜味氣體，又稱笑氣，是一種氧化劑，化學式 N_2O，在一定條件下能支持燃燒，但在室溫下穩定，有輕微麻醉作用，並能致人發笑，能溶於水、乙醇、乙醚及濃硫酸。該氣體早期被用於牙科手術的麻醉。需要注意的是，一氧化二氮是一種強大的溫室氣體，它的效果是二氧化碳的 296 倍。這種氣體是約瑟夫‧普利斯特里在 1772 年發現的。漢弗萊‧戴維自己和他的朋友，包括詩人柯爾‧律治和羅伯特‧騷塞在 16 世紀 90 年代試驗了這種氣體。他們發現一氧化二氮能使病人喪失痛覺，而且吸入後仍然可以保持意識，不會神志不清。不久後，笑氣就被當作麻醉劑使用，尤其在牙醫師領域。因為通常牙醫師無專職的麻醉師，而診療過程中常需要病患保持清醒，並能依命令做出口腔反應，故在此氣體給牙醫師帶來極大的方便。

TEST 20

Read the following passage and choose the best answer for each question.

Paying a visit to Reykjavik, in Iceland, visitors will definitely be attracted by the fabulous Harpa concert hall and conference center. In fact, Harpa Center has become not only the prime culture and art center but the most popular tourist attraction. This structure impresses people with its delicacy and elegance as well as its multifunctionality and environmental awareness.

Harpa Center was designed by the Danish firm Henning Larsen Architects in cooperation with the artist Olafur Eliasson. It is situated on the border between land and sea, which creates a better connection between the city center and the harbor. The building is made of glass and steel in a twelve-sided space-filling geometric modular system called the quasi-brick. The extensive use of glass panels allows it to be exposed to changing climatic and light effects. The crystalline structure captures and reflects the light, promoting the dialogue between the building and surrounding landscape. In addition to the visual effect, the most crucial function of the glass panels is to make use of natural light in order to reduce dependence on lamps and air conditioning. Since Iceland is generally bitterly cold, such a design helps conserve energy.

The center features an arrival and foyer area in the front of the building, four halls in the middle and a backstage area with offices, a rehearsal hall and a changing room in the back of the building. The three large halls are placed next to each other. As for the fourth hall, it is a multifunctional one, serving as a venue for more intimate performances and banquets. Visitors access the main foyer from a south-facing entrance, while staff and performers enter the backstage area from the north.

The spectacular Harpa Center is indeed a masterpiece of architecture, uniquely combining world-class acoustics and distinctive architecture; no wonder it won the 2013 European Union Prize for Contemporary Architecture, the Mies van der Rohe Award.

1. Where would this article most likely be found?

   (A) A travel brochure.

   (B) A science journal.

   (C) A language-learning book.

   (D) Mythology.

2. What is the main function of the extensively used glass panels?

(A) To add exotic flavor to the building.

(B) To decrease the use of air-conditioning in the building.

(C) To provide visitors with a great night view of the city.

(D) To capture visitor's attention and make the building a popular tourist attraction.

3. Which of the following descriptions of Harpa Center is CORRECT?

(A) The performers' entrance to the backstage area is on the south side of Harpa Center.

(B) Every room in Harpa Center is multifunctional.

(C) A rehearsal room lies in the foyer area.

(D) Glass and steel are the main components of Harpa Center's structure.

4. According to the article, which of the following statements is TRUE?

(A) Olafur Eliasson founded the Danish firm Henning Larsen Architects.

(B) Harpa Center is located in the city center.

(C) Harpa Center attracts people because of its spectacular structure and its multiple functions.

(D) Harpa Center won the European Union Prize for Contemporary Architecture three years in a row.

TEST 20 詳解

Paying a visit to Reykjavik, in Iceland, visitors will *definitely* be attracted *by the fabulous Harpa concert hall **and** conference center.*

遊覽冰島的雷克雅維克，遊客一定會被很棒的哈帕音樂廳和會議中心所吸引。

* ***pay a visit to*** 拜訪；遊覽
Reykjavik〔ˋrekjəˏvik〕*n.* 雷克雅維克【冰島的首都】
Iceland〔ˋaɪslənd〕*n.* 冰島　　visitor[2]〔ˋvɪzɪtə〕*n.* 觀光客
definitely[4]〔ˋdɛfənɪtlɪ〕*adv.* 一定　　attract[3]〔əˋtrækt〕*v.* 吸引
fabulous[6]〔ˋfæbjələs〕*adj.* 很棒的　　Harpa〔ˋhɑepə〕*n.* 哈帕
concert[3]〔ˋkɑnsɝt〕*n.* 音樂會　　***concert hall*** 音樂廳
conference[4]〔ˋkɑnfərəns〕*n.* 會議　　center[1]〔ˋsɛntə〕*n.* 中心

In fact, Harpa Center has become ***not only*** the prime culture ***and*** art center ***but*** the *most* popular tourist attraction.

事實上，哈帕中心不只成為雷克雅維克主要的文化藝術中心，也是最受歡迎的觀光景點。

Harpa Center

* prime[4]〔praɪm〕*adj.* 主要的　　culture[2]〔ˋkʌltʃə〕*n.* 文化
popular[3]〔ˋpɑpjələ〕*adj.* 受歡迎的
tourist[3]〔ˋturɪst〕*n.* 觀光客　*adj.* 觀光的
attraction[4]〔əˋtrækʃən〕*n.* 吸引力；吸引人的事物
tourist attraction 觀光景點

This structure impresses people *with its delicacy **and** elegance **as well as** its multifunctionality **and** environmental awareness.*

這座建築物的精緻和優雅，以及多功能和環保意識，使許多人印象深刻。

* structure³〔'strʌktʃɚ〕*n.* 建築物
impress³〔ɪm'prɛs〕*v.* 使印象深刻　　delicacy〔'dɛləkəsɪ〕*n.* 精緻
elegance〔'ɛləgəns〕*n.* 優雅　　***as well as*** 以及
multifunctionality〔'mʌltɪ,fʌnkʃə'nælɪtɪ〕*n.* 多功能
environmental³〔ɪn,vaɪrən'mɛntḷ〕*adj.* 環境的
awareness³〔ə'wɛrnɪs〕*n.* 察覺；意識
environmental awareness 環境意識的

Harpa Center was designed *by the Danish firm Henning Larsen*
Architects in cooperation with the artist Olafur Eliasson.

哈帕中心是由丹麥公司「亨寧・拉森建築師事務所」和藝術家奧拉弗・伊里亞森合作設計的。

* design²〔dɪ'zaɪn〕*v.* 設計　　Danish〔'dænɪʃ〕*adj.* 丹麥的
firm²〔fɝm〕*n.* 公司
Henning Larsen⁵〔'hɛnɪŋ 'larsən〕*n.* 亨寧・拉森
architect⁵〔'arkə,tɛkt〕*n.* 建築師
cooperation⁴〔ko,apə'reʃən〕*n.* 合作
in cooperation with 與…合作　　artist²〔'artɪst〕*n.* 藝術家
Olafur Eliasson〔'olafɚ 'ɪ'laɪəsn̩〕*n.* 奧拉弗・伊里亞森

It is situated *on the border between land **and** sea, **which** creates a*
*better connection between the city center **and** the harbor.*
它位於陸地和海洋的交界，這讓市中心和港口有更好的連結。

* situate〔'sɪtʃʊ,et〕*v.* 使位於　　***be situated on*** 位於
border³〔'bɔrdɚ〕*n.* 邊界　　create²〔krɪ'et〕*v.* 創造
connection³〔kə'nɛkʃən〕*n.* 連結　　harbor³〔'harbɚ〕*n.* 港口

The building is made *of glass **and** steel in a twelve-sided*

space-filling geometric modular system called the quasi-brick.

這棟建築是由玻璃和鋼材打造，以被稱爲準磚的十二邊形空間填充幾何模型的系統所建造。

space-filling

quasi-brick

* glass[1]〔glæs〕*n.* 玻璃　　steel[2]〔stil〕*n.* 鋼
  space-filling *n.* 空間填充
  geometric[5]〔,dʒɪə'mɛtrɪk〕*adj.* 幾何學的
  modular〔'mɑdʒələ〕*adj.* 模件的
  system[3]〔'sɪstəm〕*n.* 系統
  quasi〔'kwesaɪ〕*adj.* 類似的；半的；準的
  brick[2]〔brɪk〕*n.* 磚頭
  quasi-brick〔'kwesaɪ'brɪk〕*n.* 準磚

The extensive use *of glass panels* allows it to be exposed to changing climatic **and** light effects.

大量的使用玻璃面板，使得建築物能夠暴露在氣候變換和光線變化的影響中。

* extensive[5]〔ɪk'stɛnsɪv〕*adj.* 大規模的；大量的
  panel[4]〔'pænḷ〕*n.* 面板　　allow[1]〔ə'laʊ〕*v.* 允許；讓
  expose[4]〔ɪk'spoz〕*v.* 暴露；使接觸
  climatic〔klaɪ'mætɪk〕*adj.* 氣候的　　effect[2]〔ɪ'fɛkt〕*n.* 影響

The crystalline structure captures **and** reflects the light, *promoting*

*the dialogue between the building **and** surrounding landscape.*

晶體結構可以捕捉並且反射光源，促進建築物和周圍景觀之間的對話。

* crystalline〔'krɪstḷ,aɪn〕*adj.* 水晶似的；透明的【crystal[5] *n.* 水晶】
  capture[3]〔'kæptʃə〕*v.* 捕捉　　reflect[4]〔rɪ'flɛkt〕*v.* 反射

promote[3]〔prə'mot〕*v.* 促進　　dialogue[3]〔'daɪə,lɔg〕*n.* 對話
surrounding[4]〔sə'raʊndɪŋ〕*adj.* 周圍的
landscape[4]〔'lænd,skep〕*n.* 風景

In addition to the visual effect, the *most* crucial function *of the glass*

panels is to make use of natural light *in order to reduce dependence on*

*lamps **and** air conditioning.* ***Since*** *Iceland is generally bitterly cold*,

such a design helps conserve energy.

除了視覺效果之外，玻璃面板最重要的功能，是利用自然光線，以減少
對燈光及空調的依賴。因為冰島通常是酷寒的，所以這樣的設計可以節
省能源。

　　* ***in addition to*** 除了…之外（還有）
　　visual[4]〔'vɪʒʊəl〕*adj.* 視覺的　　crucial[6]〔'kruʃəl〕*adj.* 非常重要的
　　function[2]〔'fʌŋkʃən〕*n.* 功能　　natural[2]〔'nætʃərəl〕*adj.* 自然的
　　reduce[3]〔rɪ'djus〕*v.* 減少　　dependence[4]〔dɪ'pɛndəns〕*n.* 依賴
　　lamp[1]〔læmp〕*n.* 燈　　***air conditioning*** 空調
　　generally[2]〔'dʒɛnərəlɪ〕*adv.* 通常
　　bitterly[2]〔'bɪtəlɪ〕*adv.* 嚴寒地；寒冷入骨地
　　conserve[4]〔kən'sɝv〕*v.* 節省　　energy[2]〔'ɛnədʒɪ〕*n.* 能源

The center features an arrival ***and*** foyer area *in the front of the*

building, four halls *in the middle **and*** a backstage area *with offices*, a

rehearsal hall ***and*** a changing room *in the back of the building.* The

three large halls are placed *next to each other*.

中心是以建築物前方入口處與門廳的區域爲特色，四個大廳在中間和有辦公室的後台，一間排練廳和更衣室在築建物的後方。三個大廳緊密相連。

* feature³〔ˋfitʃɚ〕v. 以…爲特色　　arrival³〔əˋraɪvl̩〕n. 到達
  foyer〔ˋfɔɪɚ〕n. 門廳　　area¹〔ˋɛrɪə〕n. 地區
  hall²〔hɔl〕n. 大廳　　middle¹〔ˋmɪdl̩〕n. 中間
  backstage〔ˋbækˋstedʒ〕n. 後台　　rehearsal⁴〔rɪˋhɝsl̩〕n. 排練
  place¹〔ples〕v. 放置；安置　　**next to** 在…旁邊

As for the fourth hall, it is a multifunctional one, *serving as a venue*

*for more intimate performances **and** banquets.*

至於第四間大廳，是個多功能的大廳，可當成私人表演和宴會的會場。

* **as for** 至於　　multifunctional〔͵mʌltɪˋfʌŋkʃənl̩〕adj. 多功能的
  serve as 充當；當作　　venue〔ˋvɛnju〕n. 會場
  intimate⁴〔ˋɪntəmɪt〕adj. 親密的；私人的
  performance³〔pɚˋfɔrməns〕n. 表演
  banquet⁵〔ˋbæŋkwɪt〕n. 宴會

Visitors access the main foyer *from a south-facing entrance, **while***

staff **and** performers enter the backstage area *from the north*.

訪客從南面入口進入主要大廳，而工作人員和表演者則從北邊進入後台。

* access⁴〔ˋæksɛs〕v. 接近　　main²〔men〕adj. 主要的
  south-facing adj. 面向南方的　　entrance²〔ˋɛntrəns〕n. 入口
  staff³〔stæf〕n. 全體工作人員
  performer⁵〔pɚˋfɔrmɚ〕n. 表演者　　north¹〔nɔrθ〕n. 北方

The spectacular Harpa Center is *indeed* a masterpiece *of*

*architecture, uniquely combining world-class acoustics **and** distinctive*

architecture; *no wonder* it won the 2013 European Union Prize for

Contemporary Architecture, *the Mies van der Rohe Award.*

壯觀的哈帕中心確實是一座建築傑作，獨特地結合了世界級的音響效果和有特色的建築風格；難怪它會贏得2013年歐盟當代建築大獎，密斯‧凡德羅獎。

* spectacular⁶〔spɛkˈtækjələ〕*adj.* 壯觀的
  indeed³〔ɪnˈdid〕*adv.* 的確；真正地
  masterpiece⁵〔ˈmæstəˌpis〕*n.* 傑作
  architecture⁵〔ˈɑrkəˌtɛktʃə〕*n.* 建築學
  uniquely⁴〔juˈniklɪ〕*adv.* 獨特地　　combine³〔kəmˈbaɪn〕*n.* 結合
  acoustics〔əˈkustɪks〕*n. pl.* 音響效果；音質
  distinctive⁵〔dɪˈstɪŋktɪv〕*adj.* 有特色的；獨特的
  no wonder 難怪　　***European Union*** 歐盟
  prize²〔praɪz〕*n.* 獎
  contemporary⁵ *adj.*〔kənˈtɛmpəˌrɛrɪ〕當代的
  Mies van der Rohe〔ˈmis vɑn dəˈroə〕*n.* 密斯‧凡德羅【德國知名建築師，全名為 Ludwig Mies van der Rohe（1886-1969），亦是最著名的現代主義建築大師之一】
  award³〔əˈwɔrd〕*n.* 獎

1.（**A**）這篇文章最有可能在哪裡被發現？
  (A) 旅遊手冊。　　　　　　　(B) 科學期刊。
  (C) 語言學習書。　　　　　　(D) 神話集。
  * article²,⁴〔ˈɑrtɪkḷ〕*n.* 文章　　travel²〔ˈtrævḷ〕*n.* 旅行
    brochure⁶〔broˈʃʊr〕*n.* 小冊子　　journal³〔ˈdʒɜnḷ〕*n.* 期刊
    mythology⁶〔mɪˈθɑlədʒɪ〕*n.* 神話；神話集

2.(**B**) 大量使用玻璃面板的主要功能是什麼？

    (A) 爲建築物添加異國風情。

    (B) <u>爲減少建築物裡空調的使用。</u>

    (C) 爲提供遊客一個很棒的城市夜景。

    (D) 爲吸引遊客的注意，並讓這棟建築物成爲受歡迎的觀光景
       點。

    * extensively[5] 〔 ɪk'stɛnsɪv 〕 *adv.* 大規模地；大量地
    exotic[6] 〔 ɛg'zɑtɪk 〕 *adj.* 有異國風味的
    flavor[3] 〔 'flevɚ 〕 *n.* 味道；風味   decrease[4] 〔 dɪ'kkris 〕 *v.* 減少
    provide[2] 〔 prə'vaɪd 〕 *v.* 提供   view[1] 〔 vju 〕 *n.* 景色
    capture[3] 〔 'kæptʃɚ 〕 *n.* 捕捉；引起（注意）
    attention[2] 〔 ə'tɛnʃən 〕 *n.* 注意

3.(**D**) 關於哈帕中心的敘述，下列何者正確？

    (A) 表演者進入後台的入口是在哈帕中心的南側。

    (B) 哈帕中心的每個房間都是多功能的。

    (C) 排練室是在門廳的區域。

    (D) <u>玻璃和鋼鐵是哈帕中心建築物的主要建材。</u>

    * description[3] 〔 dɪ'skrɪpʃən 〕 *n.* 描述
    lie in 位於   component[6] 〔 kəm'ponənt 〕 *n.* 成分

4.(**C**) 根據本文，下列敘述何者爲眞？

    (A) 奧拉弗・伊里亞森成立了丹麥的公司亨寧・拉森建築師事
       務所。

    (B) 哈帕中心位於市中心。

    (C) <u>哈帕中心會吸引人是因爲它壯觀的建築和多重的用途。</u>

    (D) 哈帕中心連續三年贏得歐盟當代建築大獎。

    * found[3] 〔 faʊnd 〕 *v.* 建立   ***be located in*** 位於
    multiple[4] 〔 'mʌltəpḷ 〕 *adj.* 多重的   ***in a row*** 連續地

TEST 21

Read the following passage and choose the best answer for each question.

Statistics show left-handed people are more likely to suffer from a wide range of physical and mental disabilities, or to die young. So if evolutionary theory dictates survival of the fittest, why do lefties still exist? Researchers in France recently discovered a disproportionately high number of left-handed athletes who thrive in sports involving direct one-on-one contact, such as baseball (think Babe Ruth), tennis (think John McEnroe) and boxing (think Oscar de la Hoya or the fictional Rocky Balboa). From this interesting discovery, they formed a hypothesis about left-handedness.

They assumed that, back in the days when fighting was an important part of survival and winning mates, the rare left-hander may have come out on top more often. The rationale was that most left-handed people would be practiced in fighting right-handed people, since right-handed people make up the majority, while most right-handed fighters would not be as prepared to fight someone who favors his left side. This gives an advantage to lefties: a surprise effect.

To prove their theory, the researchers surveyed nine primitive societies in five separate continents. Through a mix of direct observation and existing data, they estimated the number of left-handed people within each population. They also looked at murder rates, thinking that those communities with higher murder rates might have populations with more left-handed people. The more violence, the more chances lefties would have at issuing their unexpected left blow, or other such weapon, and come out on top.

They found strong support for the idea that, at least in primitive societies with higher levels of violence, lefties thrive. For example, among the Dioula of Burkina Faso in West Africa, the murder rate was only 0.013 murders per 1,000 residents each year and only 3.4 percent of the population were left-handers. Meanwhile, data from the Eipo of Indonesia showed three murders per 1,000 people each year with 27 percent of the population being left-handed. The researchers then formed a new theory: what left-handed people may lack in fitness, they make up by being different.

1. What is the purpose of the passage?
   (A) To inform readers of a new theory on left-handedness.
   (B) To entertain readers with sports celebrities.
   (C) To warn readers about violent lefties.
   (D) To introduce primitive societies to readers.

2. What was the assumption about lefties' survival based on?

   (A) Right-handed people had little experience in fighting left-handers.
   (B) Left-handed people know how to produce a surprise effect.
   (C) Right-handed fighters favor their right sides in combat.
   (D) Left-handed athletes seem to excel at one-on-one sports.

3. How did researchers prove their theory?

   (A) By having interviews with lefties in primitive societies.
   (B) By associating murder rates and the population of lefties in primitive societies.
   (C) By holding a combat contest for left-handed people and right-handed people.
   (D) By using only the existing data of primitive societies.

4. According to the last paragraph, which of the following statements is true?

   (A) Researchers collected data only from Africa and Asia.
   (B) Lefties thrive in societies with a larger population.
   (C) Research found that lefties may thrive by being different.
   (D) Data from the primitive societies can barely support the hypothesis.

TEST 21 詳解

Statistics show *left-handed people are more likely to suffer from a wide range of physical **and** mental disabilities, **or** to die young.*

統計數字顯示，左撇子的人較可能罹患各式各樣身體或心理上的殘疾，或是英年早逝。

* statistics[5] 〔stə'tɪstɪks〕 *n. pl.* 統計數字
  left-handed 〔'lɛft'hændɪd〕 *adj.* 慣用左手的　　***suffer from*** 罹患
  wide[1] 〔waɪd〕 *adj.* 寬的　　range[2] 〔rendʒ〕 *n.* 範圍
  a wide range of 各式各樣的　　physical[4] 〔'fɪzɪk!〕 *adj.* 身體的
  mental[3] 〔'mɛnt!〕 *adj.* 心理的　　disability[6] 〔‚dɪsə'bɪlətɪ〕 *n.* 殘疾

***So if** evolutionary theory dictates survival of the fittest*, why do lefties *still* exist?

所以，如果進化論認爲適者生存，那爲何左撇子仍然存在呢？

* evolutionary[6] 〔‚ɛvə'luʃən‚ɛrɪ〕 *adj.* 進化的
  theory[3] 〔'θiərɪ〕 *n.* 理論
  dictate[6] 〔'dɪktet〕 *v.* 口授；規定；命令
  survival[3] 〔sə'vaɪv!〕 *n.* 生存　　fit[2] 〔fɪt〕 *adj.* 適合的
  the survival of the fittest 適者生存　　lefty 〔'lɛftɪ〕 *n.* 左撇子
  exist[2] 〔ɪg'zɪst〕 *v.* 存在

Researchers *in France recently* discovered a *disproportionately* high number *of left-handed athletes **who** thrive in sports involving direct* *one-on-one contact, such as baseball (think Babe Ruth), tennis (think*

*John McEnroe) **and** boxing (think Oscar de la Hoya **or** the fictional*

Rocky Balboa).

最近，法國的研究人員發現，在一對一接觸的運動比賽中，左撇子運動員的人數，多到不成比例，像是棒球（想想貝比‧魯斯）、網球（想想約翰‧麥肯羅）和拳擊（想想奧斯卡‧德拉霍亞，或虛構的人物洛基‧巴布亞）。

* researcher[4]〔ri'sɝtʃɚ〕*n.* 研究人員
recently[2]〔'risn̩tlɪ〕*adv.* 最近　　discover[1]〔dɪ'skʌvɚ〕*v.* 發現
disproportionately〔ˌdɪsprə'porʃənɪtlɪ〕*adv.* 不成比例地
【proportion[5] *n.* 比例】
athlete[3]〔'æθlit〕*n.* 運動員（= *sportsman*[4]）
thrive[6]〔θraɪv〕*v.* 興旺；繁榮；成功（= *succeed*[2]）
sport[1]〔sport〕*n.* 運動；競賽
involve[4]〔ɪn'vɑlv〕*v.* 牽涉；和⋯有關
direct[1]〔də'rɛkt〕*adj.* 直接的
one-on-one *adj.* 一對一的
contact[2]〔'kɑntækt〕*n.* 接觸
Babe Ruth〔'beb 'ruθ〕*n.* 貝比‧魯斯

Babe Ruth

【1985-1948，是美國職棒史上 1920、30 年代的洋基強打者，跟著洋基在取得 4 次世界大賽冠軍。曾經紅襪取得 3 次世界大賽冠軍，是美國棒球史上最有名的人，被球迷暱稱「棒球之神」】
John McEnroe〔'dʒɑn ˌmæk'ɛnro〕*n.* 約翰‧馬克安諾【1959 年 2 月 16 日出生，是已退役的美國男子網球運動員，最高世界排名單打雙打同時排名世界第一，7 座大滿貫男單桂冠得主，國際網球名人堂成員】

John McEnroe

boxing[5] (ˈbɑksɪŋ) *n.* 拳擊

Oscar de la Hoya (ˈɑskə ˌdə lə ˈhojə) *n.*
奧斯卡・德拉霍亞【1973 年 2 月 4 日出生，
前世界拳王，有「金童」之稱，出生於美國
加州的一個拳擊世家，曾奪得 1992 年奧運會
輕量級金牌】

Oscar de la Hoya

fictional[4] (ˈfɪkʃənl̩) *adj.* 虛構的；小說的

Rocky Balboa (ˈrɑkɪ ˌbælˈboə) *n.* 洛基・
巴布亞【重量級拳擊手，是席維斯史特龍
洛基系列電影中的角色】

From this interesting discovery, they formed a hypothesis *about*

left-handedness.

從這個有趣的發現，他們做出對於慣用左手的假設。

* discovery[3] (dɪˈskʌvərɪ) *n.* 發現　　form[2] (fɔrm) *v.* 形成
hypothesis (haɪˈpɑθəsɪs) *n.* 假說
left-handedness (ˈlɛftˈhændɪdnɪs) *n.* 慣用左手

They assumed *that*, [*back in the days when fighting was an*

important part of survival and winning mates], the rare left-hander

may have come out on top *more often*.

他們認為，當打鬥還是生存和贏得配偶很重要的一部分的時代，
罕見的左撇子可能更常拔得頭籌。

* assume[4] (əˈsjum) *v.* 假定；認為
back[1] (bæk) *adv.* 過去；以前 (= *in the past*)
days[1] (dez) *n. pl.* 時期；時代　　fight[1] (faɪt) *v.* 打架

mate² 〔 met 〕 *n.* 配偶　　win¹ 〔 wɪn 〕 *v.* 贏得
rare² 〔 rɛr 〕 *adj.* 稀有的　　left-hander 〔 'lɛft'hændɚ 〕 *n.* 左撇子
come out 結果；得…（成績或名次）　　top¹ 〔 tɑp 〕 *n.* 頂端
on top 勝利地；領先地

The theory was ***that*** *most left-handed people would be practiced in*

fighting right-handed people, ***since*** *right-handed people make up the*

majority, ***while*** most right-handed fighters would not be *as* prepared

to fight someone ***who*** *favors his left side.* This gives an advantage

to lefties: *a surprise effect.*

這個理論是，大部分的左撇子會練習和右撇子打鬥，因為右撇子佔大多
數，所以慣用右手的鬥士，不會做好準備來攻擊喜歡使用左手的人。這
給了左撇子一個優勢：一個攻其不備的效果。

* practice¹ 〔 'præktɪs 〕 *v.* 訓練；使練習
right-handed 〔 'raɪt'hændɪd 〕 *adj.* 慣用右手的　　***make up*** 組成
majority³ 〔 mə'dʒɔrətɪ 〕 *n.* 大多數　　while¹ 〔 hwaɪl 〕 *conj.* 然而
fighter² 〔 'faɪtɚ 〕 *n.* 戰士　　as¹ 〔 æz 〕 *adv.* 一樣地；同樣地
prepared¹ 〔 prɪ'pɛrd 〕 *adj.* 有準備的　　favor² 〔 'fevɚ 〕 *v.* 偏好
advantage³ 〔 əd'væntɪdʒ 〕 *n.* 優點；優勢
surprise¹ 〔 sə'praɪz 〕 *adj.* 令人驚訝的；使人感到意外的
effect² 〔 ɪ'fɛkt 〕 *n.* 效果

To prove their theory, the researchers surveyed nine primitive

societies *in five separate continents.*

為了要證明這樣的理論，研究人員調查了五大洲的九個原始社群。

* prove[1] 〔 pruv 〕 v. 證明　　survey[3] 〔 sə've 〕 v. 調查
primitive[4] 〔 'prɪmətɪv 〕 adj. 原始的　　society[2] 〔 sə'saɪətɪ 〕 n. 社會
separate[2] 〔 'sɛpərɪt 〕 adj. 個別的；不同的
continent[3] 〔 'kɑntənənt 〕 n. 洲；大陸

*Through a mix of direct observation **and** existing data*, they estimated

the number *of left-handed people within each population.*

透過結合直接觀察和現有的資料，他們估算出每個種族的左撇子人數。

* mix[2] 〔 mɪks 〕 n. 混合；結合　　observation[4] 〔 ,ɑbzɜ'veʃən 〕 n. 觀察
existing[2] 〔 ɪg'zɪstɪŋ 〕 adj. 現存的　　data[2] 〔 'detə 〕 n. pl. 資料
estimate[4] 〔 'ɛstə,met 〕 v. 估計　　within[2] 〔 wɪð'ɪn 〕 prep. 在⋯之內
population[2] 〔 ,pɑpjə'leʃən 〕 n. 人口；（居住在某地的）一群人

They *also* looked at murder rates, *thinking **that** those communities*

with higher murder rates might have populations with more

left-handed people.

他們還看了謀殺率，認爲謀殺率較高的社區人口中，有較多的左撇子。

* ***look at*** 察看；考慮　　murder[3] 〔 'mɜdə 〕 v. n. 謀殺
rate[3] 〔 ret 〕 n. 比率　　community[4] 〔 kə'mjunətɪ 〕 n. 社區

The more violence, ***the more*** chances *lefties would have at issuing their*

unexpected left blow, ***or*** other such weapon, ***and*** come out on top.

越多暴力，左撇子就有越多的機會，能夠出其不意地揮出左鉤拳，或是其他類似這樣的武器，來取得勝利。

* violence[3] 〔'vaɪələns 〕 *n.* 暴力　　issue[5] 〔'ɪʃjʊ 〕 *v.* 發出
  unexpected[2] 〔ˌʌnɪk'spɛktɪd 〕 *adj.* 突如其來的
  blow[1] 〔 blo 〕 *n.* 打；擊　　***left blow*** 左鉤拳
  other[1] 〔'ʌðɚ 〕 *adj.* 別的；其他的
  such[1] 〔 sʌtʃ 〕 *adj.* 這種的；這樣的　　weapon[2] 〔'wɛpən 〕 *n.* 武器

They found strong support *for the idea **that**, at least in primitive*

societies with higher levels of violence, lefties thrive.

　　他們發現有力的證據能證實他們的想法，至少在暴力程度較高的原始社會中，有很多左撇子。

* strong[1] 〔 strɔŋ 〕 *adj.* 有說服力的；強有力的
  support[2] 〔 sə'port 〕 *n.* 證據；根據　　idea[1] 〔 aɪ'diə 〕 *n.* 想法
  at least 至少　　level[1] 〔'lɛvḷ 〕 *n.* 程度

For example, among the Dioula of Burkina Faso in West Africa, the

murder rate was only 0.013 murders *per 1,000 residents each year*

***and** only 3.4 percent of the population were left-handers.*

舉例來說，在西非布基納法索裡的迪烏拉，每年謀殺率為0.013，每一千個居民當中，只有3.4%的人是左撇子。

* Dioula 〔 dɪ'ulə 〕 *n.* 迪烏拉
  Burkina Faso 〔 bɚ'kɪnə 'faso 〕 *n.* 布基納法索
  West Africa 西非　　per[2] 〔 pɚ 〕 *prep.* 每…
  resident[5] 〔'rɛzədənt 〕 *n.* 居民　　percent[4] 〔 pɚ'sɛnt 〕 *n.* 百分之…

Meanwhile, data *from the Eipo of Indonesia* showed three murders *per*

1,000 people each year with 27 percent of the population being

left-handed.

同時，來自印尼艾波的資料顯示，每年每一千個人裡，有三個謀殺犯，
而其中有27%的人是左撇子。

> * meanwhile[3] 〔ˈmin͵hwaɪl〕*adv.* 同時　　Eipo 〔ˈaɪpḷ〕*n.* 艾波
> Indonesia 〔͵ɪndoˈniʃə〕*n.* 印尼

The researchers *then* formed a new theory: ***what** left-handed people*

may lack in fitness, they make up by being different.

然後研究人員就有了新的理論：左撇子可能在體能方面有所欠缺，但是
卻藉由和其他人的不同來彌補這個缺點。

> * lack[1] 〔læk〕*v.* 缺乏　　fitness[2] 〔ˈfɪtnɪs〕*n.* 健康；體能
> ***make up*** 彌補；補足

1. (**A**) 本文的目的是什麼？

   (A) 告知讀者一個關於左撇子的新理論。
   (B) 以運動名人來娛樂讀者。
   (C) 警告讀者關於暴力的左撇子。
   (D) 向讀者介紹原始社群。

   > * inform[3] 〔ɪnˈfɔrm〕*v.* 通知　　on[1] 〔ɑn〕*prep.* 關於
   > entertain[4] 〔͵ɛntəˈten〕*v.* 娛樂　　sports[1] 〔sports〕*adj.* 運動的
   > celebrity[5] 〔səˈlɛbrətɪ〕*n.* 名人　　warn[3] 〔wɔrn〕*v.* 警告
   > violent[3] 〔ˈvaɪələnt〕*adj.* 暴力的；粗暴的
   > introduce[2] 〔͵ɪntrəˈdjus〕*v.* 介紹；引進

2. (**A**) 對於左撇子生存的推測是根據什麼？

    (A) 慣用右手的人很少有和左撇子打鬥的經驗。

    (B) 慣用左手的人知道如何製造令人驚訝的效果。

    (C) 慣用右手的鬥士在戰鬥時偏好他們的右邊。

    (D) 慣用左手的運動員似乎能在一對一的運動中勝出。

    * assumption[6] (ə'sʌmpʃən) *n.* 假定；推測
    produce[2] (prə'djus) *v.* 生產；製造
    combat[5] ('kɑmbæt) *n.* 戰鬥；格鬥
    excel[5] (ɪk'sɛl) *v.* 突出；勝過他人

3. (**B**) 研究人員如何證明他們的理論？

    (A) 在原始社群中訪問左撇子。

    (B) 把謀殺率和原始社群中左撇子的人數做聯結。

    (C) 爲慣用左手者和慣用右手者舉行格鬥比賽。

    (D) 只用原始社群的現有資料。

    * interview[2] ('ɪntɚ,vju) *n.* 面試；訪問
    associate[4] (ə'soʃɪ,et) *v.* 把…聯想在一起
    hold[1] (hold) *v.* 舉行   contest[4] ('kɑntɛst) *n.* 比賽

4. (**C**) 根據最後一段，下列敘述何者爲眞？

    (A) 研究人員只從非洲和亞洲收集資料。

    (B) 左撇子在人口較多的社會中較有機會生存。

    (C) 研究發現，左撇子可藉由與他人的不同而成功。

    (D) 原始社群的資料幾乎不能證明這項假設。

    * collect[2] (kə'lɛkt) *v.* 收集   Asia ('eʃə) *n.* 亞洲
    barely[3] ('bɛrlɪ) *adv.* 幾乎不

TEST 22

Read the following passage and choose the best answer for each question.

Caffeine, a substance in tea, coffee, and some other drinks that makes people feel more active, was reported to be the cause of the death of an Ohio teenager named Logan. Logan's death was probably related to a caffeine overdose, for bags of caffeine powder were found in his room. In addition, a coroner revealed that Logan had 70 micrograms of caffeine per milliliter of blood in his system while a typical coffee drinker would have merely 3 to 5 micrograms.

This tragedy highlighted the risks of caffeine powder, which is currently not regulated by the FDA (U.S. Food and Drug Administration) because it is now categorized as a dietary supplement. The use of caffeine in products is strictly controlled; its quantity and its effect are monitored. With many products, the serving size is one-sixteenth of a teaspoon of caffeine powder, which yields about 250 milligrams of caffeine, equal to the caffeine in two large cups of coffee. So if one consumes a single teaspoon of caffeine powder at one time, the amount of caffeine is the equivalent of that in around 30 cups of coffee. Too much caffeine will make the heart too stimulated to beat regularly, and one is very likely to suffer from heart arrhythmia and a seizure and die. What's more, the reactions to caffeine vary from person to person. Some people are more sensitive than others. It is generally warned that taking 5 to 10 grams of the stimulant could be fatal. Nevertheless, if one has an undiagnosed medical condition, even a small amount of caffeine may lead to undesirable consequences.

Because of this incident, the FDA has been paying more attention to the increasing amount of caffeine in a whole range of foods. The agency has worked on research to better understand potential health effects of caffeine and potential safe levels of consumption. Yet, according to doctors, it is highly recommended to avoid the consumption of caffeine. The best energy boost is actually a healthy diet, sleep and regular exercise.

1. How much caffeine may a large cup of coffee contain?
   (A) 10 milligrams.   (B) 125 milligrams.
   (C) 250 milligrams.   (D) 500 milligrams.

2. According the passage, why was Logan's death speculated to be associated with a caffeine overdose?

(A) The concentration of caffeine in his blood was a lot higher than that in a coffee drinker's.

(B) His record of purchasing caffeine powder online was tracked down.

(C) A receipt for caffeine powder was found in his room.

(D) He was caught red-handed consuming caffeine powder.

3. Why is the use of caffeine in products strictly regulated?

(A) Caffeine is a dietary supplement.

(B) It is categorized as medicine.

(C) It may affect the performance of athletes.

(D) Too much caffeine may cause bad, even lethal reactions.

4. What can be inferred from the passage?

(A) The FDA will prohibit the use of caffeine in products in the near future.

(B) The FDA will keep a watchful eye on the use of caffeine.

(C) The FDA will surely find a replacement for caffeine powder.

(D) The FDA will include more doctors in the administration.

TEST 22 詳解

Caffeine, *a substance in tea, coffee,* **and** *some other drinks* **that**

makes people feel more active, was reported to be the cause *of the*

death of an Ohio teenager named Logan.

　　咖啡因是一種茶類、咖啡、及其他會使人感到更活躍的飲料裡的一種物質，根據報導咖啡因是俄亥俄州一名叫羅根的青少年的死亡原因。

* caffeine[6] ('kæfiɪn) *n.* 咖啡因　　substance[3] ('sʌbstəns) *n.* 物質
drink[1] (drɪŋk) *n.* 飲料　　active[2] ('æktɪv) *adj.* 活躍的
cause[1] (kɔz) *n.* 原因　　Ohio (o'haɪo) *n.* 俄亥俄州
teenager[2] ('tin,edʒɚ) *n.* 青少年　　Logan ('logən) *n.* 羅根

Logan's death was *probably* related to a caffeine overdose, **for** *bags*

of caffeine powder were found in his room.

羅根的死，很可能和過量的咖啡因有關，因為在他房間裡發現好幾袋的咖啡因粉。

* probably[3] ('prɑbəblɪ) *adv.* 可能　　**be related to** 和…有關
overdose ('ovɚ,dos) *n.* 藥劑過量　　powder[3] ('paʊdɚ) *n.* 粉末

In addition, a coroner revealed **that** *Logan had 70 micrograms of*

caffeine per milliliter of blood in his system **while** *a typical coffee*

drinker would have merely 3 to 5 micrograms.

此外，驗屍官透露，羅根體內每毫升的血液，就有70微克的咖啡因，而一般會喝咖啡的人體內只有3到5微克而已。

* *in addition* 此外　　coroner〔'kɔrənɚ〕*n.* 驗屍官
reveal[3]〔rɪ'vil〕*v.* 透露　　microgram〔'maɪkro͵græm〕*n.* 微克
per[2]〔pɚ〕*prep.* 每…　　milliliter〔'mɪlɪ͵litɚ〕*n.* 毫升
blood[1]〔blʌd〕*n.* 血　　system[3]〔'sɪstəm〕*n.* 系統
one's **system** 身體；全身　　typical[3]〔'tɪpɪkl̩〕*adj.* 典型的
coffee drinker 喝咖啡的人
merely[4]〔'mɪrlɪ〕*adv.* 僅僅（= *only*[1]）

This tragedy highlighted the risks *of caffeine powder*, **which**
is currently not regulated by the FDA (U.S. Food and Drug
Administration) **because** *it is now categorized as a dietary supplement.*

　　這悲劇突顯出咖啡因粉末的風險，它沒有受到FDA（美國食品藥物管理局）的管制，因為它現在是歸類為膳食補充品。

* tragedy[4]〔'trædʒədɪ〕*n.* 悲劇　　highlight[6]〔'haɪ͵laɪt〕*v.* 強調
risk[3]〔rɪsk〕*n.* 風險　　currently[3]〔'kɝntlɪ〕*adv.* 現在
regulate[4]〔'rɛgjə͵let〕*v.* 管理　　FDA *n.* 美國食品藥物管理局
drug[2]〔drʌg〕*n.* 藥
administration[6]〔əd͵mɪnə'streʃən〕*n.* 管理；行政部門；局
categorize[5]〔'kætəgə͵raɪz〕*v.* 列入…的範疇
dietary〔'daɪə͵tɛrɪ〕*adj.* 飲食的【diet[3] *n.* 飲食】
supplement[3]〔'sʌpləmənt〕*n.* 補充
dietary supplement 膳食補充品

The use *of caffeine in products* is *strictly* controlled; its quantity **and**
its effect are monitored.
在產品中使用咖啡因是受到嚴格控管的；它的數量和效果都會被監測。

* product³〔'prɑdəkt〕*n.* 產品　　strictly²〔'strɪktlɪ〕*adv.* 嚴格地
quantity²〔'kwɑntətɪ〕*n.* 量　　effect²〔ɪ'fɛkt〕*n.* 影響；效果
monitor⁴〔'mɑnətɚ〕*v.* 監控；監測

With many products, the serving size is one-sixteenth *of a teaspoon*

of caffeine powder, **which** *yields about 250 milligrams of caffeine*,

equal to the caffeine in two large cups of coffee.

許多產品一份的量為1/16茶匙的咖啡因粉，這會產生大約250毫克的咖
啡因，相當於兩大杯咖啡中的咖啡因。

* serving⁶〔'sɝvɪŋ〕*n.* 一份　　one-sixteenth *n.* 十六分之一
teaspoon〔'ti,spun〕*n.* 茶匙　　yield⁵〔jild〕*v.* 產生
milligram〔'mɪlɪ,græm〕*n.* 毫克
equal¹〔'ikwəl〕*adj.* 相等的　　**be equal to** 等於

So if *one consumes a single teaspoon of caffeine powder at one time*,

the amount of caffeine is the equivalent *of that in around 30 cups*

of coffee.

所以，如果一次食用一茶匙的咖啡因粉，咖啡因含量相當於30杯咖啡中
的咖啡因。

* consume⁴〔kən'sjum〕*v.* 消耗；吃（喝）
single²〔'sɪŋgḷ〕*adj.* 單一的　　**at one time** 一次；同時
amount²〔ə'maunt〕*n.* 量　　equivalent⁶〔ɪ'kwɪvələnt〕*n.* 相等物
around¹〔ə'raund〕*prep.* 大約（= *about*¹）

Too much caffeine will make the heart *too* stimulated *to beat*

regularly, **and** one is *very* likely to suffer *from heart arrhythmia* **and**

a seizure **and** *die.*

太多的咖啡因會使心臟受到太多刺激，以致於無法規律跳動，而這很可能會使人罹患心律不整、心臟病發作，然後死亡。

* stimulate⁶〔'stɪmjə,let〕v. 刺激　　beat¹〔bit〕v. (心臟) 跳動
regularly²〔'rɛgjələlɪ〕adv. 規律地　　**suffer from** 罹患
arrhythmia〔ə'rɪθmɪə〕n. 心律不整
seizure〔'siʒɚ〕n. (疾病的) 發作【seize³ v. 抓住】
a heart seizure 心臟病發作

What's more, the reactions *to caffeine* vary *from person to person.*

Some people are *more* sensitive **than** *others.*

此外，每個人對咖啡因的反應都不一樣。有些人會比其他的人更敏感。

* **what is more** 此外　　reaction³〔rɪ'ækʃən〕n. 反應 < to >
vary³〔'vɛrɪ〕v. 改變；不同
vary from person to person 每個人都不同
sensitive³〔'sɛnsətɪv〕adj. 敏感的

It is *generally* warned **that** *taking 5 to 10 grams of the stimulant could*

be fatal.

一般都會警告說，攝取5到10克的興奮劑可能就會致命。

* generally¹,²〔'dʒɛnərəlɪ〕adv. 一般地
take¹〔tek〕v. 服用；攝取　　gram³〔græm〕n. 公克
stimulant〔'stɪmjələnt〕n. 刺激物；興奮劑
fatal⁴〔'fetḷ〕adj. 致命的

Nevertheless, *if one has an undiagnosed medical condition, even* a small amount *of caffeine* may lead to undesirable consequences.

然而，如果患有未被診斷出的疾病，即使是少量的咖啡因，也可能導致不良的後果。

* nevertheless[4] 〔ˌnɛvəðəˈlɛs〕 *adv.* 然而
  undiagnosed[6] 〔ˌʌndaɪəgˈnozd〕 *adj.* 尚未診斷的
  medical[3] 〔ˈmɛdɪkl̩〕 *adj.* 醫學的　　condition[3] 〔kənˈdɪʃən〕 *n.* 情況
  medical condition 疾病　　**lead to** 導致
  undesirable[2] 〔ˌʌndɪˈzaɪrəbl̩〕 *adj.* 令人不快的；討厭的；不受歡迎的
  consequence[4] 〔ˈkɑnsəˌkwɛns〕 *n.* 後果

Because of this incident, the FDA has been paying more attention *to the increasing amount of caffeine in a whole range of foods*.

因爲這起事件，美國食品藥物管理局更加注意各種食品咖啡因含量增加的情形。

* incident[4] 〔ˈɪnsədənt〕 *n.* 事件　　**pay attention to** 注意
  increasing[2] 〔ɪnˈkrisɪŋ〕 *adj.* 越來越多的；日益增加的
  whole[1] 〔hol〕 *adj.* 全部的；整個的
  range[2] 〔rendʒ〕 *n.* 種類；範圍　　**a whole range of** 各種的

The agency has worked on research *to better understand potential health effects of caffeine **and** potential safe levels of consumption*.

該局也已經在研究，更深入了解咖啡因對於健康可能造成的影響，和可能的食用安全程度。

　　　* agency[4]〔'edʒənsɪ〕*n.* 行政機構（＝*administration*[6]）
　　　work on 從事　　research[4]〔rɪ'sɝtʃ,'risɝtʃ〕*n. v.* 研究
　　　potential[5]〔pə'tɛnʃəl〕*adj.* 潛在的（＝*possible*[1]）
　　　consumption[6]〔kən'sʌmpʃən〕*n.* 吃（喝）；消耗

***Yet**, according to doctors*, it is *highly* recommended *to avoid the*

consumption of caffeine. The best energy boost is *actually* a healthy

diet, sleep ***and*** regular exercise.

然而，根據醫生的說法，非常建議避免食用咖啡因。要增強活力，最好
的其實就是健康飲食、睡覺，和規律的運動。

　　　* yet[1]〔jɛt〕*adv.* 然而　　highly[4]〔'haɪlɪ〕*adv.* 非常地
　　　recommend[5]〔,rɛkə'mɛnd〕*v.* 推薦　　avoid[2]〔ə'vɔɪd〕*v.* 避免
　　　energy[2]〔'ɛnədʒɪ〕*n.* 活力　　boost[6]〔bust〕*n.* 促進；提高
　　　energy boost 增強活力的事物（＝*energy booster*）
　　　actually[3]〔'æktʃuəlɪ〕*adv.* 實際上　　healthy[2]〔'hɛlθɪ〕*adj.* 健康的
　　　diet[3]〔'daɪət〕*n.* 飲食　　regular[2]〔'rɛgjələ〕*adj.* 規律的；定期的

1. (**B**) 一杯大杯咖啡可能含有多少咖啡因？

　　　(A) 10 毫克。　　　　　　　(B) <u>125 毫克。</u>
　　　(C) 250 毫克。　　　　　　 (D) 500 毫克。
　　　* contain[2]〔kən'ten〕*v.* 包含

2. (**A**) 根據本文，為什麼推測羅根的死和咖啡因過量有關聯？

　　　(A) <u>他血液中咖啡因的濃度比一個愛喝咖啡的人還要高。</u>
　　　(B) 他在網路上購買咖啡因粉末的紀錄被追查到。
　　　(C) 在他的房間裡找到一張咖啡因粉末的收據。
　　　(D) 他被當場抓到正在食用咖啡因粉末。
　　　* speculate[6]〔'spɛkjə,let〕*v.* 推測

associate[4] 〔ə'soʃ1,et〕*v.* 聯想　　***be associated with*** 和…有關

concentration[4] 〔,kɑnsṇ'treʃən〕*n.* 濃度

record[2] 〔'rɛkəd〕*n.* 記錄　　purchase[5] 〔'pɝtʃəs〕*v.* 購買

online 〔'ɑn'laɪn〕*adv.* 在網路上

track down 經追蹤或搜索而發現　　receipt[3] 〔rɪ'sit〕*n.* 收據

catch *sb.* ***red-handed*** 當場抓住；現場捕獲

3. (**D**) 為什麼會嚴格管制在產品中使用咖啡因？

(A) 咖啡因是一種膳食補給品。

(B) 它被歸類為藥品。

(C) 它可能會影響運動員的表現。

(D) 太多咖啡因可能會造成不良，甚至是致命的反應。

* medicine[2] 〔'mɛdəsṇ〕*n.* 藥　　affect[3] 〔ə'fɛkt〕*v.* 影響

performance[3] 〔pɚ'fɔrməns〕*n.* 表現

athlete[3] 〔'æθlit〕*n.* 運動員

lethal 〔'liθəl〕*adj.* 致命的（ = *fatal*[4]）

4. (**B**) 從本文可推論出什麼？

(A) 美國食品藥物管理局在不久的將來會禁止在產品中使用咖啡因。

(B) 美國食品藥物管理局會持續注意咖啡因的使用。

(C) 美國食品藥物管理局一定會找到咖啡因粉末的替代品。

(D) 美國食品藥物管理局將會有更多的醫生。

* infer[6] 〔ɪn'fɝ〕*v.* 推論　　prohibit[6] 〔prə'hɪbɪt〕*v.* 禁止

future[2] 〔'fjutʃɚ〕*n.* 未來　　***in the near future*** 在不久的將來

watchful[1] 〔'wɑtʃfəl〕*adj.* 警戒的；注意的

keep an eye on 留意

replacement[3] 〔rɪ'plesmənt〕*n.* 代替品

include[2] 〔ɪn'klud〕*v.* 包括；包含

TEST 23

Read the following passage and choose the best answer for each question.

Presidents have succeeded and failed in proportion to their effectiveness in making use of their ***charisma***. The most capable have been able to reduce the distance between themselves and the people.

Abraham Lincoln and Theodore Roosevelt are excellent examples. As president, Lincoln was perceived as a kind of Christ figure. He seemed to accept the torments of a blundering and sinful people, suffer for them, and redeem them with sacred virtues. He was also distinguished by his ambition and his humble upbringing, which made him the ultimate self-made man.

Theodore Roosevelt was the first of the country's 20th-century chiefs to achieve a degree of heroic status similar to that enjoyed by Washington, Jefferson, and Lincoln. He used his talents as an early public relations expert to fashion himself into one of the most popular leaders in U.S. history.

Unlike that of his heroic predecessors, Roosevelt's public allure was not an expression of sacrifice or self-fulfillment. Instead, Roosevelt's stature came from the popular fascination with his dynamic personality, which reignited national hopes for a unified America, from his articulation of common goals at home, and from his effective assertion of national ideals abroad.

Bill Clinton is an interesting example of how charisma serves a president. Despite his impeachment for misdeeds, Clinton's approval ratings remained as high as any two-term president this century. Clinton's personality included personal failings that many Americans could identify with and forgive. With the American economy consistently expanding, Clinton maintained an extraordinary hold on the public. To many, Clinton seemed to be a moderate spokesman for the national interest who was victimized by opponents.

1. Which of the following U.S. presidents was mentioned in the passage as being charged with improper conduct in office?

   (A) Abraham Lincoln   (B) Theodore Roosevelt

   (C) George Washington   (D) Bill Clinton

2. Which of the following best explains the word
   "*charisma*" in the first paragraph?

   (A) Ethical strength.

   (B) Public estimation of someone.

   (C) Personal magnetism.

   (D) A distinguishing attribute.

3. Theodore Roosevelt achieved his level of popularity
   NOT with his _____.

   (A) articulation of common goals

   (B) effective assertion of national ideals

   (C) dynamic personality

   (D) ambition and humble upbringing

4. According to the passage, why did Clinton remain
   popular despite his impeachment?

   (A) The impeachment process failed.

   (B) He was merely a victim of his opponents.

   (C) He was an American hero.

   (D) The economy was in good condition.

TEST 23 詳解

Presidents have succeeded **and** failed *in proportion to their*

*effectiveness in making use of their **charisma**.*

一個總統的成功與失敗，和能否有效利用他們的個人魅力成正比。

* president[2] 〔'prɛzədənt 〕 *n.* 總統　　succeed[2] 〔 sək'sid 〕 *v.* 成功
fail[2] 〔 fel 〕 *v.* 失敗　　proportion[5] 〔 prə'porʃən 〕 *n.* 比例
in proportion to　和…成比例
effectiveness[2] 〔 ə'fɛktɪvnɪs 〕 *n.* 有效　　***make use of***　利用
charisma 〔 kə'rɪzmə 〕 *n.* 個人魅力；超凡氣質

The *most* capable have been able to reduce the distance *between*

*themselves **and** the people.*

最能運用個人魅力的人，能夠縮短他們跟人民之間的距離。

* capable[3] 〔'kepəbḷ 〕 *adj.* 有能力的
the most capable　最有能力的人
reduce[3] 〔 rɪ'djus 〕 *v.* 降低；減少
distance[2] 〔'dɪstəns 〕 *n.* 距離

Abraham Lincoln **and** Theodore Roosevelt are excellent

examples. *As president*, Lincoln was perceived as a kind *of Christ*

figure.

　亞伯拉罕·林肯以及狄奧多·羅斯福是絕佳範例。身為總統，林肯
被視為具有基督的形象。

* Abraham Lincoln〔'ebrə,hæm 'lɪŋkən〕 *n.* 林肯【1809-1865，美國第
16位總統，任期為1861-1865年。當時美國南方可以蓄奴，美國北方
則禁止。林肯廢除奴隸制度，引發南北戰爭。但戰爭平息後，林肯卻
遭蓄奴擁護者刺殺身亡】

Theodore Roosevelt〔'θiə,dor 'rozə,vɛlt〕 *n.* 狄奧多・羅斯福
【1858-1919，美國第26任總統（1901-1909），
人稱老羅斯福，暱稱Teddy。主要政策是保護國
內資源，外交採門羅主義，不准歐洲人干預美洲
事務；開鑿巴拿馬運河擴充海運；調停日俄戰爭，
獲諾貝爾和平獎，學者認為他是現代美國的塑造者】

Theodore Roosevelt

excellent[2]〔'ɛkslənt〕 *adj.* 極好的
example[1]〔ɪg'zæmpl̩〕 *n.* 例子
perceive[5]〔pɚ'siv〕 *v.* 視為　　kind[1]〔kaɪnd〕 *n.* 種類
Christ〔kraɪst〕 *n.* 基督　　figure[2]〔'fɪgjɚ〕 *n.* 形象；人物；象徵

He seemed to accept the torments *of a blundering **and** sinful people,*

suffer *for them,* **and** redeem them *with sacred virtues.*
他似乎能接受那些犯錯、有罪的人的苦難，為他們受苦，用神聖的美德
來救贖他們。

* seem[1]〔sim〕 *v.* 似乎　　accept[2]〔ək'sɛpt〕 *v.* 接受
torment[5]〔'tɔrmɛnt〕 *n.* 痛苦；折磨
blundering[6]〔'blʌndərɪŋ〕 *adj.* 犯錯的
sinful[3]〔'sɪnfəl〕 *adj.* 有罪的　　suffer[3]〔'sʌfɚ〕 *v.* 受苦
redeem〔rɪ'dim〕 *v.* 解救；救贖　　sacred[5]〔'sekrɪd〕 *adj.* 神聖的
virtue[4]〔'vɝtʃu〕 *n.* 美德

He was *also* distinguished *by his ambition **and** his humble upbringing,*

which *made him the ultimoate self-made man.*

林肯也因為他的雄心及出身卑微而聞名，這讓他成為靠自己努力而成功的最佳典範。

* distinguished[4]〔dɪ'stɪŋgwɪʃt〕*adj.* 著名的 (= *prominent*[4])
  be distinguished by 以…而著名
  ambition[3]〔æm'bɪʃən〕*n.* 雄心；抱負
  humble[2]〔'hʌmbl̩〕*adj.* 謙卑的
  upbringing[6]〔'ʌp͵brɪŋɪŋ〕*n.* 教養
  ultimate[6]〔'ʌltəmɪt〕*adj.* 終極的；最好的
  self-made〔'sɛlf'med〕*adj.* 白手起家的；靠自己努力而成功的

Theodore Roosevelt was the first *of the country's 20th-century*

*chiefs to achieve a degree of heroic status similar to **that** enjoyed by*

*Washington, Jefferson, **and** Lincoln.*

狄奧多·羅斯福是美國二十世紀的第一位元首，享有跟華盛頓、傑佛遜，和林肯類似的英雄式地位的等級。

* century[2]〔'sɛntʃərɪ〕*n.* 世紀　　　chief[1]〔tʃif〕*n.* 元首
  achieve[3]〔ə'tʃiv〕*v.* 達到；獲得
  degree[2]〔dɪ'gri〕*n.* 程度；等級
  heroic[5]〔hɪ'roɪk〕*adj.* 英雄的　　status[4]〔'stetəs〕*n.* 地位
  similar[2]〔'sɪmələ〕*adj.* 相似的 < *to* >
  enjoy[2]〔ɪn'dʒɔɪ〕*v.* 享有
  Washington〔'wɑʃɪŋtən〕*n.* 華盛頓【1732-1799，
  　美國第一任總統，任期 1789-1797，全名喬治·華
  　盛頓 (George Washington)，在美國獨立戰爭
  　及建國過程中扮演重要角色，被譽為美國國父，
  　跟林肯並列為美國史上最偉大的兩位總統】

Washington

Jefferson〔'dʒɛfəsn̩〕*n.* 傑佛遜【1743-1826，
　　美國第三任總統（1801-1809），美國獨立宣言
　　起草人，奠定美國憲法第一條修正案的基礎。
　　全名湯瑪士‧傑佛遜（Thomas Jefferson），
　　創立現今的民主黨，以及維吉尼亞大學，被譽
　　爲美國史上最聰明的總統】

Jefferson

He used his talents *as an early public relations expert to fashion*

himself into one of the most popular leaders in U.S. history.

身爲早期的公共關係專家，他利用才能，使自己成爲美國歷史上最受歡
迎的總統之一。

> * talent[2]〔'tælənt〕*n.* 才能　　public[1]〔'pʌblɪk〕*adj.* 公共的
> relation[2]〔rɪ'leʃən〕*n.* 關係　　***public relations*** 公共關係
> expert[2]〔'ɛkspɝt〕*n.* 專家　　fashion[3]〔'fæʃən〕*v.* 把…塑造成
> popular[2,3]〔'pɑpjələ〕*adj.* 受歡迎的　　leader[1]〔'lidə〕*n.* 領導者
> history[1]〔'hɪstrɪ〕*n.* 歷史

Unlike that of his heroic predecessors, Roosevelt's public allure

was not an expression *of sacrifice **or** self-fulfillment.*

不同於英雄般的前輩，羅斯福的公衆魅力並非犧牲或自我實現的表
現。

> * unlike[1]〔ʌn'laɪk〕*prep.* 不像
> predecessor[6]〔ˌprɛdɪ'sɛsə〕*n.* 前人；前輩
> allure〔ə'lʊr〕*n.* 魅力【lure[6] *v.* 誘惑】
> expression[3]〔ɪk'sprɛʃən〕*n.* 表達；表現

sacrifice[4] ('sækrə,faɪs) *n.* 犧牲

self-fulfillment ('sɛlfʊl'fɪlmənt) *n.* 自我實現；達成自己願望

Instead, Roosevelt's stature came from the popular fascination

with his dynamic personality, **which** *reigned national hopes for a*

unified America , *from his articulation of common goals at home,* ***and***

from his effective assertion of national ideals abroad.

他的名望反而是來自於大眾對他充滿活力的性格很著迷，這魅力重新引燃了美國對於全國統一的希望，也來自於他在國內對於共同目標的明確表述，以及到國外對於國家理想的有效堅持。

* instead[3] (ɪn'stɛd) *adv.* 相反地；作爲代替

　stature[6] ('stætʃə) *n.* 名望；身高

　popular[2,3] ('pɑpjələ) *adj.* 大衆的

　fascination[6] (,fæsn̩'eʃən) *n.* 著迷；魅力

　dynamic[4] (daɪ'næmɪk) *adj.* 充滿活力的 (= *energetic*[3])

　personality[3] (,pɜsn̩'ælətɪ) *n.* 個性

　reignite (,riɪg'naɪt) *v.* 再度點燃

　national[2] ('næʃənl̩) *adj.* 全國的；國家的

　hope[1] (hop) *n.* 希望　　　unified[6] ('junə,faɪd) *adj.* 一致的；統一的

　articulation[6] (ɑr,tɪkjə'leʃən) *n.* 明確的表達

　【articulate[6] *v.* 清楚地表達　　*adj.* 清晰的】

　commom[1] ('kɑmən) *adj.* 共同的　　　goal[2] (gol) *n.* 目標

　at home 在國內　　effective[2] (ə'fɛktɪv) *adj.* 有效的

　assertion[6] (ə'sɜʃən) *n.* 斷言；主張；堅持

　ideal[3] (aɪ'diəl) *n.* 理想　　　abroad[2] (ə'brɔd) *adv.* 在國外

Bill Clinton is an interesting example *of **how** charisma serves a
President.*

比爾·柯林頓是個有趣的例子，可看出個人魅力對一位總統是多麼
有用。

Bill Clinton

* Bill Clinton〔ˈbɪl ˈklɪntn̩〕*n.* 比爾·柯林頓
  【1946-，美國第 42 任總統（1993-2001），
  美國史上第三年輕的總統，任內成功地提升
  美國經濟，以 65%的支持率結束任期，但也
  因緋聞案，遭到司法彈劾，但獲判無罪】
  serve[1]〔sɝv〕*v.* 為⋯服務；對（某人）有用

Despite his impeachment for misdeeds, Clinton's approval ratings
remained *as* high *as any two-term president this century.*

儘管因為行為不檢而遭到彈劾，他的支持率依然維持跟本世紀任何連任
兩屆的總統一樣高。

* despite[4]〔dɪˈspaɪt〕*prep.* 儘管
  impeachment〔ɪmˈpitʃmənt〕*n.* 彈劾
  misdeed〔mɪsˈdid〕*n.* 惡行；罪行【deed[3] *n.* 行為】
  approval[4]〔əˈpruvl̩〕*n.* 贊成；肯定
  rating[3]〔ˈretɪŋ〕*n.* 評分；（政治的）支持率
  remain[3]〔rɪˈmen〕*v.* 依然；保持   two-term〔ˈtuˈtɝm〕*adj.* 兩任的

Clinton's personality included personal failings ***that** many Americans
could identify with **and** forgive.*
柯林頓的性格包含了個人的缺點，受到很多美國人認同及原諒。

* include[2] 〔 ɪn'klud 〕 *v.* 包含   personal[2] 〔'pɝsn̩l 〕 *adj.* 個人的
failing[2] 〔'felɪŋ 〕 *n.* （性格的）缺點
identify[4] 〔 aɪ'dɛntə,faɪ 〕 *v.* 認同   forgive[2] 〔 fə'gɪv 〕 *v.* 原諒

With the American economy consistently expanding, Clinton

maintained an extraordinary hold *on the public.*

隨著美國經濟不斷地擴張，柯林頓對公衆的特殊影響力維持不變。

* economy[4] 〔 ɪ'kɑnəmɪ 〕 *n.* 經濟
consistently[4] 〔 kən'sɪstəntlɪ 〕 *adv.* 不斷地；一貫地
expand[4] 〔 ɪk'spænd 〕 *v.* 擴張   maintain[2] 〔 men'ten 〕 *v.* 維持
extraordinary[4] 〔 ɪk'strɔrdn̩,ɛrɪ 〕 *adj.* 特別的；不尋常的
hold[1] 〔 hold 〕 *n.* 掌握；影響力   *the public* 大衆

To many, Clinton seemed to be a moderate spokesman *for the*

*national interest **who** was victimized by opponents.*

對很多人來說，柯林頓似乎是國家利益的溫和發言人，卻因爲對手而受
害。

* moderate[4] 〔'mɑdərɪt 〕 *adj.* 溫和的
spokesman 〔'spoksmən 〕 *n.* 發言人 (= *spokesperson*[6])
interest[1] 〔'ɪntrɪst 〕 *n.* 利益
victimize[6] 〔'vɪktɪm,aɪz 〕 *v.* 使受害；使受苦
opponent[5] 〔 ə'ponənt 〕 *n.* 對手

1. (**D**) 下列哪一位美國總統是本文中提到被控在總統府有不當行爲？

     (A) 亞伯拉罕・林肯   (B) 狄奧多・羅斯福

     (C) 喬治・華盛頓   (D) <u>比爾・柯林頓</u>

* mention[3]〔'mɛnʃən〕n. 提到
improper[3]〔ɪm'prapɚ〕adj. 不適當的
conduct[5]〔'kandʌkt〕n. 行為

2. (**C**) 下列何者最能解釋第一段的 "**charisma**" ?

(A) 道德的力量。　　　　　(B) 公眾對某人的評價。

(C) 個人的魅力。　　　　　(D) 獨特的屬性。

* explain[2]〔ɪk'splen〕v. 解釋　　ethical[6]〔'ɛθɪkl̩〕adj. 道德的
strength[3]〔strɛŋθ〕n. 力量
estimation〔͵ɛstə'meʃən〕n. 評價【estimate[4] v. 估計】
magnetism〔'mæɡnə͵tɪzəm〕n. 吸引力；魅力
　　【magnetic[4] adj. 有磁力的】
distinguishing[4]〔dɪs'tɪŋɡwɪʃɪŋ〕adj. 獨特的
attribute〔'ætrə͵bjut〕n. 屬性；特質；特性

3. (**D**) 狄奧多‧羅斯福如此受歡迎不是因為他的 _____。

(A) 共同目標的明確表述　　(B) 國家理想的有效堅持

(C) 充滿活力的個性　　　　(D) 雄心及謙卑的教養

* level[1]〔'lɛvl̩〕n. 程度；水平
popularity[4]〔͵papjə'lærətɪ〕n. 受歡迎

4. (**D**) 根據本文，為什麼柯林頓儘管遭彈劾，仍然很受歡迎？

(A) 彈劾過程失敗。　　　　(B) 他只是他對手的受害者。

(C) 他是美國的英雄。　　　(D) 當時的經濟狀況良好。

* process[3]〔'prasɛs〕n. 過程
merely[4]〔'mɪrlɪ〕adv. 僅僅 (= only[1])
victim[3]〔'vɪktɪm〕n. 受害者　　hero[2]〔'hɪro〕n. 英雄
condition[3]〔kən'dɪʃən〕n. 情況

TEST 24

Read the following passage and choose the best answer for each question.

The freedom fighter Nelson Mandela, who had strived to have freedom for his people, died on December 5, 2013, at age 95. He dedicated all his life to his people and to his country. He was a hero to blacks and whites as well. He was taken as a moral compass and was South Africa's symbol of the struggle against racial oppression.

In his lifetime, he went through many stages, from a militant freedom fighter, to a prisoner, to a unifying figure, and finally to an elder statesman. He joined the African National Congress in 1944, and four years later he was engaged in resistance against apartheid, a system in which only white people had full political rights and people of other races, especially black people, were forced to go to separate schools and to live in separate areas. In 1961, Mandela adopted violent tactics to fight against segregation and was arrested the next year. Afterwards, he was accused of plotting to overthrow the government by violence and was sentenced to life imprisonment. Though he was in prison, Mandela's reputation grew steadily. He held a significant place in South Africa and became a powerful symbol in the anti-apartheid movement. In 1990, he was released as a result of years of an international outcry led by Winnie Mandela, Mandela's wife and a social worker. As Mandela walked out of prison, still upright and proud, he sent a clear message of **reconciliation**. He said, "As I walked out the door toward the gate that would lead to my freedom, I knew if I didn't leave my bitterness and hatred behind, I'd still be in prison." He negotiated a peaceful end to segregation and urged forgiveness for the white government that had imprisoned him. In 1993, he and President de Klerk were jointly awarded the Nobel Peace Prize for their work toward dismantling apartheid. Four years after his release, in South Africa's first multiracial elections, he became the nation's first black president. He indeed kept his promise to serve only one term. After leaving the presidency, he continued to champion causes such as human rights, world peace and the fight against AIDS.

Nelson Mandela was truly a very dignified and admirable person. His death was a great loss to the whole world. American President Barack Obama said, "We've lost one of the most influential, courageous and profoundly good human beings that any of us will share time with on this Earth. He no longer belongs to us—he belongs to the ages."

1. What is this article mainly about?

   (A) Mandela's married life.

   (B) Mandela's characteristics.

   (C) Mandela's military life.

   (D) Mandela's suffering and contribution.

2. Which of the following is NOT true about apartheid?

   (A) Only white people could go to school.

   (B) Black people were discriminated against.

   (C) White people and black people were separated.

   (D) Races other than white people were deprived of many rights.

3. Which of the following statements is TRUE?

   (A) Mandela was kept in prison for approximately 28 ycars.

   (B) Nelson Mandela and Winnie Mandela were awarded the Nobel Peace Prize.

   (C) Nelson Mandela was elected President of South Africa twice.

   (D) Nelson Mandela died during his presidency.

4. What does the word **reconciliation** in the second paragraph refer to?

   (A) Making up.   (B) Taking on.

   (C) Disaster.   (D) Revenge.

TEST 24 詳解

The freedom fighter *Nelson Mandela, **who** had strived to have freedom for his people,* died *on December 5, 2013, at age 95.*

自由鬥士納爾遜‧曼德拉,為了他的人民努力爭取自由,在2013年12月5日過世,享年95歲。

* freedom² ('fridəm) *n.* 自由　　fighter² ('faɪtɚ) *n.* 戰士
Nelson Mandela ('nɛlsn̩ 'mændiə) *n.* 納爾遜‧曼德拉
strive⁴ (straɪv) *v.* 努力 < *to* >

He dedicated all his life *to his people **and** to his country.* He was a hero *to blacks **and** whites as well.* He was taken as a moral compass **and** was South Africa's symbol *of the struggle against racial oppression.*

他為他的人民及國家奉獻一生。他對黑人和白人來說都是英雄。他被視為道德的指南,以及南非努力對抗種族壓迫的象徵。

* dedicate⁶ ('dɛdə,ket) *v.* 奉獻 < *to* >　　hero² ('hɪro) *n.* 英雄
blacks¹ ('mɔrəl) *n. pl.* 黑人　　whites¹ ('mɔrəl) *n. pl.* 白人
as well 也 (= *too*);同樣地　　*be taken as* 被認為是
moral³ ('mɔrəl) *adj.* 道德的　　compass⁵ ('kʌmpəs) *n.* 指南針
South Africa 南非　　symbol² ('sɪmbl̩) *n.* 象徵
struggle² ('strʌgl̩) *n.* 奮鬥;戰鬥　　against¹ (ə'gɛnst) *prep.* 對抗
racial³ ('reʃəl) *adj.* 種族的　　oppression⁶ (ə'prɛʃən) *n.* 壓迫

In his lifetime, he went through many stages, *from a militant*

*freedom fighter, to a prisoner, to a unifying figure, **and** finally to an*

elder statesman.

　　他一生中經歷了許多階段，從一個激進的自由鬥士、囚犯、民族統一人士，到最後成爲一位政界元老。

* lifetime³〔'laɪf,taɪm〕*n.* 一生　　***go through*** 經歷
  stage²〔stedʒ〕*n.* 階段　　militant⁶〔'mɪlətənt〕*adj.* 好戰的
  prisoner²〔'prɪznə〕*n.* 囚犯　　unify⁶〔'junə,faɪ〕*v.* 統一
  figure²〔'fɪgjə〕*n.* 人物　　elder²〔'ɛldə〕*adj.* 元老的；前輩的
  statesman⁵〔'stetsmən〕*n.* 政治家

He joined the African National Congress *in 1944*, ***and*** *four years later*

he was engaged in resistance *against apartheid, a system in **which***

*only white people had full political rights **and** people of other races,*

*especially black people, were forced to go to separate schools **and** to*

live in separate areas.

他在1944年加入非洲國民大會，四年之後，他參與反抗只有白人才有充分政治權力的種族隔離政策，而其他種族的人，特別是黑人，被迫上種族隔離的學校和住在隔離的區域。

* join¹〔dʒɔɪn〕*v.* 加入　　national²〔'næʃənḷ〕*adj.* 全國的
  congress⁴〔'kɑŋgrəs〕*n.* 國會
  Africa National Congress 非洲國民大會【目前南非之執政黨，其
  　宗旨是爭取種族平等】

engage[3] 〔 ɪn'gedʒ 〕 *v.* 從事；參與　　***be engaged in*** 從事；參與
resistance[4] 〔 rɪ'zɪstəns 〕 *n.* 反抗
apartheid 〔 ə'pɑrt,het 〕 *n.* 種族隔離政策
system[5] 〔 'sɪstəm 〕 *n.* 制度；體制　　full[1] 〔 fʊl 〕 *adj.* 充分的
political[3] 〔 pə'lɪtɪkḷ 〕 *adj.* 政治的　　right[1] 〔 raɪt 〕 *n.* 權利
race[1] 〔 res 〕 *n.* 種族　　especially[2] 〔 ə'spɛʃəlɪ 〕 *adv.* 尤其；特別是
force[1] 〔 fors 〕 *v.* 強迫　　separate[2] 〔 'sɛpərɪt 〕 *adj.* 分開的；單獨的
area[1] 〔 'ɛrɪə , 'erɪə 〕 *n.* 區域

In 1961, Mandela adopted violent tactics *to fight against segregation*
and was arrested *the next year*.

1961年，曼德拉採取暴力手段來對抗種族隔離政策，卻在隔年被逮捕。

* adopt[3] 〔 ə'dɑpt 〕 *v.* 採取　　violent[3] 〔 'vaɪələnt 〕 *adj.* 暴力的
tactics[6] 〔 'tæktɪks 〕 *n. pl.* 戰略
fight[1] 〔 faɪt 〕 *v. n.* 打架；對抗 < *against* >
segregation 〔 ,sɛgrɪ'geʃən 〕 *n.* 隔離　　arrest[2] 〔 ə'rɛst 〕 *v.* 逮捕

Afterwards, he was accused of plotting to overthrow the government
*by violence **and*** was sentenced to life imprisonment.

之後，他被控密謀以暴力推翻政府，而被判處終身監禁。

* afterwards[3] 〔 'æftəwədz 〕 *adv.* 後來；在…之後
accuse[4] 〔 ə'kjuz 〕 *v.* 指控 < *of* >　　plot[4] 〔 plɑt 〕 *v.* 密謀
overthrow[4] 〔 ,ovə'θro 〕 *v.* 推翻
government[2] 〔 'gʌvənmənt 〕 *n.* 政府
violence[3] 〔 'vaɪələns 〕 *n.* 暴力　　sentence[1] 〔 'sɛntəns 〕 *v.* 宣判
imprisonment[6] 〔 ɪm'prɪzṇmənt 〕 *n.* 監禁
life imprisonment 終身監禁

Though *he was in prison*, Mandela's reputation grew *steadily*.

雖然曼德拉在坐牢，但是他的名聲卻持續地成長。

* prison[2] (ˈprɪzn̩) *n.* 監獄　　reputation[4] (ˌrɛpjəˈteʃən) *n.* 名聲
  steadily[3] (ˈstɛdəlɪ) *adv.* 持續地；不斷地

He held a significant place *in South Africa* ***and*** became a powerful

symbol *in the anti-apartheid movement*.

他在南非有著重要的地位，而且成為反種族隔離運動強而有力的象徵。

* significant[3] (sɪgˈnɪfəkənt) *adj.* 重要的
  place[1] (ples) *n.* 地位　　powerful[2] (ˈpaʊɚfəl) *adj.* 強有力的
  anti-apartheid　*n.* 反種族隔離政策
  movement[1] (ˈmuvmənt) *n.* 活動；運動

In 1990, he was released *as a result of years of an international*

*outcry led by Winnie Mandela, Mandela's wife **and** a social worker.*

1990年，由於曼德拉的太太溫妮・曼德拉，她也是一位社會工作者，多年來領導的國際抗議運動，所以曼德拉被釋放了。

* release[3] (rɪˈlis) *v.* 釋放　　***as a result of*** 因為 (= *because of*)
  international[2] (ˌɪntɚˈnæʃənl̩) *adj.* 國際的
  outcry (ˈaʊtˌkraɪ) *n.* 強烈抗議　　lead[1,4] (lid) *v.* 帶領
  Winnie Mandela (ˈwɪnɪ ˈmændl̩ə) *n.* 溫妮・曼德拉
  social[2] (ˈsoʃəl) *adj.* 社會的

***As** Mandela walked out of prison, **still** upright **and** proud*, he sent a

clear message *of reconciliation*.

當曼德拉走出監獄,仍然抬頭挺胸而且很驕傲,他明確地表達和解的訊息。

* upright[5] ('ʌp,raɪt) *adj.* 筆直的   proud[2] ('praʊd) *adj.* 驕傲的
clear[1] (klɪr) *adj.* 清楚的   message[2] ('mɛsɪdʒ) *n.* 訊息
reconciliation[6] (,rɛkən,sɪlɪ'eʃən) *n.* 和解;和好

He said, "*As I walked out the door toward the gate **that** would lead to*

my freedom, I knew ***if** I didn't leave my bitterness **and** hatred behind*,

I'd *still* be in prison."

他說:「當我走出去這扇通往自由的門,我知道如果我不拋下我的痛苦與憎恨,我還是在牢獄中。」

* toward[1] (tə'word) *prep.* 朝向   gate[2] (get) *n.* 大門
lead to 通往   ***leave…behind*** 拋下;遺留
bitterness[2] ('bɪtənɪs) *n.* 痛苦   hatred[4] ('hetrɪd) *n.* 憎恨

He negotiated a peaceful end *to segregation **and*** urged forgiveness

*for the white government **that** had imprisoned him.*

他透過談判讓種族隔離有和平的結果,並且主張原諒囚禁他的白人政府。

* negotiate[4] (nɪ'goʃɪ,et) *v.* 協商;談判
peaceful[2] ('pisfəl) *adj.* 和平的   end[1] (ɛnd) *n.* 結束
urge[4] (ɝdʒ) *v.* 極力主張;力勸
forgiveness[2] (fə'gɪvnɪs) *n.* 原諒
imprison[6] (ɪm'prɪzn̩) *v.* 監禁

In 1993, he *and* President de Klerk were *jointly* awarded the Nobel

Peace Prize *for their work toward dismantling apartheid.*

1993年，他與總統戴克拉克一起獲頒諾貝爾和平獎，因爲他們對廢除種族隔離政策的努力。

> * jointly² (ˈdʒɔɪntlɪ) *adv.* 共同地　　award³ (əˈwɔrd) *v.* 頒發
> Nobel (noˈbɛl) *n.* 諾貝爾　　peace² (pis) *n.* 和平
> prize² (praɪz) *n.* 獎；獎品
> dismantle⁶ (dɪsˈmæntl̩) *v.* 廢除（某種制度）

Four years after his release, in South Africa's first multiracial elections,

he became the nation's first black president.

他被釋放後的四年，在南非第一次多重族群的選舉中，他成爲國家的第一位黑人總統。

> * multiracial (ˌmʌltɪˈreʃəl) *adj.* 多種族的【multi (= *many*)】
> election³ (ɪˈlɛkʃən) *n.* 選舉　　nation¹ (ˈneʃən) *n.* 國家

He *indeed* kept his promise *to serve only one term. After leaving the*

presidency, he continued to champion causes *such as human rights,*

*world peace **and** the fight against AIDS.*

他確實遵守諾言，只擔任一任的總統。在卸任總統職位後，他繼續爲人權、世界和平，和對抗愛滋病等目標而戰。

> * indeed³ (ɪnˈdid) *adv.* 的確；眞正地　　promise² (ˈprɑmɪs) *n.* 承諾
> ***keep** one's **promise*** 信守承諾　　serve¹ (sɝv) *v.* 任（職）

term² 〔tɜm〕 *n.* 任期　　presidency⁶ 〔'prɛzədənsɪ〕 *n.* 總統的職位
continue¹ 〔kən'tɪnju〕 *v.* 持續
champion³ 〔'tʃæmpɪən〕 *v.* 公開為…戰鬥　　*n.* 冠軍
human right 人權　　AIDS⁴ 〔edz〕 *n.* 愛滋病

Nelson Mandela was *truly* a *very* dignified ***and*** admirable

person.　His death was a great loss *to the whole world.*

納爾遜・曼德拉確實是一位高貴且值得敬佩的人。他的逝世對整個
世界來說，是巨大的損失。

　　* truly¹ 〔'trulɪ〕 *adv.* 眞地
　　dignified 〔'dɪgnə,faɪd〕 *adj.* 高貴的【dignity⁴ *n.* 尊嚴；高貴】
　　admirable⁴ 〔'ædmərəbḷ〕 *adj.* 令人欽佩的　　loss² 〔lɔs〕 *n.* 損失

American President Barack Obama said, "We've lost one *of the most*

*influential, courageous **and** profoundly good human beings **that** any of*

us will share time with on this Earth.　He *no longer* belongs to us—he

belongs to the ages."

美國總統巴拉克・歐巴馬說：「我們失去一位相當具影響力、有勇氣，
而且非常好的人，他是一個我們在這世上，都很願意和他相處的人。如
今，他不再屬於我們了——他是永恆不朽的。」

　　* Barack Obama 〔'bærək o'bɑmə〕 *n.* 巴拉克・歐巴馬
　　influential⁴ 〔,ɪnflu'ɛnʃən〕 *adj.* 有影響的
　　courageous⁴ 〔kə'redʒəs〕 *adj.* 英勇的
　　profoundly⁶ 〔prə'faundlɪ〕 *adv.* 極度地　　***human beings*** 人類
　　share² 〔ʃɛr〕 *v.* 分享　　earth¹ 〔ɜθ〕 *n.* 地球　　***no longer*** 不再
　　belong to 屬於　　age¹ 〔edʒ〕 *n.* 時代

1. (**D**) 本文主要是關於什麼？

    (A) 曼德拉的婚姻生活。   (B) 曼德拉的特質。

    (C) 曼德拉的軍旅生活。   (D) <u>曼德拉的苦難和貢獻。</u>

    * article[2,4]〔ˋɑrtɪkḷ〕*n.* 文章   married[1]〔ˋmærɪd〕*adj.* 已婚的
    characteristic[4]〔͵kærəktəˋrɪstɪk〕*n.* 特質（ = *feature*[3] ）
    military[2]〔ˋmɪlə͵tɛrɪ〕*adj.* 軍事的
    suffering[3]〔ˋsʌfəɪŋ〕*n.* 苦難
    contribution[4]〔͵kɑntrəˋbjuʃən〕*n.* 貢獻

2. (**A**) 關於種族隔離政策，下列何者為非？

    (A) <u>只有白人可以去上學。</u>

    (B) 黑人被歧視。   (C) 白人和黑人被分隔。

    (D) 白人以外的種族被剝奪許多權利。

    * discriminate[5]〔dɪˋskrɪmə͵net〕*v.* 歧視 < *against* >
    deprive[6]〔dɪˋpraɪv〕*v.* 剝奪 < *of* >

3. (**A**) 下列敘述何者為真？

    (A) <u>曼德拉被關在牢中大約 28 年。</u>

    (B) 尼爾森・曼德拉和溫妮・曼德拉獲頒諾貝爾和平獎。

    (C) 尼爾森・曼德拉兩次被選為南非的總統。

    (D) 尼爾森・曼德拉死於他的總統任期。

    * approximately[6]〔əˋprɑksəmɪtlɪ〕*adv.* 大約
    elect[2]〔ɪˋlɛkt〕*v.* 選舉

4. (**A**) 第二段的 "**reconciliation**" 指的是什麼？

    (A) <u>和好。</u>   (B) 承擔。

    (C) disaster[4]〔dɪzˋæstə〕*n.* 災難

    (D) revenge[4]〔rɪˋvɛndʒ〕*n.* 報復

    * *refer to* 是指

TEST 25

Read the following passage and choose the best answer for each question.

The Pyramid Texts are a collection of ancient Egyptian religious texts from the time of the Old Kingdom, mostly inscriptions on the walls of tombs in pyramids. They depict the Egyptian view of the afterlife, and the ascent into the sky of the divine Pharaoh after death. They were written upwards of five thousand years ago; thus, they are some of the oldest known writings in the world.

The oldest of these texts come from the Pyramid of Wenis, or more popularly these days, Unas at Saqqara. However, the first Pyramid Texts that were actually discovered were from the Pyramid of Pepy I. It is difficult to date the Pyramid Texts. There has been much speculation regarding their origin, because they emerge as a fully-fledged collection of mortuary texts, without any precedent in the archaeological record. The texts, made up of distinct utterances, do not have a strict narrative sequence linking them together.

The spells are separated by a hieroglyph for house in all the pyramids with the exception of Unas, where they are marked by a horizontal line. We call these spells "utterances" because we believe they were meant to be spoken by priests in the course of the royal mortuary rituals. They are usually numbered by their position within the pyramid, progressing from the burial chamber outward.

We are not really sure in which order the spells are to be read. Some believe they started at the north wall of the sarcophagus chamber, but other scholars think they began at the entrance to the antechamber. In fact, considerable debate exists as to their actual use and the associated rituals, though there seems to be no question of their ritualistic content. It has been assumed that they were selected from a larger collection of spells for very specific reasons and arranged according to a distinctive point of view.

1. What's the writer's purpose in writing this passage?
   - (A) To introduce the structure of pyramids.
   - (B) To introduce the rituals of ancient Egypt.
   - (C) To introduce the inscriptions found in Pharaohs' tombs.
   - (D) To introduce the oldest customs in ancient civilization.

2. As to the description of the Pyramid Texts, which of the following is NOT true?

   (A) The Pyramid texts are over 5,000 years old.

   (B) The oldest texts were found in Pyramid of Wenis.

   (C) Only spells in the Unas Pyramid are written horizontally.

   (D) They describe what the lives of Pharaohs might become after their death.

3. According to the passage, which of the following is correct?

   (A) In each pyramid, the utterances are divided by a symbol for an ancient Egyptian word.

   (B) The Pyramid texts were likely uttered by those who performed religious duties in a royal funeral.

   (C) The Pyramid Texts were first found as an incomplete collection of texts.

   (D) The spells are numbered according to their meanings.

4. The only thing the archaeologists are sure of with regard to the texts' order is that _____.

   (A) the texts in Unas at Saqqara start from the north wall of the burial chamber

   (B) the texts in the Pyramid of Pepy I begin at the entrance of the pyramid

   (C) the texts in the Pyramid of Wenis initiate from where the sarcophagus lies

   (D) they were arranged in some kind of order

TEST 25 詳解

The Pyramid Texts are a collection *of ancient Egyptian religious texts from the time of the Old Kingdom, mostly inscriptions on the walls of tombs in pyramids.*

　　金字塔銘文是一系列來自古王國時期的古埃及宗教文字，多半是銘刻在金字塔墓室內部牆上的碑文。

* pyramid[5] 〔ˈpɪrəmɪd〕 *n.* 金字塔
text[3] 〔tɛkst〕 *n.* 文本；聖經文句
Pyramid Text 金字塔銘文【最早在埃及第五王朝末期出現，是專為死去的國王將來復活、升天而寫的喪葬禱文、歌謠與符咒，通常刻在金字塔墓室內部的牆上。其中以第五王朝的末代法老烏納斯的金字塔銘文最著名】
collection[3] 〔kəˈlɛkʃən〕 *n.* 蒐集品；（服裝的）系列
ancient[2] 〔ˈenʃənt〕 *adj.* 古代的
Egyptian 〔ɪˈdʒɪpʃən〕 *n.* 埃及人　　*adj.* 埃及的
religious[3] 〔rɪˈlɪdʒəs〕 *adj.* 宗教的　　kingdom[2] 〔ˈkɪŋdəm〕 *n.* 王國
the Old Kingdom 古王國時期【2686-2181 B.C.，埃及多種文化在此時期經過融合，達到第一個巔峰】　　mostly[4] 〔ˈmostlɪ〕 *adv.* 多半
inscription 〔ɪnˈskrɪpʃən〕 *n.* 銘刻；碑文　　tomb[4] 〔tum〕 *n.* 墓穴

They depict the Egyptian view *of the afterlife*, **and** the ascent *into the sky of the divine Pharaoh after death.*

這些碑文描繪埃及人對於死後世界的看法，還有神聖的法老王死後會升天。

* depict[6] 〔 dɪ'pɪkt 〕 v. 描繪　　view[1] 〔 vju 〕 n. 看法
afterlife 〔'æftɚˌlaɪf 〕 n. 來世；死後的生命
ascent 〔 ə'sɛnt 〕 n. 上升　　divine[4] 〔 də'vaɪn 〕 adj. 神聖的；神性的
Pharaoh 〔'fɛro 〕 n. 法老王　　death[1] 〔 dɛθ 〕 n. 死亡

They were written *upwards of five thousand years ago*; *thus*, they are *some of the oldest known writings in the world.*

這些碑文已超過五千年的歷史；因此，它們是世界上已知最古老的書寫文字。

* upwards[5] 〔'ʌpwɚdz 〕 adv. 向上　　**upwards of** 超過；比⋯多
writing[1] 〔'raɪtɪŋ 〕 n. 寫作；著作

The oldest *of these texts* come from the Pyramid of Wenis, *or* more *popularly these days*, Unas *at Saqqara.*

最古老的銘文來自烏納斯金字塔，最近比較廣為人知的名稱，是薩卡拉的烏納斯金字塔。

* *the Pyramid of Wenis* 烏納斯金字塔
popularly[2,3] 〔'pɑpjələlɪ 〕 adv. 普遍地　　*these days* 最近
Unas at Saqqara 薩卡拉的烏納斯金字塔【也就是 the Pyramid of Wenis，而 Saqqara（薩卡拉）是埃及境內一處大型的古代墓地，位於開羅以南，現存世上最古老的金字塔仍屹立在此。薩卡拉是古埃及首都孟菲斯（Memphis）的「死者之城」，第一王朝時已有貴族葬於該地，第二王朝開始有國王長眠於此。而烏納斯是埃及第五王朝的最後一位法老，約西元前24世紀時在位，他在位期間，埃及發生戰爭與大規模饑荒，導致第五王朝結束。他的金字塔雖是古王國時期最小型的法老金字塔，但塔內刻有已知最早的金字塔銘文，該銘文也是「死者之書」的前身】

However, the first Pyramid Texts ***that** were actually discovered* were

from the Pyramid of Pepy I.

但是，最早發現的金字塔銘文，其實來自佩皮一世金字塔。

* actually[3] 〔'æktʃʊəlɪ〕*adv.* 實際上　　discover[1] 〔dɪ'skʌvɚ〕*v.* 發現
    the Pyramid of Pepy I 佩皮一世金字塔【Pepy I 是埃及第六王朝的
        第三位法老，他的金字塔裡的金字塔銘文是最早被考古學家發現的。
        他的金字塔叫作 Mennefer，這個名字被考古學家沿用，逐漸成為我們
        現在對於古埃及城市孟菲斯的稱呼】

It is difficult *to date the Pyramid Texts*.　There has been much

speculation *regarding their origin*, ***because** they emerge as a*

fully-fledged collection of mortuary texts, without any precedent in the

archaeological record.

金字塔銘文的年代很難去追溯。關於它們的起源一直有許多臆測，因為
它們出現的樣子，已經是發展完善的一系列悼念死者的文字，而且並無
任何先前考古的記錄。

* date[1] 〔det〕*v.* 鑑定年代　　speculation[6] 〔ˌspɛkjə'leʃən〕*n.* 推測
    regarding[4] 〔rɪ'gɑrdɪŋ〕*prep.* 關於 (= *about*[1])
    origin[3] 〔'ɔrədʒɪn〕*n.* 起源　　emerge[4] 〔ɪ'mɝdʒ〕*v.* 出現
    fully-fledged 〔'fʊl'flɛdʒd〕*adj.* 充分發展的
    mortuary 〔'mɔrtʃʊˌɛrɪ〕*adj.* 紀念死者的
    precedent[6] 〔prɪ'sidn̩t〕*n.* 前例
    archaeological 〔ˌɑrkɪə'lɑdʒɪkl̩〕*adj.* 考古學的
        【archaeology *n.* 考古學】
    record[2] 〔'rɛkɚd〕*n.* 紀錄

The texts, *made up of distinct utterances*, do not have a strict narrative sequence *linking them together*.

這些文字是以特殊的言詞所組成，沒有嚴謹的敘事順序將它們連結在一起。

* distinct[4] ﹝dɪ'stɪŋkt﹞ *adj.* 獨特的；清楚的
utterance[5] ﹝'ʌtərəns﹞ *n.* 言詞；表達
strict[2] ﹝strɪkt﹞ *adj.* 嚴格的；精確的
narrative[6] ﹝'nærətɪv﹞ *adj.* 敘述性的
sequence[6] ﹝'sikwəns﹞ *n.* 順序；關聯　　link[2] ﹝lɪŋk﹞ *v.* 使連結

The spells are separated *by a hieroglyph for house in all the pyramids with the exception Unas*, **where** *they are marked by a horizontal line*.

在所有金字塔中，這些咒文是被一個代表「房間」的埃及象形文字所分隔，但烏納斯金字塔例外，那裡的銘文是用橫線來標記。

* spell[1] ﹝spɛl﹞ *n.* 咒語　　separate[2] ﹝'sɛpə,ret﹞ *v.* 使分開
hieroglyph ﹝'haɪərə,glɪf﹞ *n.* (古埃及等的) 象形文字
exception[4] ﹝ɪk'sɛpʃən﹞ *n.* 例外　　mark[2] ﹝mark﹞ *v.* 做記號；標記
horizontal[5] ﹝,hɔrə'zɑntl̩﹞ *adj.* 水平的；橫向　　line[1] ﹝laɪn﹞ *n.* 線

We call these spells "utterances" **because** *we believe they were meant to be spoken by priests in the course of the royal mortuary rituals*.

我們稱這些咒文爲「言詞」，因爲一般認爲，這些字一定是在皇室的葬禮儀式中由祭司口述。

* ***be meant to be*** 目的是為了　　priest[3] 〔 prist 〕 *n.* 祭司
course[1] 〔 kors 〕 *n.* 過程；經過
in the course of 在⋯期間 (= *during*[1])
royal[2] 〔'rɔɪəl 〕 *adj.* 皇室的　　ritual[6] 〔'rɪtʃʊəl 〕 *n.* 儀式

They are *usually* numbered *by their position within the pyramid,*

progressing from the burial chamber outward.

銘文通常是依照它們在金字塔裡的位置來編號，從墓室開始往外數。

* number[1] 〔'nʌmbɚ 〕 *v.* 給⋯編號　　position[1] 〔 pə'zɪʃən 〕 *n.* 位置
within[2] 〔 wɪð'ɪn 〕 *prep.* 在⋯之內　　progress[2] 〔 prə'grɛs 〕 *v.* 前進
burial[6] 〔'bɛrɪəl 〕 *n.* 埋葬　　chamber[4] 〔'tʃembɚ 〕 *n.* 房間
outward[5] 〔'autwɚd 〕 *adv.* 向外

We are not *really* sure *in **which** order* the spells are to be read.

我們無法確定，這些咒文要按照哪個順序唸。

* order[1] 〔'ɔrdɚ 〕 *n.* 順序

Some believe they started *at the north wall of the sarcophagus chamber,*

but other scholars think *they began at the entrance to the antechamber.*

有些人認為是從石棺室北面的牆開始，但有些學者認為，它們的開頭應
該是在通往前廳的入口。

* north[1] 〔 nɔrθ 〕 *n.* 北方　　*adj.* 北方的
sarcophagus 〔 sɑr'kɑfəgəs 〕 *n.* (古代的大理石) 石棺
scholar[3] 〔'skɑlɚ 〕 *n.* 學者　　entrance[2] 〔'ɛntrəns 〕 *n.* 入口
antechamber 〔'æntɪˌtʃembɚ 〕 *n.* 前廳

In fact, considerable debate exists *as to their actual use **and** the*

*associated rituals, **though** there seems to be no question of their*

ritualistic content.

事實上，關於咒文眞正的用途及相關的儀式，有相當多的爭議存在，不過對於咒文的儀式性內容，似乎沒有什麼好質疑的。

* considerable³〔kən'sɪdərəbḷ〕*adj.* 相當大的
  debate²〔dɪ'bet〕*n.* 爭論　　exist²〔ɪg'zɪst〕*v.* 存在
  as to 至於；關於　　actual³〔'æktʃuəl〕*adj.* 實際的；眞實的
  associated⁴〔ə'soʃɪˌetɪd〕*adj.* 相關的
  ritualistic〔ˌrɪtʃuəl'ɪstɪk〕*adj.* 儀式的【ritual⁶〔'rɪtʃuəl〕*n.* 儀式】
  content⁴〔'kɑntɛnt〕*n.* 內容

It has been assumed ***that** they were selected from a larger collection of*

*spells for very specific reasons **and** arranged according to a distinctive*

point of view.

一般認爲，這些銘文是爲了非常特定的理由，從更大範圍的咒文當中所選出來的，而且是根據特定的觀點來排列。

* assume⁴〔ə'sum〕*v.* 假定；認爲　　select²〔sə'lɛkt〕*v.* 挑選
  specific³〔spɪ'sɪfɪk〕*adj.* 特定的
  arrange²〔ə'rendʒ〕*v.* 安排；排列
  distinctive⁵〔dɪ'stɪŋktɪv〕*adj.* 獨特的　　***point of view*** 觀點

1. (**C**) 作者寫這篇文章的目的是什麼？
   (A) 介紹金字塔的結構。　　　　(B) 介紹古埃及的儀式。
   (C) 介紹在法老王墳墓中發現的碑文。
   (D) 介紹古代文明中最古老的習俗。

* writer[1] (ˈraɪtɚ) *n.* 作者　　introduce[2] (ˌɪntrəˈdjus) *v.* 介紹
structure[3] (ˈstrʌktʃɚ) *n.* 結構；建築物
Egypt (ˈidʒɪpt) *n.* 埃及　　custom[2] (ˈkʌstəm) *n.* 習俗
civilization[4] (ˌsɪvḷaɪˈzeʃən) *n.* 文明

2. (**C**) 關於金字塔銘文的描述，下列何者爲非？

(A) 金字塔銘文超過 5,000 年歷史。

(B) 在烏納斯金字塔中發現最古老的銘文。

(C) <u>只有在烏納斯金字塔裡的銘文是橫式書寫。</u>

(D) 它們描述法老王們死後可能的生活。

* *as to* 關於；至於　　description[3] (dɪˈskrɪpʃən) *n.* 描述
horizontally[5] (ˌhɔrəˈzɑntḷɪ) *adv.* 水平地；橫地
describe[2] (dɪˈskraɪb) *v.* 描述

3. (**B**) 根據本文，下列何者爲眞？

(A) 在每座金字塔中用代表古埃及字的符號來劃分言詞。

(B) <u>金字塔銘文可能是皇家葬禮上履行宗教職責的人所說的。</u>

(C) 金字塔銘文最早被發現時是一系列不完整的文字。

(D) 咒文是根據其意思來編號。

* divide[2] (dəˈvaɪd) *v.* 劃分　　symbol[2] (ˈsɪmbḷ) *n.* 象徵
utter[5] (ˈʌtɚ) *v.* 說出　　perform[3] (pɚˈfɔrm) *v.* 執行
duties[2] (ˈdjutɪz) *n. pl.* 職責　　funeral[4] (ˈfjunərəl) *n.* 葬禮
incomplete[2] (ˌɪnkəmˈplit) *adj.* 不完整的
meaning[2] (ˈminɪŋ) *n.* 意義

4. (**D**) 關於銘文的順序，考古學家唯一確定的是 _____。

(A) 薩卡拉的烏納斯金字塔銘文是由墓室中的北面牆開始的

(B) 佩皮一世金字塔銘文開始於金字塔的入口處

(C) 烏納斯金字塔銘文開始於石棺的所在地

(D) <u>它們是以某種順序排列</u>

* archaeologist (ˌɑrkɪˈɑlədʒɪst) *n.* 考古學家
with regard to 關於　　initiate[5] (ɪˈnɪʃɪˌet) *v.* 創始；開始
lie[1] (laɪ) *v.* 位於；在　　some[1] (sʌm) *adj.* 某個

TEST 26

Read the following passage and choose the best answer for each question.

Music can alter a space as much as lighting, fabrics and artwork, but until recently, most people relied on their own judgment when it came to sound. Now, though, an increasing number of customers are hiring personal music stylists to pick out tunes for their homes just as they might hire an interior decorator to select furnishings.

While the music industry has for decades created what it calls "audio architecture" for commercial environments, it is just in the last five years that a handful of music consultants, mostly in New York and London, have begun to specialize in creating custom domestic soundtracks. Their assignment is compiling playlists to match their clients' household atmosphere.

Coleman Feltes, a DJ known for creating mixes for fashion shows, began his music service for individuals in 2006. He and the other music stylists typically visit clients' homes or look at photographs of them to assess their decorating styles and to understand layouts. They may also peruse clients' music collections to learn the genres and artists they've liked in the past.

Stylists typically charge between $50 and $250 per hour of music, which they usually download onto iPods but which can also be delivered on CDs.

Jessica Goldberg, a housewife with two young kids, filled out a questionnaire about their daily life and their music tastes. In a phone interview, she also described their home, which has wide-plank wood floors, large windows and modern furniture. A couple of weeks later, she got a 10-hour compilation, most of the tracks on which she had previously never heard of. She is quite satisfied with the playlist, which has an overall warm sound and harmonizes with her apartment's open floor plan and casual, contemporary feel. "It is like they could read my mind," she says.

1. To compile music for their clients, music stylists will do all of the following except _____.

   (A) visit their homes
   (B) study their decorating styles
   (C) look at their music collections
   (D) discuss music with all the family members

2. According to the passage, how did people use to choose music played at home?

(A) They hired an interior decorator to do it for them.

(B) They decided on their own.

(C) They gathered information online.

(D) They follow professional suggestions.

3. How does Jessica feel about the service she got?

(A) Satisfied.

(B) Furious.

(C) Surprised.

(D) Motivated.

4. Which of the following is the best title for this article?

(A) The Impact Music Has on Your Mood

(B) The Interior Decorator, a Rising Occupation

(C) The Audio Architecture of Your House

(D) Mixing Fashion Shows with Music

TEST 26 詳解

Music can alter a space *as much **as** lighting, fabrics and artwork,*

***but** until recently,* most people relied on their own judgment ***when** it*

came to sound.

　　音樂改變空間的能力不亞於光線、布料與藝術品,但是直到最近,
一提到聲音,大家還是習慣仰賴自己的判斷。

* alter[5] 〔ˈɔltɚ〕 v. 改變　　space[1] 〔spes〕 n. 空間;場所;地區
  lighting[1] 〔ˈlaɪtɪŋ〕 n. 燈光照明
  fabric[5] 〔ˈfæbrɪk〕 n. 布料;織品
  artwork 〔ˈɑrt,wɝk〕 n. 藝術品　　recently[2] 〔ˈrisn̩tlɪ〕 adv. 最近
  rely on 依賴　　judgment[2] 〔ˈdʒʌdʒmənt〕 n. 判斷
  when it comes to 一提到

Now, though, an increasing number *of customers* are hiring personal

music stylists *to pick out tunes for their homes just **as** they might hire*

an interior decorator to select furnishings.

不過現在有愈來愈多顧客,會雇用個人的音樂設計師來幫他們的家挑選
曲目,正如同雇用室內設計師來幫他們選家具一樣。

* though[1] 〔ðo〕 adv. 然而;不過【置於句中或句尾】
  increase[2] 〔ɪnˈkris〕 v. 增加
  an increasing number of 愈來愈多的
  customer[2] 〔ˈkʌstəmɚ〕 n. 顧客　　hire[2] 〔haɪr〕 v. 雇用
  personal[2] 〔ˈpɝsn̩l̩〕 adj. 個人的　　stylist[3] 〔ˈstaɪlɪst〕 n. 設計師

pick out 挑選　　tune[3] (tjun) *n.* 曲調；歌曲
interior[5] (ɪn'tɪrɪɚ) *adj.* 內部的
decorator[2] ('dɛkə,retɚ) *n.* 裝飾者；室內裝潢業者
select[2] (sə'lɛkt) *v.* 選擇；挑選
furnishings[4] ('fɝnɪʃɪŋz) *n. pl.* (房子的) 陳設品；裝修

While the music industry has for decades created what it calls

"audio architecture" for commercial environments, it is *just in the*

last five years that a handful of music consultants, mostly in New York

and London, have begun to specialize in creating custom domestic

soundtracks.

雖然數十年來，音樂產業已經爲了商業環境創造了所謂的「影音建築」，但直到最近五年，才有少數的音樂顧問，大多在紐約與倫敦開始專門創作客製的家用原聲帶。

* while[1] (hwaɪl) *conj.* 雖然 (= *though*[1])
industry[2] ('ɪndəstrɪ) *n.* 產業　　decade[3] ('dɛked) *n.* 十年
create[2] (krɪ'et) *v.* 創造　　**what it calls** 它所謂的
audio[4] ('ɔdɪ,o) *adj.* 聽覺的
architecture[5] ('ɑrkə,tɛktsɚ) *n.* 建築
audio architecture 影音建築
commercial[3] (kə'mɝʃəl) *adj.* 商業的
environment[2] (ɪn'vaɪrənmənt) *n.* 環境
last[1] (læst) *adj.* 過去的
handful[3] ('hænd,fʊl) *n.* 一把　　**a handful of** 少數的
consultant[4] (kən'sʌltənt) *n.* 顧問；專家
mostly[4] ('mostlɪ) *adv.* 大多
specialize[6] ('spɛʃəl,aɪz) *v.* 專攻 < *in* >

custom² 〔'kʌstəm〕*adj.* 客製的
domestic³ 〔də'mɛstɪk〕*adj.* 家庭的
soundtrack 〔'saʊnd,træk〕*n.* (電影、電視的) 原聲帶

Their assignment is compiling playlists *to match their clients'*

household atmosphere.
他們的任務就是要編輯適合客戶家中氛圍的播放清單。

* assignment⁴ 〔ə'saɪnmənt〕*n.* 任務；作業
  compile⁶ 〔kəm'paɪl〕*v.* 編輯
  playlist 〔'ple,lɪst〕*n.* 播放清單
  match²,¹ 〔mætʃ〕*v.* 符合　　client³ 〔'klaɪənt〕*n.* 客戶
  household⁴ 〔'haʊs,hold〕*adj.* 家庭的
  atmosphere⁴ 〔'ætməs,fɪr〕*n.* 氣氛

Coleman Feltes, *a DJ known for creating mixes for fashion shows,*

began his music service *for individuals in 2006.*

　　因為幫時裝秀混音而聞名的DJ柯爾曼・費爾特斯，2006年開始為個
人提供音樂服務。

* Coleman Feltes 〔'kolmən 'fɛltɪz〕*n.* 柯爾曼・費爾特斯
  DJ 音樂節目主持人 (= *disc jockey*)
  be known for 以⋯有名
  mix² 〔mɪks〕*v.* 混合　*n.* 混合 (物)
  fashion³ 〔'fæʃən〕*n.* 流行；時裝
  fashion show 時裝秀
  service¹ 〔'sɝvɪs〕*n.* 服務
  individual³ 〔,ɪndə'vɪdʒʊəl〕*n.* 個人

Coleman Feltes

He **and** the other music stylists *typically* visit clients' homes **or** look
at photographs *of them to assess their decorating styles* **and** *to*
understand layouts.

他與其他的音樂設計師通常會造訪客戶的家，或是觀察他們的照片，來
評估他們家中的裝潢風格並了解格局。

* typically[3] (ˈtɪpɪklɪ) *adv.* 通常　　visit[1] (ˈvɪzɪt) *v.* 拜訪
look at 觀察；研究　　photograph[2] (ˈfotə͵græf) *n.* 照片
assess[6] (əˈsɛs) *v.* 評估　　decorating[2] (ˈdɛkə͵retɪŋ) *adj.* 裝飾的
style[3] (staɪl) *n.* 風格；方式　　layout[6] (ˈle͵aʊt) *n.* 格局

They may *also* review clients' music collections *to learn the genres*
and *artists they've liked in the past.*

他們可能也會檢視客戶的音樂收藏，以得知顧客以前喜歡的音樂類型與
藝人。

* review[1] (rɪˈvju) *v.* 複習；審查
collection[3] (kəˈlɛkʃən) *n.* 收集；收藏品
learn[1] (lɜn) *v.* 知道　　genre (ˈʒɑnrə) *n.* 類型
artist[2] (ˈɑrtɪst) *n.* 表演藝術家　　**in the past** 以前

Stylists *typically* charge between $50 **and** $250 *per hour of*
music, **which** *they usually download onto iPods* **but which** *can also be*
delivered on CDs.

　　音樂設計師的收費標準，一般是每小時的音樂50美元到250美元之間，他們通常會把這些音樂下載在iPod上或是發行CD。

* charge[2] 〔tʃɑrdʒ〕 v. 收費　　per[2] 〔pɚ〕 prep. 每…
download[4] 〔'daʊn,lod〕 v. 下載
onto[3] 〔'ɑntə〕 prep. 到…之上　　deliver[2] 〔dɪ'lɪvɚ〕 v. 發行；發佈

Jessica Goldberg, *a housewife with two young kids*, filled out a
questionnaire *about their daily life **and** their music tastes.*

　　有兩個年幼小孩的家庭主婦潔西卡・戈德堡填了一份問卷，回答一些關於日常生活與音樂品味的問題。

* Jessica Goldberg 〔'dʒɛsɪkə 'goldbɝg〕 n. 潔西卡・戈德堡
housewife[4] 〔'haʊs,waɪf〕 n. 家庭主婦
young[1] 〔jʌŋ〕 adj. 年幼的　　kid[1] 〔kɪd〕 n. 小孩
fill out 填寫　　questionnaire[6] 〔,kwɛstʃən'ɛr〕 n. 問卷
daily life 日常生活　　taste[1] 〔test〕 n. 品味；愛好

In a phone interview, she *also* described their home, ***which** has*
*wide-plank wood floors, large windows **and** modern furniture.*

在電話訪問中，她也描述了他們的家，裡面有著寬厚的木地板、大型窗戶，以及現代化的家具。

* interview[2] 〔'ɪntɚ,vju〕 n. 訪問　　describe[2] 〔dɪ'skraɪb〕 v. 描述
wide[1] 〔waɪd〕 adj. 寬的　　plank 〔plæŋk〕 n. 厚板
wood[1] 〔wʊd〕 adj. 木製的　　floor[1] 〔flɔr〕 n. 地板
modern[2] 〔'mɑdɚn〕 adj. 現代化的；摩登的
furniture[3] 〔'fɝnɪtʃɚ〕 n. 家具

A couple of weeks later, she got a 10-hour compilation, *most of the*

tracks on **which** *she had previously never heard of.*

幾週過後,她收到了一份十小時的合輯,裡面有很多曲目是她之前從來
沒有聽過的。

> * *a couple of* 幾個 　 ompilation⁶〔͵kɑmpḷ'eʃən〕*n.* 編輯
> track²〔træk〕*n.* 音軌;曲目
> previously³〔'prɪvɪəslɪ〕*adv.* 以前 (= *in the past*)
> *hear of* 聽說

She is *quite* satisfied with the playlist, ***which*** *has an overall warm*

sound **and** *harmonizes with her apartment's open floor plan* **and**

casual, contemporary feel. "It is like *they could read my mind*," she

says.

她對這份播放清單相當滿意,裡面的音樂都有溫暖的音調,和她的公寓
開闊的格局很協調,達到一種悠閒而現代的感覺。「這就像他們知道我
在想什麼一樣,」她說。

> * quite¹〔kwaɪt〕*adv.* 相當 　 satisfied²〔'sætɪs͵faɪd〕*adj.* 滿意的
> *be satisfied with* 對…滿意 　 overall⁵〔'ovɚ͵ɔl〕*adj.* 整體的
> warm¹〔wɔrm〕*adj.* 溫暖的
> harmonize⁴〔'hɑrmən͵aɪz〕*v.* 和諧;一致;協調
> apartment²〔ə'pɑrtmənt〕*n.* 公寓
> *floor plan* 樓面平面圖 　 *open floor plan* 開放式平面圖
> casual³〔'kæʒuəl〕*adj.* 休閒的;非正式的
> contemporary⁵〔kən'tɛmpə͵rɛrɪ〕*adj.* 當代的
> *read one's mind* 看出某人的想法

1.(**D**) 音樂設計師爲了要爲他們的客戶編輯音樂，會做下列全部的
　　　　事，除了 ＿＿＿＿＿＿＿ 。
　　　　(A) 參觀他們的房子　　　　(B) 研究他們的裝潢風格
　　　　(C) 看他們的音樂收藏
　　　　(D) 與他們所有的家庭成員討論音樂
　　　　* except[1] (ɪk'sɛpt) prep. 除了　　　study[1] ('stʌdɪ) v. 研究
　　　　discuss[2] (dɪ'skʌs) v. 討論　　member[2] ('mɛmbɚ) n. 成員

2.(**B**) 根據本文，過去人們在家裡是如何選擇播放的音樂？
　　　　(A) 他們僱用一位室內設計師幫他們做。
　　　　(B) 他們自己決定。　　　(C) 他們在網路上收集資訊。
　　　　(D) 他們聽從專業的建議。
　　　　* **used to** 以前　　　**interior decorator** 室內設計師
　　　　on one's **own** 自己　　　gather[2] ('gæðɚ) v. 收集
　　　　information[4] (ˌɪnfɚ'meʃən) n. 資訊
　　　　online ('ɑn'laɪn) adv. 在網路上　　follow[1] ('falo) v. 聽從
　　　　professional[4] (prə'fɛʃənl) adj. 專業的
　　　　suggestion[4] (səg'dʒɛstʃən) n. 建議

3.(**A**) 潔西卡對於她得到的服務覺得如何？
　　　　(A) **satisfied**[2] ('sætɪsˌfaɪd) adj. 滿意的
　　　　(B) furious[4] ('fjʊrɪəs) adj. 狂怒的
　　　　(C) surprised[1] (sə'praɪzɪd) adj. 驚訝的
　　　　(D) motivated[4] ('motəˌvetɪd) adj. 受到激勵的

4.(**C**) 下列何者是本文最好的標題？
　　　　(A) 音樂對心情的影響　　　(B) 室內裝潢員一個新興的職業
　　　　(C) 你家的影音建築　　　　(D) 將時裝秀與音樂相結合
　　　　* title[2] ('taɪtl) n. 標題　　article[2,4] ('ɑrtɪkl) n. 文章
　　　　impact[4] ('ɪmpækt) n. 影響 (= effect[2] = influence[2])
　　　　mood[3] (mud) n. 心情
　　　　rising[1] ('raɪzɪŋ) adj. 新興的；蓬勃成長中的
　　　　occupation[4] (ˌɑkjə'peʃən) n. 職業

TEST 27

Read the following passage and choose the best answer for each question.

Technology can now be used to determine a computer typist's age, sex, and background within 10 keystrokes by monitoring his or her speed and rhythm.

A team of researchers at the University of Newcastle have revealed that they could produce a "keyboard profile" of someone after just 10 taps, a technological feat that could be useful in tracking down online fraudsters and pedophiles.

The technique has been described by cyber crime experts, who seek to adapt the technology for use in law enforcement and forensics, as a "fantastic tool to aid intelligence gathering for crime-fighting agencies."

Computer users' fingers are hooked up to electronic sensors while the UK researchers video, monitor and record their typing patterns with an accurate clock. The speeds and rhythms provided by typing 10 numbers or letters are then analyzed to identify the typist's gender, culture, age and any hand injuries.

They timed and tracked volunteers who typed a password 400 times in a row. The results demonstrated that women tend to type quicker than men while the latter are a little more heavy-handed.

"We are looking at the application of the research, particularly in relation to internet grooming," said the British report, adding that the new technique could be used to prevent fraud at cash machines as well. "We have also had interest from the private sector, which is keen to see whether this technology can be used as an additional tool for identity verification, such as in online banking."

The "keyboard profile" method enjoys an accuracy rate of 95 percent, similar to that of trustworthy verification tools such as fingerprints and the lie detector.

1. What's the writer's purpose in writing this passage?
   (A) To facilitate the typing speed of computer users.
   (B) To help the police arrest runaway criminals.
   (C) To explain the consequences of using a computer too much.
   (D) To introduce a new crime-fighting technique.

2. What is the 4th paragraph about?

(A) Whether this technology can be used as an additional tool for identity verification.

(B) Why the "keyboard profile" enjoys a low rate of accuracy.

(C) How a computer user's profile is identified by using the new technique.

(D) How cyber crime experts use the technique in law enforcement and forensics.

3. When it comes to fingerprints, the lie detector, and keyboard profile, which functions better?

(A) They function equally well as trustworthy verification tools.

(B) Fingerprints are out of date while the other two are in fashion.

(C) The keyboard profile is superior to the other two.

(D) They are all one hundred percent accurate as verification tools.

4. What were volunteers asked to do?

(A) Key in their age, gender and background.

(B) Learn about Internet grooming.

(C) Provide their fingerprints and take a lie detector test.

(D) Type a password 400 times in a row.

TEST 27 詳解

Technology can *now* be used *to determine a computer typist's*

age, sex, **and** *background within 10 keystrokes by monitoring his* **or**

her speed **and** *rhythm.*

　　科技現在只要監測一個人打字的速度跟節奏，就可以在十個鍵之
內，測定電腦打字者的年齡、性別，還有背景資料。

* technology³ 〔tɛk'nɑlədʒɪ〕 *n.* 科技
　 determine³ 〔dɪ'tɝmɪn〕 *v.* 決定；測定
　 typist⁴ 〔'taɪpɪst〕 *n.* 打字者　　sex³ 〔sɛks〕 *n.* 性別
　 background³ 〔'bæk͵graʊnd〕 *n.* 背景
　 within² 〔wɪð'ɪn〕 *prep.* 在…之內
　 keystroke 〔'ki͵strok〕 *n.* 敲一次鍵盤
　 monitor⁴ 〔'mɑnətɚ〕 *v.* 監視；追蹤
　 speed² 〔spid〕 *n.* 速度　　rhythm⁴ 〔'rɪðəm〕 *n.* 節奏

A team *of researchers at the University of Newcastle* have

revealed **that** *they could produce a "keyboard profile" of someone*

after just 10 taps, a technological feat **that** *could be useful in tracking*

down online fraudsters **and** *pedophiles.*

　　新堡大學的研究小組發現，敲十下鍵盤，就可以揭露某人的「鍵盤
使用概況」，這種科技大發明，可用來追蹤網路上的詐欺犯還有戀童癖
者。

* team[2] 〔 tim 〕 *n.* 團隊；小組　　researcher[4] 〔 rɪˈsɝtʃɚ 〕 *n.* 研究人員

Newcastle 〔ˈnuˌkæsḷ〕 *n.* 新堡【英格蘭的港口城市】

University of Newcastle 新堡大學【英格蘭歷史悠久的名校之一，
　位於新堡，1834年創校，醫學院尤其有名】

reveal[3] 〔 rɪˈvil 〕 *v.* 透露；揭發

produce[2] 〔 prəˈdjus 〕 *v.* 生產；製造

keyboard[3] 〔ˈkiˌbord 〕 *n.* 鍵盤

profile[5] 〔ˈprofaɪl 〕 *n.* 輪廓；概況；數據圖表

keyboard profile 鍵盤使用特徵【利用打字的速度及節奏，可分辨
　打字者的性別、年齡或是身分背景的技術，可用於預防網路犯罪或
　是網路誘拐】　　tap[4,3] 〔 tæp 〕 *n.* 敲打聲

technological[4] 〔ˌtɛknəˈlɑdʒɪkḷ 〕 *adj.* 科技的

feat 〔 fit 〕 *n.* 功績；偉業；絕技　　useful[1] 〔ˈjusfəl 〕 *adj.* 有用的

track[2] 〔 træk 〕 *v.* 追蹤；查出　　***track down*** 追蹤；查出

online 〔ˈɑnˌlaɪn 〕 *adj.* 線上的；網路上的

fraudster 〔ˈfrɔdstɚ 〕 *n.* 詐欺犯　　pedophile 〔ˈpidəˌfaɪl 〕 *n.* 戀童癖

The technique has been described *by cyber crime experts,* **who**

seek to adapt the technology for use in law enforcement **and** *forensics,*

as a "fantastic tool to aid intelligence gathering for crime-fighting

agencies."

想把這項技巧改造成可用在執法單位與鑑識方面的網路犯罪專家說，這
項科技是「非常棒的工具，可以幫助打擊犯罪的政府機關收集情報。」

* technique[3] 〔 tɛkˈnik 〕 *n.* 技術；技巧

describe[2] 〔 dɪˈskraɪb 〕 *v.* 描述

cyber 〔ˈsaɪbɚ 〕 *adj.* 虛擬的；網路的

crime[2] 〔ˈkraɪm 〕 *n.* 罪；犯罪　　expert[2] 〔ˈɛkspɝt 〕 *n.* 專家

seek[3] ﹝ sik ﹞ *v.* 尋求　　***seek to*** 尋求；試圖
adapt[4] ﹝ ə'dæpt ﹞ *v.* 使適應；改造　　law[1] ﹝ lɔ ﹞ *n.* 法律
enforcement[4] ﹝ ɪn'dɔrsmənt ﹞ *n.* 執行
law enforcement 執法　　forensics ﹝ fə'rɛnsɪks ﹞ *n.* 鑑識學
fantastic[4] ﹝ fæn'tæstɪk ﹞ *adj.* 很棒的　　tool[1] ﹝ tul ﹞ *n.* 工具
aid[2] ﹝ ed ﹞ *v.* 幫助　　intelligence[4] ﹝ ɪn'tɛlədʒəns ﹞ *n.* 情報
gather[2] ﹝ 'gæðə ﹞ *v.* 聚集　　***intelligence gathering*** 情報收集
crime-fighting ﹝ 'kraɪm'faɪtɪŋ ﹞ *adj.* 打擊犯罪的
agency[4] ﹝ 'edʒənsɪ ﹞ *n.* 政府機關

Computer users' fingers are hooked up *to electronic sensors*
while the UK researchers video, monitor *and* record their typing
patterns *with an accurate clock.*

　　電腦使用者的手指跟電子感應器連結在一起，同時備有精準的時
鐘，英國的研究員錄影、監看並記錄他們的打字模式。

* user[2] ﹝ 'juzə ﹞ *n.* 使用者　　hook[4] ﹝ hʊk ﹞ *v.* 以鉤掛住
hook up to 使接線到…上
electronic[3] ﹝ ɪ,lɛk'trɑnɪk ﹞ *adj.* 電子的　　sensor ﹝ 'sɛnsə ﹞ *n.* 感應器
the UK 英國 (= *the United Kingdom*)
video[2] ﹝ 'vɪdɪ,o ﹞ *v.* 錄影　　record[2] ﹝ rɪ'kɔrd ﹞ *v.* 記錄
type[2] ﹝ taɪp ﹞ *v.* 打字　　pattern[2] ﹝ 'pætən ﹞ *n.* 模式
accurate[3] ﹝ 'ækjərɪt ﹞ *adj.* 正確的

The speeds *and* rhythms *provided by typing 10 numbers or letters* are
then analyzed *to identify the typist's gender, culture, age and any*
hand injuries.

然後藉由分析打十個數字或字母的速度跟節奏，來辨識打字者的性別、文化、年齡，以及手上是否有傷。

* provide[2] 〔 prə'vaɪd 〕 v. 提供　　letter[1] 〔'lɛtɚ 〕 n. 字母
analyze[4] 〔'ænl̩,aɪz 〕 v. 分析　　identify[4] 〔 aɪ'dɛntə,faɪ 〕 v. 辨試
gender[5] 〔'dʒɛndɚ 〕 n. 性別　　culture[2] 〔'kʌltʃɚ 〕 n. 文化
injury[3] 〔'ɪndʒərɪ 〕 n. 傷害

They timed *and tracked volunteers **who** typed a password 400 times in a row.*

研究人員計時並追蹤連續輸入密碼四百次的自願者。

* time[1] 〔 taɪm 〕 v. 計時　 n. 次數
volunteer[4] 〔,vɑlən'tɪr 〕 n. 自願者
password[3] 〔'pæs,wɝd 〕 n. 密碼
row[1] 〔 ro 〕 n. 排　　 ***in a row*** 連續地

The results demonstrated ***that** women tend to type quicker **than** men **while** the latter are a little more heavy-handed.*

結果證明女人打字普遍比男人快，而男人手腳比較笨拙。

* result[2] 〔 rɪ'zʌlt 〕 n. 結果
demonstrate[4] 〔'dɛmən,stret 〕 v. 證明；說明
tend to 傾向於　　 latter[3] 〔'lætɚ 〕 n. 後者
heavy-handed 〔'hɛvɪ'hændɪd 〕 adj. 手腳笨拙的

"We are looking at the application *of the research, particularly in relation to Internet grooming,*" said the British report, *adding **that*** *the new technique could be used to prevent fraud at cash machines as*

well.

「我們正觀察這項研究的應用，特別是關於網路誘拐行為。」這份英國的報告指出，又補充說，這項新技術也能被用來預防提款機詐騙。

* application⁴〔͵æplə'keʃən〕 n. 應用
  research⁴〔rɪ's͵t͵ʃ, 'ris͵tʃ〕 v. n. 研究
  particularly²〔pə'tɪkjələlɪ〕 adv. 尤其；特別是
  relation²〔rɪ'leʃən〕 n. 關係　　*in relation to* 關於
  Internet⁴〔'ɪntə͵nɛt〕 n. 網際網路
  groom〔grum〕 v. 打扮；修飾；調教（人）成為…
  Internet grooming 網路誘拐【在網路上接近兒童，意圖對兒童做出性騷擾行為。grooming 表與兒童建立友誼，解除戒心的過程，不只是網路，日常生活也有可能發生。而 Internet grooming 特別指網路上的誘拐行為】
  British〔'brɪtɪʃ〕 adj. 英國的　　report¹〔rɪ'port〕 n. 報告
  add¹〔æd〕 v. 補充說　　prevent³〔prɪ'vɛnt〕 v. 防止；預防
  fraud⁶〔frɔd〕 n. 詐欺
  cash machine【英】提款機（= *ATM* = *automated teller machine*）
  as well 也（= *too*）

"We have *also* had interest *from the private sector,* *which is keen to*

*see **whether** this technology can be used as an additional tool for*

identity verification, such as in online banking."

某些私人企業對這項技術也很有興趣，他們很想要看這項技術能否用來作為一項附加的身分認證工具，像是用在網路銀行業務。」

* private[2]〔'praɪvɪt〕 *adj.* 私人的　　sector[6]〔'sɛktɚ〕 *n.* 部門；領域

keen[4]〔kin〕 *adj.* 渴望的　　***be keen to*** 積極於…

additional[3]〔ə'dɪʃənl̩〕 *adj.* 額外的

identity[3]〔aɪ'dɛntətɪ〕 *n.* 身分

verification〔,vɛrəfɪ'keʃən〕 *n.* 證實；證明

such as 像是　　online〔,ɑn'laɪn〕 *adj.* 線上的；網路的

banking[1]〔'bæŋkɪŋ〕 *n.* 銀行業務

online banking 網路銀行業務

The "keyboard profile" method enjoys an accuracy rate *of 95 percent,* similar to ***that*** *of trustworthy verification tools such as fingerprints* ***and*** *the lie detector.*

「鍵盤使用概況」方法有百分之九十五的準確度，類似指紋機或測謊機等可靠的認證工具。

* method[2]〔'mɛθəd〕 *n.* 方法　　enjoy[2]〔ɪn'dʒɔɪ〕 *v.* 享受；享有

accuracy[4]〔'ækjərəsɪ〕 *n.* 正確性；精準性

rate[3]〔ret〕 *n.* 比率　　percent[4]〔pɚ'sɛnt〕 *n.* 百分之…

similar[2]〔'sɪmələ〕 *adj.* 類似的 < *to* >

trustworthy〔'trʌst,wɜðɪ〕 *adj.* 可信的；可靠的

fingerprint〔'fɪŋgɚ,prɪnt〕 *n.* 指紋

detector[2]〔dɪ'tɛktɚ〕 *n.* 偵測器　　***lie detector*** 測謊機

1. (**D**) 作者寫本文的主要目的是什麼？

　　(A) 增進電腦使用者的打字速度。

　　(B) 幫助警方逮捕逃跑的罪犯。

　　(C) 解釋太常使用電腦的後果。

　　(D) <u>介紹新的打擊犯罪的技術。</u>

* writer[1] 〔'raɪtɚ 〕 *n.* 作者　　purpose[1] 〔'pɝpəs 〕 *n.* 目的
facititate[6] 〔fə'sɪlə,tet 〕 *v.* 使便利；促進；幫助
arrest[2] 〔ə'rɛst 〕 *v.* 逮捕　　runaway 〔'rʌnə,we 〕 *adj.* 逃跑的
criminal[3] 〔'krɪmənḷ 〕 *n.* 罪犯　　explain[2] 〔ɪk'splen 〕 *v.* 解釋
consequence[4] 〔'kɑnsə,kwɛns 〕 *n.* 後果
introduce[2] 〔,ɪntrə'djus 〕 *v.* 介紹

2. (**C**) 第四段是關於什麼？

　　(A) 這項科技是否能被當成一種身份認證的附加工具。

　　(B) 爲什麼「鍵盤使用概況」準確率很低。

　　(C) 如何以這項新技術辨認電腦使用者的概況。

　　(D) 網路犯罪專家如何在執法單位和鑑識方面使用這項技術。

3. (**A**) 當提到指紋、測謊機，和鍵盤使用概況時，哪一項的效果較好？

　　(A) 作爲可靠的認證工具，它們的效果一樣好。

　　(B) 指紋已過時，而另外兩項正流行。

　　(C) 鍵盤使用概況比另外兩項優秀。

　　(D) 作爲認證工具，它們全都是百分之百準確。

　　* function[2] 〔'fʌŋkʃən 〕 *v.* 運作
　　equally[1] 〔'ikwəlɪ 〕 *adv.* 相等地
　　out of date 過時的　　*in fashion* 流行的
　　superior[3] 〔sə'pɪrɪɚ 〕 *adj.* 較優秀的 < *to* >

4. (**D**) 自願者被要求做什麼？

　　(A) 輸入他們的年齡、性別，和背景。

　　(B) 學習關於網路誘拐。

　　(C) 提供他們的指紋，並且接受測謊機測驗。

　　(D) 連續輸入密碼四百次。

　　* *key in* 輸入　　*take a test* 接受測驗

TEST 28

Read the following passage and choose the best answer for each question.

Imagine the following scenario. In the rush to get to work, you drop a piece of toast on the floor. You hesitate over whether or not to pick it up. Then you pick it up and eat it like nothing happened. Well, should you? Most people would probably follow their instinct to pick up the food because they believe that food is still safe to eat if you pick it up within five seconds of dropping it—the so-called "five-second rule." To many people, it seems a waste of food to throw the food into the trash can rather than put it into their mouth. However, you may want to think again next time you do it.

Scientists now warn that five seconds are all it takes for food to become **contaminated** with just enough bacteria to make you sick. Bacteria lead to all kinds of diseases. Some bacteria are known to grow on food. If the food is eaten, common symptoms like vomiting and diarrhea may occur. The question is, exactly how threatening can bacteria be to our life? One of the food-borne bacteria called salmonella, for instance, makes 1.4 million people sick every year. Salmonella is often found in raw eggs and chicken. It is therefore advised to cook these kinds of foods thoroughly before eating them. Also, to prevent infection, it is important to keep household surfaces clean, for salmonella could stay for weeks.

So remember: next time you drop a small piece of your food on the floor, no matter how tasty it appears to be or how expensive it is, the best thing seems to be to toss it out rather than eat it.

1. According to the passage, which of the following statements is **False**?
   (A) The "five-second rule" dealing with dropped morsels is not wise.
   (B) Thoroughly cooked foods reduced the risk of getting infected by bacteria.
   (C) It takes more than five seconds for bacteria to attach to foods.
   (D) Salmonella is a kind of food-borne bacterium.

2. What is the purpose of the passage?

(A) To explain the process of how bacteria attach to food.

(B) To warn of the danger of getting sick after eating dropped food.

(C) To highlight the importance of cooking foods thoroughly.

(D) To provide measures for killing household bacteria.

3. The word **contaminated** in the second paragraph is closest in meaning to _____.

(A) polluted

(B) stale

(C) delicious

(D) rough

4. According to the conclusion, the best way to deal with dropped food is to _____.

(A) pick it up within five seconds

(B) pick it up immediately and wash it thoroughly

(C) throw it away

(D) cook it thoroughly to kill bacteria

TEST 28 詳解

Imagine the following scenario.

想像下列的情景。

　* imagine[2] (ɪˈmædʒɪn) *v.* 想像
　　following[2] (ˈfɑləwɪŋ) *adj.* 下列的
　　scenario (sɪˈnɛrɪo) *n.* 劇情；情景

In the rush to get to work, you drop a piece of toast *on the floor*. You hesitate *over **whether or not** to pick it up*. *Then* you pick it up **and** eat it *like nothing happened*. Well, should you?

趕著上班的你，不小心掉了一片吐司在地上。你在猶豫是否要撿起來。然後你把它撿起來，接著像什麼都沒發生似地把吐司吃了。嗯，該這樣做嗎？

　* rush[2] (rʌʃ) *n.* 匆忙　　drop[2] (drɑp) *v.* 使掉落
　　piece[1] (pis) *n.* 片；張　　toast[2] (tost) *n.* 吐司
　　floor[1] (flɔr) *n.* 地板　　h esitate[3] (ˈhɛzə͵tet) *v.* 猶豫
　　whether or not 是否　　**pick up** 撿起

Most people would *probably* follow their instinct *to pick up the food* **because** they believe **that** food is still safe to eat **if** you pick it up *within five seconds of dropping it*—the so-called "five-second rule."

大部分的人可能都會遵循本能撿起食物，因為他們相信，只要在掉到地上的五秒之內把食物撿起來，吃這個食物就還是安全的──這就是所謂的「五秒法則」。

> * probably[3] 〔'prɑbəblɪ〕 *adv.* 可能　　follow[1] 〔'falo〕 *v.* 遵循
> instinct[4] 〔'ɪnstɪŋkt〕 *n.* 本能
> within[2] 〔wɪð'ɪn〕 *prep.* 在…之內
> second[1] 〔'sɛkənd〕 *n.* 秒　　so-called *adj.* 所謂的
> rule[1] 〔rul〕 *n.* 規則

To many people, it seems a waste *of food to throw the food into the*

*trash can **rather than** put it into their mouth.* *However*, you may want

to think *again **next time** you do it.*

對很多人來說，比起把掉下的食物塞進嘴裡，把食物丟進垃圾桶似乎是種浪費。然而，下次你這麼做之前，可能需要再多想想。

> * waste[1] 〔west〕 *n.* 浪費　　throw[1] 〔θro〕 *v.* 丟
> ***trash can*** 垃圾桶　　***rather than*** 而不是
> ***put…into*** 把…放進　　mouth[1] 〔mauθ〕 *n.* 嘴巴

Scientists *now* warn ***that*** *five seconds are all it takes for food to*

*become **contaminated** with just enough bacteria to make you sick.*

科學家們現在警告，五秒鐘已經足夠讓致病的細菌污染你的食物。

* scientist[2]〔'saɪəntɪst〕 *n.* 科學家　　warn[3]〔wɔrn〕*v.* 警告
take[1]〔te〕*v.* 需要
contaminated[5]〔kən'tæmə,netɪd〕 *adj.* 被污染的
bacteria[3]〔bæk'tɪrɪə〕*n. pl.* 細菌
sick[1]〔sɪk〕*adj.* 生病的

Bacteria lead to all kinds *of diseases*.　Some bacteria are known to

grow *on food*.　***If the food is eaten***, common symptoms *like vomiting*

and *diarrhea* may occur.

細菌會導致各種疾病。已知有些細菌會在食物上生長繁殖。如果受污染
的食物被吃下肚，常見的症狀，像是嘔吐和腹瀉，就可能會發生。

* ***lead to*** 導致；造成　　kind[1]〔kaɪnd〕*n.* 種類
disease[3]〔dɪ'ziz〕*n.* 疾病　　grow[1]〔gro〕*v.* 生長
common[1]〔'kɑmən〕*adj.* 常見的
symptom[6]〔'sɪmptəm〕*n.* 症狀
vomit[6]〔'vɑmɪt〕*v.* 嘔吐（= *throw up*）
diarrhea〔,daɪə'riə〕*n.* 腹瀉
occur[2]〔ə'kɝ〕*v.* 發生

The question is, *exactly how* threatening can bacteria be *to our life*?
問題是，細菌對於我們的生活，究竟多麼具有威脅性？

* problem[1]〔'prɑbləm〕*n.* 問題
exactly[2]〔ɪg'zæktlɪ〕*adv.* 確切地；究竟
threatening[3]〔'θrɛtn̩ɪŋ〕*adj.* 威脅的

One *of the food-borne bacteria called salmonella, for instance,* makes

1.4 million people sick *every year.*

舉例來說，一種叫作沙門氏桿菌的細菌能透過食物傳播，每年讓一百四十萬人生病。

> * food-borne *adj.* 食源性的 (= *foodborne*)
> 【bear-borne-borne *v.* 生；具有；帶有；傳遞】
> salmonella〔͵sælmə'nɛlə〕*n.* 沙門氏桿菌
> *for instance* 例如 (= *for example*)
> million² ('mɪljən) *n.* 百萬

Salmonella is *often* found *in raw eggs **and** chicken.* It is *therefore*

advised to cook these kinds *of foods thoroughly before eating them.*

沙門氏桿菌常常見於生雞蛋和生雞肉，因此建議食用前先把這類食物煮熟。

> * raw³〔rɔ〕*adj.* 生的　therefore²('ðɛr͵fɔr) *adv.* 因此
> advise³〔əd'vaɪz〕*v.* 勸告　cook¹〔kuk〕*v.* 煮
> thoroughly⁴('θɝolɪ) *adv.* 徹底地

Also, to prevent infection, it is important *to keep household surfaces*

*clean, **for** salmonella could stay for weeks.*

此外，為預防感染，保持居家環境外觀衛生也很重要，因為沙門氏桿菌能停留數週。

> * also¹('ɔlso) *adv.* 此外　prevent³(prɪ'vɛnt) *v.* 預防

infection[4] (ɪnˈfɛkʃən) *n.* 感染
household[4] (ˈhaʊsˌhold) *adj.* 家庭的
surface[2] (ˈsɝfɪs) *n.* 表面

So remember: ***next time*** *you drop a small piece of your food on*

the floor, ***no matter*** *how tasty it appears to be* ***or*** *how expensive it is,*

the best thing seems to be to toss it *out* ***rather than*** *eat it.*

所以請記住，下次你不小心掉了一小塊食物在地上，無論那食物看起來多好吃或是多麼昂貴，最好的做法似乎就是把它丟掉，而不是吃下肚。

* tasty[2] (ˈtestɪ) *adj.* 好吃的　　appear[1] (əˈpɪr) *v.* 看起來
toss[3] (tɔs) *v.* 投擲；扔

1. (**C**) 根據本文，下列敘述何者為非？
   (A) 以「五秒法則」來處理掉落的食物是不明智的。
   (B) 完全煮熟的食物減低被細菌感染的風險。
   (C) <u>細菌附著在食物上需要多於五秒的時間。</u>
   (D) 沙門氏桿菌是一種經由食物傳播的細菌。

   * statement[1] (ˈstetmənt) *n.* 敘述
   deal with 應付；處理　　wise[2] (waɪz) *adj.* 聰明的
   reduce[3] (rɪˈdjus) *v.* 減少　　risk[1] (rɪsk) *n.* 風險
   infect[4] (ɪnˈfɛkt) *v.* 感染
   attach[4] (əˈtætʃ) *v.* 附著 < *to* >
   bacterium (bækˈtɪrɪəm) *n.* 細菌【複數形為 bacteria[3]】

2. (**B**) 本文的目的是什麼？

(A) 解釋細菌如何附著在食物上的過程。

(B) <u>警告在吃掉落食物後會生病的危險。</u>

(C) 強調將食物完全煮熟的重要性。

(D) 提供殺死居家細菌的措施。

* purpose¹〔'pɝpəs〕*n.* 目的　　explain²〔ɪk'splen〕*v.* 解釋
process³〔'prɑsɛs〕*n.* 過程　　***warn of*** 警告
danger¹〔'dendʒɚ〕*n.* 危險　　highlight⁶〔'haɪˌlaɪt〕*v.* 強調
provide²〔prə'vaɪd〕*v.* 提供　　measure²ˑ⁴〔'mɛʒɚ〕*n.* 措施
kill⁴〔kɪl〕*v.* 殺死

3. (**A**) 第二段 "**contaminated**" 這個字的意思和 ＿＿＿＿＿ 最接近。

(A) ***polluted***³〔pə'lutɪd〕*adj.* 受污染的

(B) stale³〔stel〕*adj.* 不新鮮的；腐壞的

(C) delicious²〔dɪ'lɪʃəs〕*adj.* 美味的

(D) rough³〔rʌf〕*adj.* 粗糙的

4. (**C**) 根據結論，最佳處理掉落食物的方法是 ＿＿＿＿＿＿。

(A) 五秒之內撿起來

(B) 馬上撿起來然後徹底洗淨

(C) <u>丟掉</u>

(D) 完全煮熟以殺死細菌

* conclusion³〔kən'kluʒən〕*n.* 結論
immediately³〔ɪ'misɪɪtlɪ〕*adv.* 立刻
wash¹〔wɑʃ〕*v.* 洗　　***throw away*** 丟掉

TEST 29

Read the following passage and choose the best answer for each question.

Are organically grown foods the best food choices?
The advantages claimed for such foods over conventionally
grown and marketed food products are now being debated.
Advocates of organic foods frequently proclaim that such
products are safer and more nutritious than others. The
growing interest of consumers in the safety and nutritional
quality of the typical North American diet is a welcome
development. However, much of this interest has been
sparked by sweeping claims that the food supply is unsafe
or inadequate in meeting nutritional needs. Although most
of these claims are not supported by scientific evidence, a
great deal of written material advancing such claims makes
it difficult for the general public to separate fact from
fiction. As a result, claims that eating a diet consisting
entirely of organically grown foods prevents or cures
disease or provides other benefits to health have become
widely publicized and form the basis for folklore.

Almost daily the public is **besieged** by claims for "no-aging" diets, new vitamins, and other wonder foods. There are numerous unconfirmed reports that natural vitamins are superior to synthetic ones, that fertilized eggs are nutritionally superior to unfertilized eggs, and the like. One thing that most organically grown food products seem to have in common is that they cost more than conventionally grown foods. But in many cases consumers are misled if they believe organic foods can maintain health and provide better nutritional quality than conventionally grown foods. So there is real cause for concern if consumers, particularly those with limited incomes, distrust the regular food supply and buy only expensive organic foods instead.

1. What is the writer's purpose in writing this passage?
   (A) To promote the benefits of eating organic foods.
   (B) To discredit the advantages of organic foods.
   (C) To call for the government's attention to organic foods.
   (D) To discuss the diseases caused by consuming organic foods.

2. The word "**besieged**" in the second paragraph is closest in meaning to _____.

(A) instructed   (B) deceived

(C) distrusted   (D) surrounded

3. Which of the following can be inferred from the passage?

(A) Natural vitamins are better than synthetic ones regarding the side effects.

(B) Eating organic foods may help reduce the risk of catching certain diseases.

(C) Scientific evidence shows that organic foods may lack some vital vitamins.

(D) More and more consumers are beginning to take what they are eating seriously.

4. Which of the following is true according to the passage?

(A) Organic foods usually cost more than conventional ones.

(B) Organic foods provide more nutrition to human bodies than conventional ones.

(C) Consumers with limited incomes tend to purchase more organic foods.

(D) Many organic foods are not certified by the government.

TEST 29 詳解

Are *organically* grown foods the best food choices?

有機栽種的食物是最好食物的選擇嗎？

* organically⁴ 〔ɔr'gænɪkl̩ɪ〕 *adv.* 有機地
【organic⁴ 〔ɔr'gænɪk〕 *adj.* 有機的】
grow¹ 〔gro〕 *v.* 種植　　choice² 〔tʃɔɪs〕 *v.* 選擇

The advantages *claimed for such foods over conventionally grown*

and marketed food products are *now* being debated.

有機食物宣稱勝過傳統方式栽種、販賣的食物的好處，目前卻頗受爭議。

* advantage³ 〔əd'væntɪdʒ〕 *n.* 優點
claim² 〔klem〕 *v. n.* 主張；宣稱
conventionally⁴ 〔kən'vɛnʃənl̩ɪ〕 *adv.* 傳統上；照慣例
market¹ 〔'mɑrkɪt〕 *v.* 販賣　　product³ 〔'prɑdəkt〕 *n.* 產品
debate² 〔dɪ'bet〕 *v.* 辯論；爭論

Advocates *of organic foods frequently* proclaim *that* such products

are safer and more nutritious than others.

有機食物的倡導者經常聲明有機的產品比較安全，也比其他食物來得營養。

* advocate⁶ 〔'ædvəkɪt〕 *n.* 提倡者
frequently³ 〔'frikwəntlɪ〕 *adv.* 經常

proclaim〔pro'klem〕v. 聲明

nutritious[6]〔nju'trɪʃəs〕adj. 有營養的

The growing interest *of consumers* | *in the safety* **and** *nutritional*

quality of the typical North American diet | is a welcome development.

消費者越來越關注典型北美飲食的安全和營養品質，這是個可喜的發
展。

* growing[1]〔'groɪŋ〕adj. 日益增加的
  interest[1]〔'ɪntrɪst〕n. 興趣；關心 <*in*>
  consumer[4]〔kən'sumə,-'sjumə〕n. 消費者
  safety[2]〔'seftɪ〕n. 安全　　nutritional[6]〔nju'trɪʃənḷ〕adj. 營養的
  quality[2]〔'kwɑlətɪ〕n. 品質；特質　　typical[3]〔'tɪpɪkḷ〕adj. 典型的
  North America 北美的　　diet[3]〔'daɪət〕n. 飲食
  welcome[1]〔'wɛlkəm〕adj. 受歡迎的；令人高興的
  development[2]〔dɪ'vɛləpmənt〕n. 發展

However, much *of this interest* has been sparked | *by sweeping claims*

that *the food supply is unsafe* **or** *inadequate in meeting nutritional*

needs.

然而，許多的關注都是因為廣泛的聲稱所引起，像是食品供給不安全，
或是不足以滿足營養需求。

* spark[4]〔spɑrk〕v. 引起　　sweeping[2]〔'swipɪŋ〕adj. 廣泛的
  supply[2]〔sə'plaɪ〕v. 供給　　unsafe[1]〔ʌn'sef〕adj. 不安全的
  inadequate[4]〔ɪn'ædəkwɪt〕adj. 不足的
  meet[1]〔mit〕v. 滿足（需求）　　need[1]〔nid〕n. 需求

Although most of these claims are not supported by scientific evidence, a great deal of written material *advancing such claims* makes it difficult *for the general public to separate fact from fiction.*

雖然這些言論大部份沒有科學證據支持，但有很多提出這些言論的書面資料，使一般大眾相當難分辨事實和虛構。

> * support[2] 〔sə'port〕 v. 支持
> scientific[3] 〔,saɪən'tɪfɪk〕 adj. 科學的
> evidence[4] 〔'ɛvədəns〕 n. 證據　　*a great deal of* 相當多的
> material[2,6] 〔mə'tɪrɪəl〕 n. 資料　　advance[2] 〔əd'væns〕 v. 提出
> general[1,2] 〔'dʒɛnərəl〕 adj. 一般的
> public[1] 〔'pʌblɪk〕 adj. 公共的；公開的
> *the general public* 一般大眾
> separate[2] 〔'sɛpə,ret〕 v. 使分開；區別
> fiction[4] 〔'fɪkʃən〕 n. 小說；虛構的事

As a result, claims *that eating a diet consisting entirely of organically grown foods* prevents *or* cures disease *or* provides other benefits *to health* have become *widely* publicized *and* form the basis *for folklore.*

因此，完全只吃有機栽培的食物就能預防或治癒疾病，或是供給健康其他益處的說法，就被廣為宣傳，並形成民間說法的基礎。

> * *as a result* 因此 (= *therefore*)
> *consist of* 由…組成 (= *be made up of*)
> entirely[2] 〔ɪn'taɪrlɪ〕 adv. 完全地　　prevent[3] 〔prɪ'vɛnt〕 v. 預防

cure² (kjur) *v.* 治療　　disease³ (dɪ'ziz) *n.* 疾病
provide² (prə'vaɪd) *v.* 提供　　benefit³ ('bɛnəfɪt) *n.* 利益；好處
health¹ (hɛlθ) *n.* 健康　　widely¹ ('waɪdlɪ) *adv.* 廣泛地
publicize⁵ ('pʌblɪˌsaɪz) *v.* 宣傳　　form² (fɔrm) *v.* 形成
basis² ('besɪs) *n.* 基礎；根據　　folklore⁵ ('fokˌlor) *n.* 民間傳說

Almost daily the public is **besieged** *by claims for* "*no-aging*"

*diets, new vitamins, **and** other wonder foods.*

　　幾乎每天，大眾被一堆聲稱「不老」飲食、新維他命，或是其他神
奇食物所包圍。

　　* daily² ('delɪ) *adv.* 每天　　besiege⁶ (bɪ'sidʒ) *v.* 包圍
　　age¹ (edʒ) *v.* 變老　　vitamin³ ('vaɪtəmɪn) *n.* 維他命
　　wonder² ('wʌndɚ) *adj.* 驚人的；奇妙的

There are numerous unconfirmed reports *that* natural vitamins are

*superior to synthetic ones, **that** fertilized eggs are nutritionally superior*

*to unfertilized eggs, **and** the like.*

有許多未經證實的報告指出，天然的維他命優於人工合成的維他命，或
是受精的蛋比未受精的蛋來得好，諸如此類的。

　　* numerous⁴ ('njumərəs) *adj.* 許多的
　　unconfirmed (ˌʌnkən'fɝmd) *adj.* 未證實的
　　　【confirm² *v.* 證實；確認】
　　report¹ (rɪ'port) *n.* 報告；報導
　　natural² ('nætʃərəl) *adj.* 天然的
　　be superior to 比…好；勝過
　　synthetic⁶ (sɪn'θɛtɪk) *adj.* 合成的

fertilize〔'fɜtl̩͵aɪz〕*v.* 使受精（↔ unfertilize *v.* 未受精）
nutritionally[6]〔nju'trɪʃənl̩ɪ〕*adv.* 在營養上

One thing *that* most organically grown food products seem to have in

common is *that* they cost more *than* conventionally grown foods.

大部分有機栽培食物的共通點，似乎就是它們比用傳統方式栽培的食物還要貴。

But in many cases consumers are misled *if* they believe organic foods

can maintain health *and* provide better nutritional quality *than*

conventionally grown foods.

但在很多情況下，如果消費者相信，有機食物能夠維持人體健康，且能提供比傳統方式栽培的食物更好的營養品質的話，那他們就被誤導了。

* case[1]〔kes〕*n.* 情況；例子　　mislead[4]〔mɪs'lid〕*v.* 誤導
maintain[2]〔men'ten〕*v.* 維持

So there is real cause *for concern* *if* consumers, *particularly those*

with limited incomes, distrust the regular food supply *and* buy *only*

expensive organic foods *instead.*

所以如果消費者，特別是那些收入有限的消費者，不相信一般的食物供
給，反而只購買昂貴的有機食物，那就真的會令人擔心。

* real[1] (ˈriəl) *adj.* 真的　　cause[1] (kɔz) *n.* 原因；理由
  concern[3] (kənˈsɝn) *n.* 擔心；關心
  particularly[2] (pɚˈtɪkjələlɪ) *adv.* 尤其；特別是
  limit[2] (ˈlɪmɪt) *adj.* 有限的　　income[2] (ˈɪnˌkʌm) *n.* 收入
  distrust[6] (dɪsˈtrʌst) *v.* 不相信
  regular[2] (ˈrɛgjələ) *adj.* 一般的
  instead[3] (ɪnˈstɛd) *adv.* 反而；作為代替

1. (**B**) 作者寫本文的目的是什麼？

   (A) 推廣吃有機食物的好處。

   (B) 懷疑有機食物的優點。

   (C) 呼籲政府注意有機食物。

   (D) 討論因吃有機食物而造成的疾病。

   * writer[1] (ˈraɪtɚ) *n.* 作者　　purpose[1] (ˈpɝpəs) *n.* 目的
     promote[3] (prəˈmot) *v.* 提倡
     discredit[3] (dɪsˈkrɛdɪt) *v.* 懷疑；不信任
     call for 呼籲　　government[2] (ˈgʌvɚnmənt) *n.* 政府
     attention[2] (əˈtɛnʃən) *n.* 注意 < *to* >
     discuss[2] (dɪˈskʌs) *v.* 討論
     consume[4] (kənˈsum) *v.* 吃；喝

2. (**D**) 第二段的 "**besieged**" 的意思和 ＿＿＿＿＿＿ 最接近。

   (A) instruct[4] (ɪnˈstrʌkt) *v.* 教導

   (B) deceive[5] (dɪˈsiv) *v.* 欺騙

   (C) distrust[6] (dɪsˈtrʌst) *v.* 不相信

   (D) ***surround***[3] (səˈraʊnd) *v.* 包圍；環繞

   * meaning[2] (ˈminɪŋ) *n.* 意義

3.(**D**) 從本文可以推論出下列何者？

(A) 關於副作用，天然維他命較人工合成的維他命好。

(B) 吃有機食物可能幫助減少得到某些特定疾病的風險。

(C) 科學證據顯示，有機食物可能缺乏某些重要的維他命。

(D) <u>越來越多的消費者開始認真看待他們所吃的東西。</u>

*infer[6] 〔 ɪn'fɝ 〕*n.* 推論

regarding[4] 〔 rɪ'gɑrdɪŋ 〕*prep.* 關於（ = *concerning*[4]）

side[1] 〔 saɪd 〕*n.* 邊　　effect[2] 〔 ɪ'fɛkt 〕*n.* 影響

side effect 副作用

reduce[3] 〔 rɪ'djus 〕*v.* 減少　　risk[3] 〔 rɪsk 〕*n.* 風險

catch[1] 〔 kætʃ 〕*v.* 罹患　　lack[1] 〔 læk 〕*v.* 缺乏

vital[4] 〔 'vaɪtḷ 〕*adj.* 非常重要的；維持生命所必需的

seriously[2] 〔 'sɪrɪəslɪ 〕*adv.* 嚴重地；嚴肅地

take* sth. *seriously 認真看待某事

4.(**A**) 根據本文，下列何者為真？

(A) <u>有機食物通常要比傳統栽培的食物貴。</u>

(B) 有機食物比傳統栽培的食物提供更多的營養給人體。

(C) 收入有限的消費者傾向於購買較多的有機食物。

(D) 許多有機食物沒有被政府認證。

*nutrition[6] 〔 nju'trɪʃən 〕*n.* 營養

human[1] 〔 'hjumən 〕*adj.* 人類的

conventional[4] 〔 kən'vɛnʃənḷ 〕*adj.* 傳統的

tend to V. 易於；傾向於

purchase[5] 〔 'pɝtʃəs 〕*v.* 購買（ = *buy*[1]）

certify[6] 〔 'sɝtə,faɪ 〕*v.* 證明；認證

TEST 30

Read the following passage and choose the best answer for each question.

There are many theories about the beginning of drama in ancient Greece. The one most widely accepted today is based on the assumption that drama evolved from ritual. In the beginning, human beings viewed the natural forces of the world, even the seasonal changes, as unpredictable, and they sought, through various means, to control these unknown and feared powers. Those measures which appeared to bring the desired results were then retained and repeated until they hardened into fixed rituals. Eventually stories about the mysteries of the rites arose. As time passed, some rituals were abandoned, but the stories, later called myths, persisted and provided material for art and drama.

Those who believe that drama evolved out of ritual also argue that those rites contained the seed of theater because music, dance, masks, and costumes were almost always used. In addition, there were performers, and, since considerable importance was attached to avoiding mistakes in the enactment of rites, religious leaders usually assumed that task. Wearing masks and costumes, they often impersonated other people, animals, or supernatural beings, and mimed the desired effect, such as success in a hunt or battle, the arrival of rain, and the revival of the sun. Eventually such dramatic representations were separated from religious activities. Another theory traces the theater's origin to the human interest in storytelling. According to this view, tales are gradually elaborated, at first through the use of action and dialogue by a narrator and then through the assumption of each of the roles by a different person. A closely related theory traces theater to those dances that are primarily rhythmical and gymnastic or that are imitations of animal movements and sounds.

1. How did stories about the mysteries of the rituals get started?
   (A) Humans felt angry about the consequences of natural disasters.
   (B) Humans spread good news so as to avoid bad things.
   (C) Humans desired to control the natural forces and the unknown.
   (D) Religious leaders used the stories to remember their roles.

2. Which of the following is NOT true according to the passage?

   (A) Stories told repeatedly about rituals provided material for drama and art.

   (B) The ancient rituals also employed music, dance, masks and costumes.

   (C) Humans knew how to control the weather with certain measures centuries ago.

   (D) Humans' interest in telling stories also contributed to the formation of drama.

3. Which of the following is not mentioned as a drama effect appearing in the rituals?

   (A) The sun.   (B) The moon.

   (C) Animals.   (D) Rain.

4. Why were the performers in the rites usually religious leaders?

   (A) It was quite difficult to find professional actors at that time.

   (B) Religious leaders were familiar with how a ritual proceeded.

   (C) Religious leaders back then were also qualified actors.

   (D) The church ordered the priests to play the lead roles.

TEST 30 詳解

There are many theories *about the beginning of drama in ancient Greece.*

有許關於古希臘戲劇的起源多理論。

* theory[3] (ˈθiərɪ) *n.* 理論　　beginning[1] (bɪˈgɪnɪŋ) *n.* 起源
drama[2] (ˈdrɑmə, ˈdræmə) *n.* 戲劇
ancient[2] (ˈenʃənt) *adj.* 古代的　　Greece (gris) *n.* 希臘

The one *most widely accepted today* is based on the assumption *that drama evolved from ritual.*

最被普遍接受的說法，是以戲劇是由儀式所演變而來的假定。

* widely[1] (ˈwaɪdlɪ) *adv.* 廣泛地；普遍地
accept[2] (əkˈsɛpt) *v.* 接受　　*be based on* 根據；以…爲基礎
assumption[6] (əˈsʌmpʃən) *n.* 假定；擔任
evolve[6] (ɪˈvɑlv) *v.* 演化　　ritual[6] (ˈrɪtʃʊəl) *n.* 儀式

In the beginning, human beings viewed the natural forces *of the world, even the seasonal changes*, as unpredictable, *and* they sought, *through various means, to control these unknown **and** feared powers.*

一開始，人類把全世界的大自然力量，甚至是季節的轉變，都視爲是不可預測的，所以他們就透過不同的方式，試圖要掌控這些未知且令人感到畏懼的力量。

* ***human beings*** 人類

view A as B 把 A 視爲 B (= *see A as B = regard A as B*)

natural[2] 〔'nætʃərəl 〕 *adj.* 自然的   force[1] 〔 fors 〕 *n.* 力量

seasonal[1] 〔'siznl 〕 *adj.* 季節的

unpredictable[4] 〔͵ʌnprɪ'dɪktəbḷ 〕 *adj.* 不可預測的

seek[3] 〔 sik 〕 *v.* 尋求【三態變化：seek-sought-sought】

through[2] 〔 θru 〕 *prep.* 透過

various[3] 〔'vɛrɪəs 〕 *adj.* 各式各樣的

means[2] 〔 minz 〕 *n. pl.* 方法；手段

unknown[1] 〔 ʌn'non 〕 *n.* 未知   feared[1] 〔 fɪrd 〕 *adj.* 令人畏懼的

Those measures ***which*** *appeared to bring the desired results* were

then retained ***and*** repeated ***until*** *they hardened into fixed rituals.*

Eventually stories *about the mysteries of the rites* arose.

那些似乎能帶來渴求結果的措施就被保留下來，並且一再地被重複，直到它們確定成爲固定儀式爲止。最後，關於這些儀式的謎團就產生了。

* measure[2,4] 〔'mɛʒɚ 〕 *n.* 措施   appear[1] 〔 ə'pɪr 〕 *v.* 似乎

desired[2] 〔 dɪ'zaɪrd 〕 *adj.* 如所願的；預期的；想得到的

result[2] 〔 rɪ'zʌlt 〕 *n.* 結果   retain[4] 〔 rɪ'ten 〕 *v.* 保留

repeat[2] 〔 rɪ'pit 〕 *v.* 重複   harden[4] 〔'hɑrdn 〕 *v.* 變得確定

fixed[2] 〔 fɪkst 〕 *adj.* 固定的   eventually[4] 〔 ɪ'vɛntʃuəlɪ 〕 *adv.* 最後

mystery[3] 〔'mɪstrɪ 〕 *n.* 奧秘；謎   rite[6] 〔 raɪt 〕 *n.* 儀式

arise[4] 〔 ə'raɪz 〕 *v.* 產生【三態變化：arise-arose-arisen】

As time passed, some rituals were abandoned, ***but*** the stories, *later*

called myths, persisted ***and*** provided material *for art **and** drama.*

隨著時間的過去，有些儀式雖然被摒棄，但是這些故事後來被稱爲神話，反而繼續存在，而且爲藝術和戲劇提供了題材。

> * abandon[4]〔ə'bændən〕 v. 拋棄　　later[1]〔'letə〕 adv. 後來
> myth[5]〔mɪθ〕 n. 神話　　persist[5]〔pə'zɪst〕 v. 持續；繼續存在
> provide[2]〔prə'vaɪd〕 v. 提供　　material[2,6]〔mə'tɪrɪəl〕 n. 材料
> art[1]〔ɑrt〕 n. 藝術

Those *who believe **that** drama evolved out of ritual also argue **that** those rites contained the seed of theater **because** music, dance, masks, **and** costumes were almost always used.*

那些相信戲劇是從儀式演變而來的人同時也主張，那些儀式包含了戲劇的起源，因爲音樂、舞蹈、面具，和服裝，幾乎都會被使用到。

> * argue[2]〔'ɑrgju〕 v. 主張；爭論　　contain[2]〔kən'ten〕 v. 包含
> seed[1]〔sid〕 n. 種子；根源　　theater[2]〔'θiətə〕 n. 戲院；戲劇
> mask[2]〔mæsk〕 n. 面具　　costume[4]〔'kɑstjum〕 n. 服裝

In addition, there were performers, **and**, **since** considerable importance was attached to avoiding mistakes in the enactment of rites, religious leaders *usually* assumed that task.

此外，也有表演者，而且因爲在制定儀式時避免犯錯是相當重要的，所以宗教領袖通常都會擔任這項任務。

> * performer[5]〔pə'fɔrmə〕 n. 表演者

considerable³〔kən'sɪdərəbļ〕adj. 相當大的
attach⁴〔ə'tætʃ〕v. 附上；認爲…有重要性＜to＞
avoid²〔ə'vɔɪd〕v. 避免
enactment⁶〔ɪn'æktmənt〕n. 制定【enact⁶ v. 制定】
religious³〔rɪ'lɪdʒəs〕adj. 宗教的　　leader¹〔'lidɚ〕n. 領袖
assume⁴〔ə's(j)um〕v. 承擔　　task²〔tæsk〕n. 工作；任務

*Wearing masks **and** costumes*, they *often* impersonated other people,

animals, *or* supernatural beings, **and** mimed the desired effect, *such*

*as success in a hunt **or** battle, the arrival of rain, **and** the revival of the*

sun.

他們通常穿戴著面具和服裝，來模仿其他人、動物，或是超自然生物，
並且用默劇的方式演出想要的效果，例如在狩獵或是戰鬥中的勝利、降
雨，或是太陽的復活。

　　* impersonate〔ɪm'pɝsn̩͵et〕v. 扮演；模仿
　　supernatural〔͵supɚ'nætʃərəl〕adj. 超自然的
　　being³〔'biɪŋ〕n. 生物　　mime〔maɪm〕v. 用默劇演出
　　effect²〔ɪ'fɛkt〕n. 效果　　success²〔sək'sɛs〕n. 成功
　　hunt²〔hʌnt〕v. 打獵　　battle²〔'bætļ〕n. 戰役
　　arrival³〔ə'raɪvļ〕n. 到達
　　revival⁶〔rɪ'vaɪvļ〕n. 復活【revive⁵ v. 復活】

Eventually such dramatic representations were separated *from*

religious activities.

最後，這些戲劇化的演出，就從宗教活動中分隔開來了。

> * dramatic³〔drəˈmætɪk〕*adj.* 戲劇的
> representation⁴〔ˌrɛprɪzɛnˈteʃən〕*n.* 演出
> separate²〔ˈsɛpəˌret〕*v.* 使分開；區別
> activity³〔ækˈtɪvətɪ〕*n.* 活動

Another theory traces the theater's origin *to the human interest in storytelling*.

另一個理論把戲劇的起源追溯到人類對說故事的興趣。

> * trace³〔tres〕*v.* 追溯　　origin³〔ˈɔrədʒɪn〕*n.* 起源
> storytelling〔ˈstɔrɪˌtɛlɪŋ〕*n.* 說故事

According to this view, tales are *gradually* elaborated, *at first through the use of action **and** dialogue by a narrator **and** then through the assumption of each of the roles by a different person.*

根據這個看法，故事逐漸地被詳細闡述，起先是透過一個敘事者的動作和對話，然後再由另外一個不同的人擔任故事中的角色。

> * view¹〔vju〕*n.* 看法　　tale¹〔tel〕*n.* 故事
> gradually³〔ˈgrædʒuəlɪ〕*adv.* 逐漸地
> elaborate⁵〔ɪˈlæbəˌret〕*v.* 詳盡闡述　　***at first*** 起初
> action¹〔ˈækʃən〕*n.* 行動；動作　　dialogue³〔ˈdaɪəˌlɔg〕*n.* 對話
> narrator⁶〔ˈnæretɚ〕*n.* 敘述者　　role²〔rol〕*n.* 角色

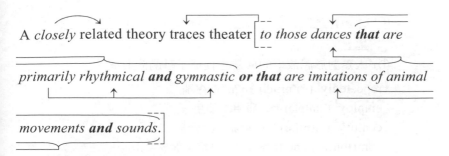

A *closely* related theory traces theater *to those dances **that** are primarily rhythmical **and** gymnastic **or that** are imitations of animal movements **and** sounds.*

一個密切相關的理論，將戲劇追溯到那些強調節奏性及體操性的舞蹈，或是模仿動物的動作及聲音的舞蹈。

> * ***closely related*** 密切相關的
> primarily³ ('praɪ,mɛrəlɪ) *adv.* 主要地
> rhythmical⁶ ('rɪðmɪk!) *adj.* 有節奏的【rhythm⁴ *n.* 節奏】
> gymnastic (dʒɪm'næstɪk) *adj.* 體操的【gymnastics *n.* 體操】
> imitation⁴ (,ɪmə'teʃən) *n.* 模仿
> movement¹ ('muvmənt) *n.* 動作

1. (**C**) 關於謎樣儀式的故事是如何開始的？

　　(A) 人類對於天然災害造成的後果感到生氣。

　　(B) 人類散佈好消息，以避免壞事。

　　(C) 人類渴望控制自然的力量和未知的事物。

　　(D) 宗教領袖用這些故事來記得他們的任務。

> * consequence⁴ ('kɑnsə,kwɛns) *n.* 後果
> disaster⁴ (dɪz'æstə) *n.* 災難
> spread² (sprɛd) *v.* 散播
> ***so as to V.*** 以便於…

2. (**C**) 根據本文，下列何者為非？

　　(A) 有關儀式的故事不停地被講述，給戲劇和藝術提供素材。

　　(B) 古代的儀式也使用音樂、舞蹈、面具，和服裝。

(C) 人類在幾個世紀之前，就懂得如何用特定的措施控制天氣。

(D) 人類對於說故事的興趣也促成了戲劇的形成。

* repeatedly[2] 〔 rɪ'pitɪdlɪ 〕 adv. 重複地

  employ[3] 〔 ɪm'plɔɪ 〕 v. 雇用；使用

  century[2] 〔 'sɛntʃərɪ 〕 n. 世紀

  contribute[4] 〔 kən'trɪbjut 〕 v. 貢獻；促成 < to >

  formation[4] 〔 fɔr'meʃən 〕 n. 形成

3. (**B**) 下列何者不是本文所提出，出現在儀式中的戲劇性效果？

　(A) 太陽。　　　　　　　　(B) 月亮。

　(C) 動物。　　　　　　　　(D) 雨。

4. (**B**) 為什麼在儀式中的表演者，通常是宗教領袖？

　(A) 在那時候要找專業演員相當困難。

　(B) 宗教領袖熟悉儀式如何進行。

　(C) 那時的宗教領袖也是合格的演員。

　(D) 教會命令神職人員扮演主角。

* quite[1] 〔 kwaɪt 〕 adv. 相當地

  professional[4] 〔 prə'fɛsənḷ 〕 adj. 職業的；專業的

  actor[1] 〔 'æktɚ 〕 n. 演員

  familiar[3] 〔 fə'mɪljɚ 〕 adj. 熟悉的 < with >

  proceed[4] 〔 prə'sid 〕 v. 前進；進行

  qualified[5] 〔 'kwɑlə,faɪd 〕 adj. 合格的

  church[1] 〔 tʃɝtʃ 〕 n. 教堂；教會　　order[1] 〔 'ɔrdɚ 〕 v. 命令

  priest[3] 〔 prist 〕 n. 神職人員　　play[1] 〔 ple 〕 v. 扮演

  lead[1] 〔 lid 〕 adj. 領導的　　*lead role* 主要角色；主角

高三同學要如何準備「升大學考試」

考前該如何準備「學測」呢？「劉毅英文」的同學很簡單，只要熟讀每次的模考試題就行了。每一份試題都在7000字範圍內，就不必再背7000字了，從後面往前複習，越後面越重要，一定要把最後10份試題唸得滾瓜爛熟。根據以往的經驗，詞彙題絕對不會超出7000字範圍。每年題型變化不大，只要針對下面幾個大題準備即可。

準備「詞彙題」最佳資料：

背了再背，背到滾瓜爛熟，讓背單字變成樂趣。

考前不斷地做模擬試題就對了！

你做的題目愈多，分數就愈高。不要忘記，每次參加模考前，都要背單字、背自己所喜歡的作文。考壞不難過，勇往直前，必可得高分！

練習「模擬試題」，可參考「學習出版公司」出版的「7000字學測試題詳解」。我們試題的特色是：
①以「高中常用7000字」為範圍。 ②經過外籍專家多次校對，不會學錯。③每份試題都有詳細解答，對錯答案均有明確交待。

「克漏字」如何答題

　　第二大題綜合測驗（即「克漏字」），不是考句意，就是考簡單的文法。當四個選項都不相同時，就是考句意，就沒有文法的問題；當四個選項單字相同、字群排列不同時，就是考文法，此時就要注意到文法的分析，大多是考連接詞、分詞構句、時態等。「克漏字」是考生最弱的一環，你難，別人也難，只要考前利用這種答題技巧，勤加練習，就容易勝過別人。

準備「綜合測驗」（克漏字），可參考「學習出版公司」出版的「7000字克漏字詳解」。

　　本書特色：

1. 取材自大規模考試，英雄所見略同。
2. 不超出7000字範圍，不會做白工。
3. 每個句子都有文法分析。一目了然。
4. 對錯答案都有明確交待，列出生字，不用查字典。
5. 經過「劉毅英文」同學實際考過，效果極佳。

「文意選填」答題技巧

　　在做「文意選填」的時候，一定要冷靜。你要記住，一個空格一個答案，如果你不知道該選哪個才好，不妨先把詞性正確的選項挑出來，如介詞後面一定是名詞，選項裡面只有兩個名詞，再用刪去法，把不可能的選項刪掉。也要特別注意時間的掌控，已經用過的選項就劃掉，以免重複考慮，浪費時間。

準備「文意選填」，可參考「學習出版公司」出版的「7000字文意選填詳解」。

特色與「7000字克漏字詳解」相同，不超出7000字的範圍，有詳細解答。

「閱讀測驗」的答題祕訣

① 尋找關鍵字——整篇文章中，最重要就是第一句和最後一句，第一句稱為主題句，最後一句稱為結尾句。每段的第一句和最後一句，第二重要，是該段落的主題句和結尾句。從「主題句」和「結尾句」中，找出相同的關鍵字，就是文章的重點。因為美國人從小被訓練，寫作文要注重主題句，他們給學生一個題目後，要求主題句和結尾句都必須有關鍵字。

② 先看題目、劃線、找出答案、標題號——考試的時候，先把閱讀測驗題目瀏覽一遍，在文章中掃瞄和題幹中相同的關鍵字，把和題目相關的句子，用線畫起來，便可一目了然。通常一句話只會考一題，你畫了線以後，再標上題號，接下來，你找其他題目的答案，就會更快了。

③ 碰到難的單字不要害怕，往往在文章的其他地方，會出現同義字，因為寫文章的人不喜歡重覆，所以才會有難的單字。

④ 如果閱測內容已經知道，像時事等，你就可以直接做答了。

準備「閱讀測驗」，可參考「學習出版公司」出版的「7000字閱讀測驗詳解」，本書不超出7000字範圍，每個句子都有文法分析，對錯答案都有明確交待，單字註明級數，不需要再查字典。

「中翻英」如何準備

可參考劉毅老師的「英文翻譯句型講座實況DVD」，以及「文法句型180」和「翻譯句型800」。考前不停地練習中翻英，翻完之後，要給外籍老師改。翻譯題做得越多，越熟練。

「英文作文」怎樣寫才能得高分？

① 字體要寫整齊，最好是印刷體，工工整整，不要塗改。

② 文章不可離題，尤其是每段的第一句和最後一句，最好要有題目所說的關鍵字。

③ 不要全部用簡單句，句子最好要有各種變化，單句、複句、合句、形容詞片語、分詞構句等，混合使用。

④ 不要忘記多使用轉承語，像 *at present*（現在），*generally speaking*（一般說來），*in other words*（換句話說），*in particular*（特別地），*all in all*（總而言之）等。

⑤ 拿到考題，最好先寫作文，很多同學考試時，作文來不及寫，吃虧很大。但是，如果看到作文題目不會寫，就先寫測驗題，這個時候，可將題目中作文可使用的單字、成語圈起來，寫作文時就有東西寫了。但千萬記住，絕對不可以抄考卷中的句子，一旦被發現，就會以零分計算。

⑥ 試卷有規定標題，就要寫標題。記住，每段一開始，要內縮5或7個字母。

⑦ 可多引用諺語或名言，並注意標點符號的使用。文章中有各種標點符號，會使文章變得更美。

⑧ 整體的美觀也很重要，段落的最後一行字數不能太少，也不能太多。段落的字數要平均分配，不能第一段只有一、兩句，第二段一大堆。第一段可以比第二段少一點。

準備「英文作文」，可參考「學習出版公司」出版的：